D1417387

Policy Making by Plebiscite:
School Referenda

Lexington Books Politics of Education Series
Frederick M. Wirt, Editor

Michael W. Kirst, Ed., *State, School, and Politics: Research Directions*

Joel S. Berke, Michael W. Kirst, *Federal Aid to Education: Who Benefits? Who Governs?*

Al J. Smith, Anthony Downs, M. Leanne Lachman, *Achieving Effective Desegregation*

Kern Alexander, K. Forbis Jordan, *Constitutional Reform of School Finance*

George R. LaNoue, Bruce L.R. Smith, *The Politics of School Decentralization*

David J. Kirby, T. Robert Harris, Robert L. Crain, Christine H. Rossell, *Political Strategies in Northern School Desegregation*

Philip K. Piele, John Stuart Hall, *Budgets, Bonds, and Ballots: Voting Behavior in School Financial Elections*

John C. Hogan, *The Schools, the Courts, and the Public Interest*

Jerome T. Murphy, *State Education Agencies and Discretionary Funds*

Howard D. Hamilton, Sylvan H. Cohen, *Policy Making by Plebiscite: School Referenda*

Policy Making by Plebiscite: School Referenda

Howard D. Hamilton
Kent State University

Sylvan H. Cohen
Slippery Rock State College

Lexington Books
D.C. Heath and Company
Lexington, Massachusetts
Toronto   London

Library
I.U.P.
Indiana, Pa.

379.15   H18p

C 1

Library of Congress Cataloging in Publication Data

Hamilton, Howard Devon, 1920-
 Policy making by plebiscite: school referenda.

 1. Education—United States—Finance. 2. School bonds—United
States. 3. Referendum—United States. I. Cohen, Sylvan H., joint
author. II. Title.
LB2825.H23   379'.15'0973   73-19725
ISBN 0-669-90969-6

Copyright © 1974 by D.C. Heath and Company

All rights reserved. No part of this publication may be reproduced or trans-
mitted in any form or by any means, electronic or mechanical, including
photocopy, recording, or any information storage or retrieval system, without permission in writing from the publisher.

Published simultaneously in Canada.

Printed in the United States of America.

International Standard Book Number: 0-669-90969-6

Library of Congress Catalog Card Number: 73-19725

Contents

List of Figures

List of Tables

Preface

This volume is the product of seven years of collecting data, running surveys, interviewing, and observing school elections in one of the states with the largest volume of school referenda. Our interest was whetted by being participant-observers in two communities where a series of tax levy defeats culmimated in an acute school crisis, with schools suspended for a month in one community.

Another reason for our interest in this subject is that it is the most extensive practice of direct legislation in America and perhaps the world. The approximately one thousand school bond, two thousand school budget, and five thousand tax levy elections annually exceed the combined number of referenda in city, county, and state governments. The place to see direct democracy is in our school districts, and this is a study of referenda as a political process, one considerably more extensive and important than the political science guild has recognized.

The contents reflect the interests and perspectives of students of politics, and consist of: (1) an inventory of the various state referenda systems; (2) analysis of trends and the determinants of election outcomes; (3) examination of tax levy and bond election campaigns; (4) comprehensive analysis of voting behavior in referenda, those "elections" with issues rather than candidates and parties, using the data of nine case studies in addition to our own; (5) application of Q analysis methodology to the study of voting behavior; (6) examination of the effects of the referenda system on community conflict and public administration; (7) a theoretical consideration of the efficacy of referenda as a public policy decision-making instrument in the light of various theoretical decision-making models; and (8) a tentative overall appraisal of the institution and its future.

Although this is not a handbook for running school election campaigns, the contents surely are of more than academic interest to school board members, school administrators, state officials, and education associations. At the risk of falling between stools, we have tried to make the contents as useful for professional educators as for political scientists. We thought there was some need for a solid reference work.

No man is an island and our debts are numerous since this volume is a synthesis of the research, largely unpublished, that has been done in this field. It would not have been possible without the spadework by the authors of the case studies listed in Chapter 8. We are particularly grateful to the authors of three monographs from which we extracted so much information, Professors Alan Clem, University of South Dakota, Roberta A. Sigel, SUNY Buffalo, and R. V. Smith, Eastern Michigan University, and to the authors of a school election handbook, Professors Michael Y. Nunnery and Ralph B. Kimbrough, University of Florida.

This volume would have been far less comprehensive and accurate without the assistance by officials of the various state departments of education and state teacher associations, who were generous in supplying statistics and other information: Frank W. Cannady, research supervisor, Arkansas; Melvin W. Gipe, consultant, California; assistant commissioner Edwin Steinbrecher, Colorado; Ray Bazell, administrator of school finance, Florida; Roger C. Mowrey, administrative assistant, Delaware; associate superintendent O. H. Joiner, Georgia; Fred Bradshaw, director of finance, Illinois; superintendent D. F. Engelking, Idaho; Gayle C. Obrecht, chief of plant facilities, Iowa; Dale M. Dennis, director of school finance, Kansas; Joe M. Alsip, director of finance, Kentucky; Ethel Bailey, supervisor of data collection, Louisiana; Walter Harvey, research director, Minnesota; Ruby M. Thompson, supervisor of finance, Mississippi; Robert W. Stockton, supervisor of state aid, Montana; Phillip T. Frangos, school law information, Michigan; assistant commissioner Harold Y. Bills, New Jersey; David D. Billmyer, bureau of educational finance research, New York; A. C. Davis, controller, North Carolina; assistant superintendent Cecil E. Foulkes, Oklahoma; Lloyd Thomas, coordinator of statistical services, Oregon; Gale D. Schlueter, director of statistical services, South Dakota; Maynard J. Mathison, director of school fiscal services, Washington; assistant superintendent Aaron Rapking, Jr., West Virginia. Similar valuable assistance was furnished by Charles F. Gaienne, Jr., director, Louisiana State Bond Commission; George C. Brown, assistant executive secretary, Michigan Educational Association; Reginald Cickajlo, assistant to the superintendent, Detroit Board of Education; Marvin Shamburger, director of research, Missouri State Teachers Association; D. D. Cooper, executive secretary, Montana Education Association; Boyd Wright, director, Bureau of Governmental Affairs, University of North Dakota; and Mark A. Peterson, research assistant, Wyoming Taxpayers Association.

Additionally, we are grateful for the counsel of Frederick M. Wirt, editor of the Lexington Books Politics of Education Series; Byron Marlowe, research director, Ohio Education Association; and our colleague, Richard Taylor, for his valuable criticism of the manuscript.

Policy Making by Plebiscite:
School Referenda

Maybe Year–Maybe Forever

By TOM RYAN

A Majority Affirmative
Vote is Necessary for Passage.

VOTE BALLOT WITH AN "X"

Detroit schools do have one more chance!

Schools Lose 13 Of 22 Bids For More Money

Area Voters Pass 3 Bond Issues, 6 New Levies

12 Mills Given Approval On Youngstown Ballot

Teachers protest

NEA Imposes Sanctions On W. Va. County

Reject Six Mills For Operation; New Vote Slated

School Fund, Bond Issues Are Defeated

Washtenaw County Voters Turn Down Five Proposals

Schools' Future To Face Board

Evergreen Levy Defeated 3rd Time

THE ONLY TIME HE GETS A CHANCE IS ON School Millage!

Levy-Loss Plan Set In Fremont

Schools Close Nov. 14 If Voters Turn Down 9.6-Mill Tax At Polls

Won't Cut Busing, Athletics

Twinsburg Avoids Angering Parents

Records Shattered By Special Elections

Brighton Calls Levy Record 'Worst Defeat Of The Decade'

VOTE YES ON SCHOOL MILLAGE

20-Teacher Cut Slated In Erie

Levy Defeat Results In Budget Pacing

Third Millage Vote

SUPPORT ROOTSTOWN SCHOOLS— VOTE NO

400 At Napoleon Join Bond Drive

Half-Day School Possible If Issue Fails, Official Says

Springfield Trying New Way To Explain Tax Proposal

Voters Defeat School Tax

1,400 Local Issues Facing Voters

1

Origin, Types, and Frequencies of School Referenda

The importance of school fiscal referenda—bond, tax levy, and budget "elections"—is evident in daily newspaper headlines which report school crises in communities across the nation: defeats of school budgets and bond proposals; schools operating on double sessions or using portable facilities; tax levies defeated four, five, or six times; teacher strikes and mass resignations; picketing by parents in opposition to cutbacks in transportation and other school programs; Detroit schools on the brink of closing; Oklahoma City school threatened; and actual school closings in Youngstown, Dayton, Independence, Portland, and a score of smaller communities. The common element of all the news is that schools are "in trouble," because the voters have said No at school elections.

The news, of course, is quite unrepresentative of reality, as only the dramatic crises reach the news wires and make headlines nationally. The school closings, actually suspensions of a few days or weeks, affect only an infinitesimal portion of the sixteen thousand school systems; most schools are not in a state of crisis, and the voters say Yes to school financial requests far more frequently than they say No. In fact, during the last decade, they said Yes to $19 billion in school bonds, and every year they endorse four or five thousand property tax levies. Twenty-five billion dollars of school revenue is derived annually from the general property tax, of which a large portion, nearly all in some states, is authorized in voting booths. The fiscal decisions of the "peepul" manifestly are not penny ante ones.

It cannot be gainsaid that the voters' tolerance of school tax rate increases and bond issues has declined markedly since the 1950s, when school proposals rarely lost. Numerous referenda have generated intense community conflict and have produced authentic crises for some school systems. From the standpoint of the schools, the referendum system is not working well in many communities, although how much better off the schools would be in the long run without it is uncertain. Teacher associations and school officials in some states are trying to abolish the system, thus far with scant success.

Scope and Purpose

This is the first comprehensive treatment of school fiscal referenda, which

1

include all school plebiscites except those concerned with district reorganization and such occasional idiosyncratic considerations as ''Shall kindergartens be established in Lane District 4?'' Reorganization elections tend to be episodic, occurring in most states in waves of school consolidation, about a generation apart in time (although it has been calculated that a reorganization election occurs somewhere in Michigan every forty hours[1]). And, since consolidation has already reduced the number of school districts to 16,515, reorganization referenda will be infrequent henceforth.

We propose to do these things: (1) inventory the rich variety of fiscal referenda systems in the nation; (2) examine the processes of bond and levy elections—the issues, strategies, and campaigns; (3) analyze election statistics in search of variables that affect the outcome of school elections; (4) marshal a large corpus of survey data and investigate voting behavior; (5) explain and illustrate Q analysis, a promising method of voting behavior research, which is particularly useful for referenda and other local elections, and which may also be of practical use by school officials; (6) scrutinize the results of this system of direct democracy—community conflict and the effects on school operations and revenue; (7) present a theoretical analysis of fiscal referenda as a policy making process; and (8) assay the system and its future.

Recent decision making literature provides some new tools for analysis of political structures; we will employ these for appraising the efficacy of referenda. We will then go on to a comparative analysis of the referendum system—the Populist model of decision making—by reference to other useful analytical models: the Rationalist or technocratic model, the Pluralist model, and an Economics model.

The content selection is guided by two criteria. One is our aim to be comprehensive. There is a paucity of convenient information of this subject; most of it is either unpublished or in obscure places—''fugitive literature.'' This dearth of accessible information is due in part to the strange neglect of school referenda by political scientists, who rarely have regarded schools as political systems deserving their attention. Much of the data herein derives from our own research during the past seven years.

The other selection criterion is to make this volume useful, and possibly interesting, to three audiences, above all public officials: school board members, superintendents, and legislators. Possibly it contains sufficient political science to be of some value to our own guild and social studies teachers, particularly those interested in voting behavior or local government. We also harbor the hope that it may be of some utility for other people with an exceptional interest in our schools, such as activists in the League of Women Voters and parent-teacher associations.

Geographic Distribution

The annual frequencies of bond, tax levy, and school budget elections in each state are posted on the map of Figure 1-1. The entries are averages of the last three years, except the authors' estimates for those states without records of levy elections.[2] Bond elections occur in all states except Alabama, Hawaii, and Indiana; however some school systems are exempt from referenda in fourteen states.[3] In both frequency and amounts, the principal bond election states are California, Texas, Michigan, Ohio, and Illinois in that order. During the 1962-1971 decade, schools in those states conducted seven thousand bond elections authorizing $9 billion in bonds—about half the amount for the entire nation.[4]

Tax levy elections occur in varying degrees and a host of forms in twenty-seven states, including the five states with school budget elections, which are functional equivalents of levy elections, those of Colorado and Oregon being avowedly so. Little change has occurred in the distribution and frequency of elections since the 1930s when several states instituted referendum systems. North Carolina discontinued referenda in 1967 and Minnesota began in 1971.

Historical circumstances largely explain the distinct pattern in the geographic distribution of levy referenda. New England has few independent school districts and no tax levy elections; school budgets and taxes have always been voted at town or school meetings or by city councils and town boards. New York and New Jersey have school districts, but the school meeting tradition has been retained by annual budget elections in the districts outside the large cities. West of the Appalachians, whether or not a state has fiscal referenda depends on whether an antiproperty tax movement ever developed sufficient strength to write tax rate limits into the state constitution or statutes.

Origin

It has been widely presumed that school referenda are a legacy of the progressive movement, which promoted popular initiative and referendum laws.[5] They also have been said to be a residuum of Jacksonian democracy,[6] but neither of those explanations has much validity. Possibly school budget elections in New York and New Jersey owe something to Jacksonism as a reinforcement of the New England town meeting tradition, and the populist and progressive movements may have been contributory influences in a few states where fiscal referenda began in that era, e.g., Oklahoma 1907, Ohio 1910, and Oregon 1916.

Actually, plebiscitary democracy in school districts was the unintended handiwork of conservative political forces rather than Jacksonian democrats or Progressives. It was a classic instance of unplanned parenthood. Direct democracy was not adopted for its own sake on its own merits; it was an unplanned byproduct of debt and tax limitation statutes and constitutional provisions which originated in the 1870s and spread until the First

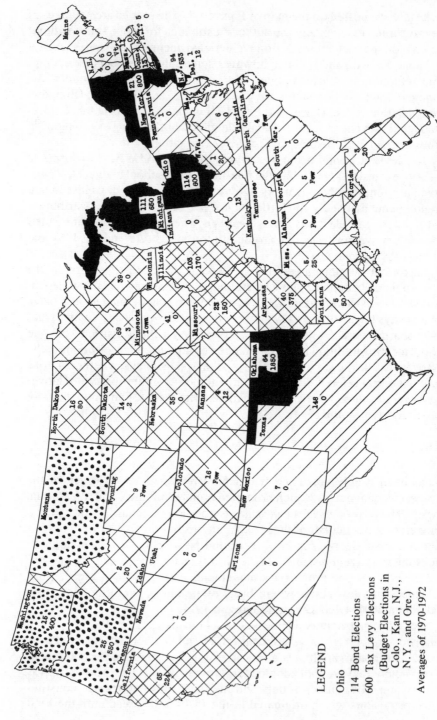

Figure 1-1. Annual Number of School Bond, Tax Levy, and Budget Elections in Each State

LEGEND

Ohio

114 Bond Elections

600 Tax Levy Elections
(Budget Elections in
Colo., Kan., N.J.,
N.Y., and Ore.)

Averages of 1970-1972

World War. Their purpose was to inhibit bond issues by requiring referenda and to clamp a tight lid on property tax rates by state law. Some of the laws were the classified limits type, a schedule of maximum rates for cities, counties, townships, and school districts. Others were the overall limit type, i.e., that the aggregate amount of tax levied on any parcel of land should not exceed so many mills. The depression of the 1930s triggered another wave of agitation against property taxes and a half dozen more states adopted "dollar-and-a-half" laws or "fifteen-mills" amendments.[7]

In most states such laws added the referendum option, sometimes after a brief unpleasant experience, out of deference to the tradition of local autonomy and to provide a modicum of flexibility. The electorate of a county or school district could authorize special levies above or "outside" the statutory of constitutional rate limits. Some of the laws clearly showed that their purpose was not more democracy by restricting the suffrage to property owners, "taxpayers"—and the spouses of taxpayers in Michigan—and by requiring supramajorities for authorizing bond issues or tax levies. It was presumed, of course, that "extramillage" would be voted infrequently, but that proved not to be the case in most states.

The device of passing a law against debt and taxes turned out to have important consequences, but most of the consequences were unanticipated ones and the intended ones were not fully achieved. How much they have inhibited debt and taxation is impossible to determine with any precision, but patently they have not been very effective. The unanticipated results have been quite obvious. The initial effect in most states was an acute shortage of revenue for schools and other local governments, in some states "chaos" and a "widespread breakdown in local government,"[8] which led to the next unanticipated consequence, a radical revision of state-local fiscal relations and state revenue structures. To bail out the schools and other local governments, states enacted sales taxes and devised a variety of grants and tax sharing arrangements. Thus the tax limitation schemes begat fiscal policy centralization and a web of state-local fiscal relationships and interdependence.

The state largess notwithstanding, schools and other local units have been obliged to use the referendum option to raise tax rates as the legal limits proved unrealistic, in part because of that favorite American shell game, competitive property tax underassessment, which makes the legal limits fictitious. For example the 30 percent assessment ratio in Ohio makes the 10 mills maximum actually only 3 mills. Few of the legal maxima, particularly those embalmed in constitutions thirty years or more ago, would be adequate with full value assessment; the underassessment game has made them ludicrous.

It cannot be denied that the quixotic tax limitation devices have added a lot of color to local politics—so much voting, school crises, and an abundance of fictions and anomalies. The actual tax rates have been substantially higher than the "legal" rates for years, four or five times over in some states. For elementary school districts of California, the statutory maximum is 9 mills, but to qualify for the state equalization program an elementary district must levy 10 mills. No land may be taxed more than 10 mills in Ohio, says the constitution, but a school district with a rate of less than 20 mills will not get a penny of the state foundation program. The Oklahoma constitution proclaims 15 mills, but schools must levy 35 mills in order to benefit fully from the "Incentive Aid" grant program—an irresistible carrot. Other times, other laws.

Another absurdity has emerged in Ohio and perhaps elsewhere. Two generations of voting tax levies has nurtured the idea that the only legitimate taxes are those enacted in the voting booth. Hence a referendum is required for a city payroll or a county sales tax. If a local body ventures to adopt an excise unilaterally, the opposition will shout that it is "unconstitutional" without a plebiscite—a potent propaganda gambit.

A prominent theme in political science currently is a renewed attention to political symbolism. It is said that the symbolic "outputs" of political systems are as important as the material ones.[9] The durability of the hoary property tax limitations is a vivid demonstration of the potency of symbols. The Michigan "Fifteen-Mills Amendment" of 1932 was retained in the constitution of 1962 after extensive deliberation at the convention.[10] The convention evidently chose not to risk defeat of its handiwork. The incident attests to the reputation of the property tax (worse than it deserves), to the intensity of antitaxation sentiment, and to the power of political symbols.

Frequency

Nobody knows how many school referenda occur in this country. The U.S. Office of Education collects statistics only of bond elections. Detailed records of tax levy elections are kept in several states by the department of education or the state teachers association, but in some states there are no records. Unfortunately, data available from a HEW-sponsored study[11] of voter turnout in school referenda, in which a huge national sample of school districts was used, did not prove a useful tool for estimating the missing information on tax levy elections. Our estimates are based on perusal of state statutes and documents and the questioning of state officials and teacher organizations.

Currently, there are about seven thousand tax levy and budget elections across the country, with eight states accounting for over five thousand. The consolidation movement surely has reduced the volume of elections considerably, but not their importance. Each year the voters pass judgment on more than three billion dollars in bonds, but it is impossible to make a firm estimate of the dollar volume of their decisions on operating budgets and tax levies. Essentially, all property taxes are voted in a few states, and all school budgets are voted in Oregon and the noncity districts of New York.

One of the most striking aspects of Figure 1-1 is the amazing differences in the frequency of levy elections. Oklahomans vote in more than eighteen hundred such elections each year; New York has eight hundred budget elections; and there are six hundred tax levy referenda in Ohio and Michigan; while other states have less than a dozen!

One of the authors has observed the contrasts. There were no referenda in his native Indiana, but in Michigan he got to vote on numerous interesting things—tax levies, school construction, reapportionment, and colored margarine. Later when he moved to Ohio, in May 1966 he voted on a school operating levy and reapportionment; in November on a levy for retarded children, a proposal to rebuild the county infirmary, a big operating levy for the school, and a small one for Penta County vocational school; and in December he was summoned back to the polls for a repeat of the defeated Penta County levy. It was quite a year for the sovereigns of Bowling Green, who seemed to be making more decisions than their officials.

Evidently school referenda systems are not identical. Why does Illinois have only a fourth as many elections as Michigan and Ohio? Why are high frequencies concentrated in two regions, the North Central and Pacific coast states? The frequency for a state may be a function of several variables:

The size of school districts—a thousand in California but only sixty county systems in Florida and Louisiana.

The proportion of operating revenue derived from local sources—70 percent in North Dakota but only 25 percent in Alabama.

The level of the "legal" maximum school tax rate (the "within" millage)—30 mills in Idaho but less than 5 mills in West Virginia.

The assessment ratio and whether the legal maximum applies to the assessment figures of the local assessors or to a state adjusted or equalized valuation, as in Michigan after 1962.

The school share of the "within" millage in states that have an overall type of legal limit.

The minimum school tax mandated by statute, either directly as Louisiana's archaic 5 mills "constitutional tax," or indirectly by the eligibility requirements of state grant programs—16 mills in Utah, 20 in Ohio, 25 mills in Idaho, and 35 in Oklahoma.

The time length of voted levies—only one year in Arkansas, Oklahoma, Washington, and the three annual budget election states, up to five years in North Dakota and West Virginia, ten in Louisiana, but indefinitely in several states.

The authority of school boards to call repeat elections—none in Arkansas, two in New York and Ohio, but any number in Michigan and Oregon.

The frequency with which schools are impelled by levy defeats to schedule repeats.

A low volume of elections occurs in states where the period of authorizations is indefinite, and thus essentially permanent. Levy elections occur only when the school board proposes to change the rate, which is to say it wants more revenue. (There are a few authentic instances when the proposal is a rate reduction; there are one or two in California each year, some of which have been defeated!) Louisiana has quasi-permanent ten-year levies which supply 70 percent of the property tax revenue.

For those states with the busiest voters, the explanation is the concatenation of numerous school districts and a few legal provisions, such as the practice of annual budget elections in New York and Oregon and voting the tax levy at the annual school meeting in Arkansas. If a proposed budget is defeated in Oregon, elections are repeated until it is approved—as many as four or five times. In New York there may be a second and possibly a third round. Repeats also are numerous in Michigan, although rarely more than once, and in Ohio, where three attempts may be made in a calendar year—a three strikes law.

The combination of numerous districts, a low constitutional maximum rate, and short-term levies assures frequent elections in Michigan, Ohio, Oklahoma, and Washington, the latter two states having only single-year levies. California and Ohio have a mix of term and indefinite levies, but mostly term. In two-thirds of the cases, California officials forego the (legal) opportunity to request indefinite levies—a self-restraint quite possibly related to the distinctly lower passage rate of indefinite proposals. The self-restraint of Ohio officials is understandable, since the citizenry had been voting short-term levies for two generations before indefinite ones were permissible.

Referenda in Metropolises

School referenda occur less frequently in metropolitan areas. Recently, the Ohio cities, the few west coast cities, Kansas City, St. Louis, Oklahoma City, and Detroit are the only cities that have held tax levy elections. This is partly an accident of geography; many metropolises are in nonlevy states. It also is because the metropolis often is the subject of special legislation, e.g., the tax rate for the Chicago school district essentially is fixed by the legislature, and Orleans parish has a special legal tax rate so large that New Orleans is the one school system in Louisiana not dependent on voted millage. The school boards of New York City and the other metropolises of that state are dependent on the generosity of city councils rather than the electorate, obtaining their funds by appropriation.

This suggests that the referendum system may be less suitable for the metropolis; some logic and evidence point in that direction. Patently the physical feasibility of direct democracy is inverse to scale. School elections usually interest an even smaller proportion of the populace in the metropolis than elsewhere.[12] Size handicaps communication between school officials and the electorate. The proportion of adults that are parents of schoolchildren is smaller in the core city. In two recent Detroit levy elections, critical ones for the schools, the turnout rate was only 30 percent of the registered voters.[13]

If adequacy and stability of school revenue and the avoidance of community conflict and crises are important values, then there is no dearth of evidence that the referendum system is not working ideally in metropolises. With a few exceptions, notably Cleveland, metropolitan school systems lately have been losing a lot of levy and bond elections—two or more recently in Dayton, St. Louis, Los Angeles, Portland, Kansas City, and Detroit. Seattle has had to close some schools and a repeat election was required in 1971 to pass the annual levy. Repeated efforts of Kansas City schools to raise the rate have failed. Four straight levy defeats in two years closed Dayton schools briefly in 1971. The 1971-1972 school year was abbreviated in Portland after a budget increase was defeated three times. Detroit made three futile levy efforts in 1972, and the system would have closed in the Spring of 1973 but for an emergency statute authorizing a levy without a referendum.

Schoolmen have long held that schools fare better financially where schools are fiscally independent rather than dependent on city council appropriations. With respect to metropolises, the validity of the argument for fully autonomous schools has become progressively more dubious. A recent study of the eighteen largest cities in the nation found that the revenue per pupil in the dependent school systems is no less than in the independent systems.[14] In practice, the so-called independent systems are nearly always restricted by special statutory rate ceilings or dependent on voter approval of operating levies and bonds. They do not, therefore, enjoy a revenue advantage over dependent districts, because "the public is not so open-handed with regard to educational expenditures as has been assumed."[15]

The vicissitudes of metropolitan schools are not past and the portents are unfavorable for the systems that are dependent on plebiscites for operating revenue and authorization of large capital outlays. For winning fiscal referenda, the metropolitan schools have three peculiar and acute handicaps: a shrinking tax base, necessitating higher tax rates just to keep going,[16] racial conflict, and the shrinking proportion of parents of schoolchildren. The latter handicap was cited by a Washington legislative study commission. "The decreasing numbers of parents with school-age children in Seattle may soon lead to school levy failures," which in turn "would spur an even greater exodus of parents and a still worse atmosphere for levy passage." For dealing with the perceived problem, the commission did not propose discontinuance of referenda nor exemption of Seattle by special legislation. Instead, it suggested the novel idea of a metropolitan educational finance district. "The suburbs would obtain the advantage of Seattle's larger tax base and Seattle would be able to shore up its support for special levies with suburban parents."[17]

Racial conflict has been a conspicuous factor in several recent school crises. In Cleveland, which has a habit of endorsing bonds and levies by landslides, a levy narrowly escaped defeat when it coincided with an intense fracas between the school board and civil rights groups over segregation.[18] When Oklahoma City schools were under a court order to integrate in 1970, the opponents of busing threatened to close down the schools by defeating the school levies—and nearly succeeded.[19] The context of the Dayton school closing also was intense resistance to the school board's integration plan.[20] In Detroit in 1972, a novel system of regional school boards had just been established by act of the legislature, an arrangement strongly desired by some blacks and some white neighborhoods, and denounced by other whites and blacks as a segregation scheme.[21] Simultaneously, Detroit was mandated by a federal court to eliminate de facto school segregation by merging with all the school systems of Wayne County, the biggest school busing plan to date. That was the scenario for Detroit's five school levy defeats in 1972. In May, the school board placed a renewal and a 5 mills new levy on the ballot; the new levy was defeated badly and even the renewal lost by a slight margin. A special election was called in August, and both proposals were defeated badly. By November the vicissitudes of the Detroit schools were augmented by the simultaneous presence on the ballot of two constitutional amendments, proposed by the state teachers association, to replace the local property tax by state financing from income tax revenue. The beleaguered board placed only the 5 mills renewal on the ballot and even it lost. School financial referenda provide convenient means for disgruntled individuals and interest groups to vent their displeasure with school policies or taxes and to exert leverage or inflict retribution on a school board. The racial cold war in the cities is not helpful for school referenda.

Notes

1. Nicholas A. Masters et al., *State Politics and the Public Schools* (New York: Knopf, 1964), p. 243.

2. Bond election results are published annually by the U.S. Office of Education, but no effort is made to collect data on tax levy and school budget elections. Consequently the authors gathered data by correspondence with officials in the various states, those listed in the preface, and the state teacher associations in Michigan, Missouri, and Ohio. The officials were wonderfully cooperative; some had detailed statistics, others had none. The data base for these averages is indicated in our descriptions of the referendum systems in each state in Chapter 2.

3. See the footnote of Appendix Table B-2. Most of the Kentucky school bonds are revenue bonds issued with a referendum.

4. Appendix Table B-2.

5. E.g., Frederick M. Wirt and Michael W. Kirst, *The Political Web of American Schools* (Boston: Little, Brown, 1972), p. 96.

6. Scott Greer, *Governing the Metropolis* (New York: John Wiley, 1962), p. 124.

7. See *State Constitutional and Statutory Restrictions on Local Taxing Powers* (Washington: United States Advisory Commission on Intergovernmental Relations), ch. 3.

8. Ibid., p. 51.

9. Cf. Murray Edelman, *The Symbolic Uses of Politics* (Urbana: University of Illinois Press, 1964).

10. *State Constitutional and Statutory Restrictions*, pp. 32-34 and sec. IX-6 of the Michigan constitution.

11. Richard F. Carter and William G. Savard, *Influence of Voter Turnout on School Bond and Tax Elections* (Washington: U. S. Office of Education, 1961), p. 10

12. Ibid., p. 12.

13. Elections in May and August 1972.

14. T. Edward Hollander, "Fiscal Independence and Large City School Systems," in *Educating an Urban Population*, ed. by Marilyn Gittell (Beverly Hills, California: Sage Publications, 1967), pp. 103-116.

15. Ibid., p. 112.

16. The inevitable necessity of tax increases has been advanced as a reason why New York City should retain the fiscally dependent school board arrangement. Hollander, op. cit., p. 113.

17. Temporary Special Levy Study Commission, *Summary Report and Research Reports* (March 1971), vol. 1, p. 45.

18. Louis Masotti, "Patterns of White and Nonwhite School Referenda Participation and Support: Cleveland 1960-64," in Gittel, op. cit., p. 253.

19. Associated Press dispatch in *The Blade*, Toledo, Ohio, January 28, 1970, p. 3.

20. Akron *Beacon Journal*, October 10, 1971, p. B1.

21. Cf. Joel D. Aberbach and Jack L. Walker, "Citizen Desires, Policy Outcomes, and Community Control," paper presented at Midwest Political Science Association meeting, September 7, 1971.

2

Federalism in Bloom: The Various State Systems

American government textbooks used to emphasize that experimentation and diversity are great virtues of a federal system. It permits each state to tailor public policies to fit its own conditions and the tastes of its citizens. "We have forty-eight laboratories" was a favorite cliche. Since about 1940 those themes have been muted and supplanted by others. The states, it is said, have ceased to be very innovative and American politics are being homogenized by mighty economic and social forces of national scope which are rapidly eroding differences among the states. "Federalism is dead." Scrutiny of the school referenda systems across the country reveals amazing interstate differences; the school referenda system of each state is different, a justification of that textbook refrain "but the practice varies from state to state." Here is luxuriant federalism.

There are, of course, some discernible patterns, which can be better understood after one has scanned the various state systems. The following descriptions are conspicuously uneven in length, in part because of the variations in state record keeping, but also because some pigs are more equal than others. School referenda are far more consequential in some states than others. The focus in this chapter is on operating levy and budget elections; the fewer variations of bond referenda will be noted later.

This inventory of the state systems, with data never previously assembled, may be the most useful part of our enterprise for some officials and research agencies, but for some readers it may be wearily tedious. The latter may elect to skip to the concluding generalizations at the end of the chapter.

California: Term and Indefinite Levies

Although the volume of tax elections is less in California than in some states, because of indefinite period levies, levy elections are mighty important for California schools. More than $2 billion of annual school revenue is derived from local property taxes, many of which are voted levies. The statutory maximum rates without a referendum range from 75¢ to $1.65 (7½ to 16½ mills) according to the type of school, but most districts (804 of 1094 in 1969) have voted higher rates. Indeed in numerous instances the "override" rate is double the statutory maximum. In California the proposition is, not to levy an additional 3 mills but to raise the school general fund tax to $2.95, for example,[1] which "overrides" the statutory $1.65.

The annual volume of elections fluctuates considerably, but there is less variation in the number of levies approved. The passage rate is related to the frequency of going to the well. The mean since 1966 has been 206 proposals annually, with a 52 percent approval rate. It should be noted, however, that a few proposals are decreases and several are for continuation of the prevailing rate (a fourth of the ballots in 1972), which pass easily. The overall passage rate may be less significant, because of renewals, than the approval rate for increases. Thus the overall passage rate of 50 percent in 1972 was about par, but that was a poor year for California schools as the passage rate of increases slid to 33 percent.

There is a surprisingly wide range in the size of the tax increases proposed each year. Some are a few cents and some exceed $2.00, the median in 1972 being 55¢. Although the association between increase size and approval rate is erratic for any single year, when a few years are pooled, as in Table 2-2, a monotonic correlation appears. As the proposed rate hikes exceed 40¢, the mortality rate increases, but perhaps equally significant is the fact that nearly a third of the large increases are approved. The size of the increase is not an index of the tax rate that is being proposed. Possibly there is a greater correlation between levy success and the size of the proposed rate than between levy success and the size of the increase. Unfortunately California's extensive statistics do not contain the data for that computation.

California is one of the few states where school boards have unlimited discretion in selecting the time length of levy authorizations. Hence it is interesting to see what periods are selected and how much of a factor length of period is in the judgments of the electorate. Not surprisingly, the preference of the school boards is for indefinite, i.e., permanent levies; obviously California voters do not share that preference. Three-fifths of the term levies were approved in 1972, while only 35 percent of the indefinite levies were approved. The three-year term, although most often proposed, was the least successful, in 1972, of any term less than six years. The electorate's lack of enthusiasm for levies longer than five years suggests that California school boards will be waging levy campaigns for the foreseeable future.

The participation rates in California cover the spectrum from 10 to 90 percent of the registered voters. The annual patterns are consistently right-skewed normal distributions. A fifth of the tax referenda attract 60 percent of the electorate. The median turnout rate is 42 percent and the mean is 45 percent, which although not high, is distinctly better than the 36 percent reported for a national sample,[2] and much higher than the voting in New York budget elections.

Table 2-1
California School Tax Elections

School Year	Elections	Levies Passed	Percent Passed	Increases Passed	Pct.
1967	209	101	48	74	42
1968	122	83	68	55	59
1969	234	122	52	93	45
1970	254	120	47	92	40
1971	240	125	52	na	na
1972	177	89	50	43	33
Mean	206	107	52	71	43

Data source: California Department of Education.

Table 2-2
Tax Size and Success of California Levies
(percent passed)

Tax Size	1967	1968	1969	1970	1967-70	N
Lower	50	100	100	67	83	12
Same	96	96	100	98	98	105
Increase	42	59	45	40	44	709
1-20¢	47	53	62	50	53	55
21-40	42	68	60	54	53	178
41-60	48	57	49	41	47	211
61-80	33	64	54	31	42	103
Over 80	21	46	23	34	30	162

Data source: California Department of Education

Table 2-3
Duration of Levies and Success, 1971-72 Elections

Years Duration	Levies Proposed	Levies Passed	Pct. Passed
One	0	—	—
Two	15	11	74
Three	52	30	58
Four	6	5	83
Five	26	16	62
Six & over	7	2	29
Indefinite	71	25	35

Data source: California Department of Education.

Table 2-4
Voting Rates and Levy Success in California, 1968-1972

Turnout Rate	Elections in			Three Years	Pct. of Elections	Levies Approved in		
	1968	1970	1972			1968	1970	1972
0-19.9	8	13	11	32	6%	87%	69%	72%
20-39.9	53	91	66	210	39	70	42	64
40-59.9	30	113	47	180	33	73	50	47
60-79.9	25	41	45	111	20	52	46	23
80 & over	6	1	4	11	2	67	100	50
Median	40%	40%	43%	42%				

Turnout is percent of registered voters that voted.
Data unavailable for four elections during the period.
Data source: California Department of Education.

Another regularity of California elections is the pronounced negative correlation of turnout and election outcomes. A similar but more monotonic pattern was found in the national sample of turnout rates. These data have prompted frequent statements that turnout rate profoundly affects outcomes, i.e., that the higher the turnout the lower the probability of a levy's success. There are, however, other data which cast doubt on the validity of that inference, which will be examined in a later chapter.

Colorado: 106 Percent Budget Limitation

A unique system was inaugurated by Colorado in 1970. The general fund budgetary authority of school boards is limited by statute to 106 percent of the current year expenses per pupil in average daily attendance times the estimated attendance for the ensuing year. Increases greater than 6 percent must be approved at a special budget election in December. This restriction does not apply to expenditures for transportation, capital outlay and debt, and certain "categorical purposes." If attendance exceeds the estimate, a district may expend more than the budgeted amount by drawing on its contingency account. No information is available about the frequency and results of Colorado budget elections, since the information is not reported to the state department of education. From contextual evidence, one may infer that a few, but only a few, budget elections occur.

The arrangement was instituted by the school foundation act of 1969. Previously the legal limitation was in terms of tax rates. A district could not increase its levy by more than 5 percent without approval of the state tax commission. A department of education publication states that "One of the severe weaknesses of that approach of limiting budgetary authority for a school district was that no assured consideration was provided for districts experiencing enrollment growth."[3] Manifestly the new system is a good one for adjusting to enrollment fluctuations, but it makes no provision for another critical variable—prices. Thus it appears to share a weakness common to alternative systems of property tax limitation. Apparently the Colorado formula is working smoothly with no school financial crises and few referenda, but it might be less satisfactory in a period of rapid inflation.

Delaware: Indefinite Levy System

All school tax levies are authorized by referenda in Delaware, but the frequency is not large because authorizations are for an indefinite period, which usually means that a referendum occurs only when a tax increase is viewed as necessary by the school board. When a bond issue is voted, a tax levy for debt service is voted simultaneously.

Referenda usually are scheduled as special elections. Recently, most bond-tax proposals have been approved, but operating levies have been quite unsuccessful. In fact, the only operating levies ratified during the past two years involved no rate increase. A Delaware official notes that "a tax levy referendum system does produce some difficulties since it may cause a retrenchment in educational programs and activities when an election to authorize a tax increase fails."[4] However, less than a fifth of Delaware's school revenue is derived from the property tax.

Illinois: Indefinite Levies

A schedule of maximum rates by type of school district is prescribed by statute for general operating expense, a building fund, and the specific purposes listed in Table 2-6. Voter approval is required to exceed the limits, and such authorizations are of indefinite duration. Special levies may be imposed without referendum for a variety of purposes: debt service, retirement funds, disability insurance, junior college tuition, special education buildings, and working cash. The rate limits are exaggerations since the official assessment ratio is 50 percent of full market value, although they are less fictitious than the legal rates of several states with lower assessment ratios.

A distinctive aspect of the Illinois system is the optional referendum —in local parlance, the "backdoor referendum." Rates within the legal maximum levied by school boards are subject to referendum upon petition of one-fifth of the voters of the district. Bond issues for the working cash fund are also subject to a "backdoor referendum."

The volume of levy elections in Illinois, although substantial is surprisingly low for a state with 1174 school districts. This is accounted for, in part, by the fact that Illinois authorizations are of indefinite duration, i.e., essentially permanent. Also, the legal limits of the school board discretion are less severe in Illinois than, e.g., in Michigan and Ohio where the volume of elections is considerably greater. The passage rate has dropped precipitously recently, perhaps more than in any other state; in 1971, the passage rate slumped to 27 percent. Illinois schools are free to reschedule levies; but currently the prospect is bleak for tax increases; and, although there have been no "school crisis" headlines, evidently numerous Illinois schools are experiencing financial stringency.

Kentucky: Indefinite Levies

Levy referenda in Kentucky are principally for the building fund, and are

Table 2-5
Delaware Tax Referenda

	1970-71	71-72
Current expense	4	6
Passed	0	2
Bond issues	8	5
Passed	5	3
Total	12	11

Data source: Delaware Department of Public Instruction.

Table 2-6
Illinois Rate Limitations, 1971-1972

	Type of District	Max. rates (mills)	
		no ref.	with ref.
Educational fund	K-8, 9-12	9.2*	30.0
	K-12	16.0	40.0
Building fund	K-8, 9-12	2.5*	5.5
	K-12	3.75	7.5
Capital improv't.	All	—	0.6
Fire & Safety	All	0.5	1.0
Summer school	All	—	1.5
Transportation	All	1.2	2.0

*Subject to backdoor referendum.
Data source: *Public School Finance Programs, 1971-72.*

Table 2-7
Illinois Tax Levy Elections

Year	Number Passed			Failed	Pct. Passed
	Bldg. F.	Ed. F.	Total		
1966-67			140	109	56
1967-68	18	92	110	123	47
1968-69	26	72	98	116	46
1969-70	8	38	46	98	32
1970-71	6	30	36	94	27

Data source: Illinois Department of Public Instruction.

voted concurrently with bond authorizations, which require a two-thirds majority. Operating levy referenda are infrequent, only two or three a year, because extramillage authorizations are permanent and only a third of school revenue is derived from local sources. As of June 1972, extramillage had been voted in 31 of the 190 school districts, and 101 districts had building fund levies.

Kentucky has a unique formula for the legal taxing authority of school districts sans referendum. Each district has its own ceiling which may vary slightly from year to year. Prior to 1967, Kentucky had a conventional arrangement, a 15 mills limit for schools, when a court mandate of full-value assessment led to adoption of the present formula. The legal limit is the rate that would provide the previous year revenue plus the amount of the yield of the previous year effective rate applied to the net assessment growth (property added and deleted from tax rolls). The formula essentially froze tax rates at 110 percent of the 1965-66 level in the respective districts.[5] The system, says a state official, does not create difficulties for schools "as a usual thing," but there is some dissatisfaction among school people with the operating levy ceilings and with poor assessments.[6]

Louisiana: Ten-Year Levies

Parish boards of education in Louisiana may levy only a 5 mills "constitutional" tax without a referendum. Three optional taxes may be authorized by referenda for periods up to ten years: 5 mills for building and equipment, 7 mills for maintenance and operation, and an additional 7 mills for operation—the "special leeway" tax. These optional taxes also may be authorized by the voters of a district within a parish. Thus, in addition to the "constitutional" tax, up to 38 mills may be authorized by referendum. Permission to conduct a levy election requires approval of the state bond board. The Orleans parish board is authorized to levy 13 mills in addition to the constitutional tax, which exempts New Orleans schools from the referendum system.

Although the property tax provides an unusually small fraction of school revenue in Louisiana (about one-third), more than 70 percent of the property tax revenue is from voted levies. Information about school tax elections is fragmentary. The annual volume fluctuates between forty and eighty, inclusive of bond issues with tax levies attached.[7] The passage rate is rather high—70 percent for the last three years.

Louisiana tax and bond elections were unique in one respect until 1969. The franchise for both was restricted to property owners and passage of a measure required two majorities: a majority of the individuals voting and a majority of the assessed property, i.e., the yeasayers had to own more property than the naysayers. A voter cast two ballots, one listing his assessment. That eccentricity was terminated by a Supreme Court decision in 1969 that property ownership is an unconstitutional suffrage requirement, a decision which affected several states.[8]

Table 2-8
Kentucky Tax Levy Elections

| | Building Fund | | Operating Levies | | | Pct. |
Year	Passed	Failed	Passed	Failed	Total	Passed
1969-70	6	9	1	2	18	39
1970-71	1	12	1	0	15	13
1971-72	1	4	0	1	6	17

Data source: Kentucky Department of Education.

Table 2-9
Property Tax Revenue Louisiana School Districts, 1970-71

Tax	Parishes	Revenue (million)
Mntce. & operation	60	$29.4
Bldg. & equipment	31	11.4
Bond & interest	64	51.8
Voted by ref.		$92.4
Constitutional	66	38.1
Total		$130.5

Data source: Louisiana Department of Education.

Table 2-10
Louisiana Tax and Bond Elections

Year	Passed	Lost	Result Unknown	Total	Pct. Passed
1970	16	14	8	38	53
1971	44	10	1	55	82
1972	57	26	3	86	69
Total	117	50	12	179	70

Data source: Louisiana Bond Board.

Michigan: Short- Term Levies

"Extramillage" elections, have been a common occurrence, frequently quite animated, in every community of Michigan since the "Fifteen-Mills Amendment" of the state constitution in 1932.[9] As that overall property tax limitation initially did not exclude levies for debt service, it simultaneously instituted bond referenda. Each year the school systems sponsor six or seven hundred operating levies along with a hundred bond issues. Most are voted on school election day in June, but a few hundred levies are voted on at special elections scattered throughout the year. Every day is election day somewhere in Michigan, and repeat levy elections are common.

Initially, securing revenue via the ballot box was far from easy: only taxpayers could vote for bonds; levies required a two-thirds majority and could be authorized for no longer than five years; the supramajority rule produced numerous instances of minority rule, where the affirmative vote was between 50 and 60 percent; and the time limitation blocked bond issues for longer than five years. In 1948, levies were authorized for up to twenty years and the voting rule was changed to a simple majority. The effect was visible—$18 million of extramillage was voted in 1948, $50 million in 1951.[10] The practice of short-term levies continues, however, perhaps in part because only taxpayers and their spouses are eligible to vote on levies of more than five years.[11]

One reason for the volume of levy elections is the frequency of defeats; three attempts is not unusual for a new levy, and about a third of the renewals, entail two elections. The approval rate of additions matches the rates in California and Ohio, but renewals fare differently. Whereas renewals pass routinely in those states, they are not automatic in Michigan—146 were defeated in 1971! Defeat of a new levy may be conclusive, at least for some months, but defeat of a renewal is not final. A repeat election is scheduled promptly. When repeated, renewals nearly always win, usually by shaving the request.

Detroit is one of the largest school systems dependent on the willingness of the electorate to vote for more taxes, and that has not been a comfortable position for the Detroit school board since the 1957 levy defeat. Two efforts in 1972 to pass a new levy failed and a renewal lost three times. School would have closed six weeks earlier in 1973 but for an emergency statute authorizing the Detroit board to impose a levy sans referendum.

How could the legislature exempt the Detroit schools from the clear intent and plain language of the state constitution? The constitution of 1962 retained the venerated Fifteen-Mills section, but a sentence was added. "The foregoing limitations shall not apply to taxes imposed for the payment of principal and interest on bonds." The legislature authorized the Detroit board to issue bonds for the extraordinary purpose of current operating expense, with the bonds secured by future property and city income tax revenue. The devious statute is a patent contradiction of the intent of the Fifteen-Mills provision, but "what is the constitution among friends?", particularly when confronted with "a fact and not a theory."

Table 2-11
Michigan School Levy Elections

	1968	1969	1970	1971	1972
Renewals					
Elections	na	na	na	472	418
Approved				325	346
Percent				69	83
Additional					
Elections	na	na	na	302	207
Approved				112	92
Percent				37	45
All types					
Elections	591	659	666	774	625
Approved	374	410	441	437	438
Percent	63	62	66	57	70

Data source: Michigan Education Association.

Table 2-12
Outcomes of Michigan Levy Elections by Type of Levy, July-September 1972

Type of Levy	Won	Lost	Pct. Won	Size (mills) Range	Size (mills) Mean
Additional only	6	10	38	1-8	3.8
Renewal only	12	6	67	11-18	9.6
Combination	11	3	79	4-30	10.3

Data source: Michigan Education Association.

The frequency of levy and bond defeats became so alarming to education groups by 1968 that they launched a drive to curtail or abolish the system. A novel alternative was presented in 1969 by the ad hoc Governor's Commission on Educational Reform: a uniform state-imposed property tax instead of the existing local property taxes. The proposal was for complete state financing of the basic operating budgets of the schools, with local revenue restricted to a small optional local levy by referendum for "enrichment purposes."[12] The proposal was endorsed fulsomely by the governor but not by the legislature.

After three years of futile effort to pursuade the legislature to sponsor reform, the Michigan Education Association in 1972 used the popular initiative to place a revised proposal on the ballot. Proposal C was a mandate for the legislature "to establish a program of general state taxation and a method of distributing funds for the support of public school districts," with local support, voted in referenda for "enrichment purposes," not to exceed 6 mills. Proposal C prescribed, not a state property tax, but an overall property tax limit of 26 mills on state-equalized valuation, with all 26 mills assigned to local governments; it bore the rubric "Property Tax Reduction and Equal Educational Financing." The state was to secure the money from the state income tax, and to make that possible, Proposal C had a twin, Proposal D, authorizing graduated rates. Both went down to defeat.[13]

Missouri: Indefinite Levies

Until 1972, Missouri held about six hundred school levy elections annually. The constitutional tax limitation allows rural districts to levy only 6½ mills and urban districts 12½ mills. Until 1971, additional amounts could be authorized for one year by majority vote and for up to four years by a two-thirds majority. Since no district can operate on 12½ mills, Missouri school boards had to submit the tax levy to the electorate annually, or at least quadrennially, and it had to win approval; otherwise the rate reverted to the constitutional 12½ mills. Elections were repeated until one was successful; for example, the Hickman Mills school board announced that elections would be repeated every seventeen days.[14] In Independence, schools closed for ten days (November 1971) after a tax levy was defeated for the seventh time.[15]

In 1970, the system was revised by a constitutional amendment which permits levy authorizations without time limit. Subsequently, elections are only on rate increase proposals, and if a proposal fails, the existing rate remains in force. This reduced the volume of elections to one hundred fifty in 1972. Although it eliminated fiscal uncertainty, by stabilizing the tax rates, this amendment did not make it any easier for school boards to increase rates.

The referendum system is still a lively issue in Missouri, principally because the two-thirds majority required for a levy above 37½ mills is a high hurdle. Although fifty districts have surmounted the hurdle, repeated efforts by Kansas City and Independence schools have failed. Strenuous efforts to abolish the supramajority or to raise the amount that may be voted by a simple majority have been fruitless.[16] Either one requires constitutional amendment, always a formidable task.

New York: Annual School Budget Elections

School budgets are voted each May by residents of the school districts of New York outside the sixty-two cities. In 1962, the noncity districts con-

Library
I.U.P.
diana, Pa.

379.15 H18p
25/
C/

Table 2-13
Missouri Tax Levy Elections, April 1970

	Passed	Failed	Total	Percent Passed
Rates below 37½ mills				
Increased rate	108	37	145	72
Decreased rate	10	1	11	91
Same rate	144	14	158	91
Subtotal	262	52	314	83
Rates above 37¼ mills	14	16	30	47
Total	276	68	344	81

Note: Data are for districts which voted by April 7.
Data source: Missouri State Teachers Association.

Table 2-14
New York School Budget Elections

	1970	1971	1972
Districts voting	678	680	672
Defeats in 1st election	82	133	103
Percent voting	12	20	15

Data source: New York Department of Education

ducted eight hundred thirty-four budget elections, as more than a hundred districts voted two or three times. Only a fifth or less of the electorate chooses to participate, and the voting rate apparently fluctuates with the amount of taxpayer resistance. Observe the correlation of turnout and defeats in Table 2-14.

At the conclusion of the balloting in 1972, forty district budgets remained unratified. The law provides for that exigency. The board of education is empowered to levy a tax sufficient to defray the cost of those items specifically authorized by law and the cost of items deemed by the board to constitute "ordinary contingent expenses," an umbrella which covers salaries, supplies, utilities, and transportation—apparently about all routine expenses. There are no legal limits on the amounts of budgets or on tax rates. The community electorate is free to "buy" as much as it chooses, but evidently not always as little as it chooses if the school board disagrees and persists.

The traditions of community autonomy and direct democracy continue only in the village districts of New York, which although numerous contain only 30 percent of the state's school children. There is neither direct democracy nor autonomy in the cities, except for occasional tax rate referenda. For tax policy decision making, New York has three distinct systems. The schools of the six large cities are fiscally dependent, i.e., secure their funds by appropriation of the city council. The school budgets of the other fifty-six cities are not subject to approval by either the electorate or city councils, but those school boards are subject to tight maximum tax rates, ranging from 12½ to 20 mills, prescribed by the state constitution.

Those city districts whose legal maxima initially were below 20 mills may elevate the legal limit in increments of 2½ mills by a 60 percent majority vote in a referendum. Apparently the supramajority requirement and public attitudes make it difficult to raise the legal limits via the ballot box. As of 1970, the legal rate limits of all but eight cities were below 20 mills; but in nearly all cities the actual school levy was greater than the nominal legal limit, as budgets included items excluded by statute from the tax limit.

According to a recent publication of the New York department of education, the city districts are pressing their tax rate ceilings and are at a serious disadvantage in competition with noncity districts for hiring teachers. The department recommends that the rate limits be removed or modified and only a simple majority be required for rate increases.[17]

North Dakota: Five-Year Levies and Supramajority

The property tax is still the principal source of revenue for schools in North Dakota, and levy elections are routine, although less frequent than in some states. Referenda proposals are concerned with building funds; junior colleges; bond issues; and excess millage, which supplies a third or more of the revenue of most districts.

Counties are mandated to impose a school general fund tax of 21 mills, which school districts augment by referendum. North Dakota is one of the few states with a statutory ceiling for voted millage: no more than a 75 percent increase of the permanent county levy. The form of that statutory limit explains the peculiar units of the levy elections; a proposal is for a "50 percent increase." Most districts currently are levying a 50 percent increase, some less, and several levy 75 percent. Most authorizations are for the five years permitted by law.[18] When a levy proposal fails, it is rescheduled, usually for the same amount. Two elections usually suffice, although one district voted eight times in 1966-1967.[19] Passage rates have not declined sharply in recent years as they have in some states.

Supramajorities are required for operating levies and bond issues. A

Table 2-15
School Levy Elections in North Dakota, 1961-1970

Year	Levies	Passed	Percent
1961[a]	18	10	55.6
1962	75	55	73.3
1963	52	31	59.6
1964	88	64	72.7
1965	70	57	81.4
1966	110	68	61.8
1967	75	58	77.3
1968	93	58	62.4
1969	84	53	63.1
1970[b]	46	29	63.0

[a]July-December.
[b]January-June.
Data source: Bureau of Governmental Affairs, University of North Dakota.

Table 2-16
Impact of Sixty Percent Majority Rule, July 1961-June 1970

	Bonds	Levies
Proposals Failed	113	228
Proposals Passed	182	483
Vote about 50%	270	577
Total	295	711

Data source: Bureau of Governmental Affairs, University of North Dakota.

simple majority suffices for a 25 percent increase levy, but most proposals are large enough to require a 60 percent affirmative vote, as do bond issues. The supramajority standard has been responsible for a third of the operating levy defeats and three-fourths of the bond defeats.[20] The supramajority rule does not, however, exert a profound restraint on the volume of property taxation; its principal effects are delay and more voting. The bond issues do pass, usually without being scaled down and the schools do get built, after a year or two and after two, three, or four elections. Three-fourths of the defeated operating levy requests are also eventually authorized with no changes.

Ohio: Short-Term Levies

"Voting for levies in excess of the rate limitation has become a way of life in

Ohio. In fact, local governments—particularly school districts—could not operate effectively without recourse to excess-levy referenda."[21] The constitutional property tax maximum in Ohio is 10 mills; the prevailing tax rates are in the 30-40 mills range. No wonder every election day is tax levy day in Ohio. All classes of local government rely to some extent on extramillage, but schools are the most dependent. The property tax is the source of 60 percent of the operating revenue of the schools, supplying over a billion dollars annually.

Ohio became a leading practitioner of direct democracy quite inadvertently. The legislature enacted in 1910 an aggregate property tax limit of 15 mills, with the qualification that additional amounts might be authorized by referenda. The limitation was inserted into the constitution in 1929, and was reduced to 10 mills in 1933. Subsequently, a court ruling specified that the limitation applies to payments of debt; the tax limit thereby became also a debt limit, in the sense of requiring a referendum for all bond issues. The constitutional maximum remains an unrealistic 10 mills, but another law specifies that to qualify for state foundation grants a school district must levy at least 20 mills.

Popular control is maximized by a short tether; most levies are for brief terms. Five years was the maximum until 1959, when school districts (only) were permitted to vote indefinite-period levies of not more than 10 mills and larger levies for ten years. The bulk of levies continue to be for terms; consequently numerous ballot proposals are for extension of a prevailing rate rather than for more. Buckeyes distinguish "new" levies, "renewals," and "combinations"—a renewal at a higher rate. Half of the ballots are renewals, which are ratified perfunctorily—99 percent pass. As economists have long known, the *proper tax* is the prevailing one. The few combinations also usually win, but new levies are another matter. Although in the halcyon 1950s, Ohio voters were remarkably generous to their schools[22]—in 1954, they approved 86 percent of the bond proposals and 98 percent of the new levies—by the 1970s, the approval rate had dropped to 40 percent.

Nine-tenths of the levies are scheduled concurrently with primary and general elections in order to avoid election expense and to achieve high participation. There was an additional incentive prior to 1967 for avoiding special elections; a 55 percent majority was required. November is the preferred date, because officials are aware of the positive correlation to turnout and levy success in Ohio. There also is an incentive "to go" in May, the Ohio three strikes policy. A levy may be voted three times in a calendar year. If a levy fails in May, it can be repeated in November and, if necessary, at a December special, with the campaign theme of "the last chance to save our schools." Most specials are repeats and an unusual volume is indicative of a poor year for new levies.

Table 2-17
Ohio School Operating Levies, 1970-1972*

Year	New	Renewal	Combi-nation	All	Approved New	Approved All
1970	386	306	30	718	37%	67%
1971	238	310	19	577	42	70
1972	156	218	10	384	39	75

*Exclusive of approximately fifty special elections annually.
Data source: Ohio Education Association.

Table 2-18
Size and Volume of New School Levies, Ohio

Year	Number Below 5 Mills	Number Over 5 Mills	Percent Passed Below 5 Mills	Percent Passed Over 5 Mills
1964	260	43	71	51
1965	165	22	41	59
1966	185	43	51	58
1967	172	57	60	47
1968	175	129	68	59
1969	146	146	42	42

Data source: James S. Ginocchio, *Fiscal Policy Making by Plebiscite: Local Tax and Bond Referenda in Ohio* (thesis, Bowling Green State University, 1971), p.46.

The amount of additional taxation approved annually has not declined as much as the shrinking new levy passage rate suggests, because of a simultaneous trend of larger levies. Currently the average, including renewals, is 8 mills. Surprisingly in this period of increasing taxpayer resistance, statewide, large levies have been as successful as small ones.

The importance of Ohio tax elections was publicized nationally by the spectacular wave of school "closings" in the 1967-1971 period, when a score of systems, including Dayton and Youngstown, exhausted their treasuries and suspended operation for a few weeks. The fiscal condition of the schools has since been ameliorated without changing the system. The supramajority voting requirement for levies at special elections was discontinued; the qualifying millage for state aid was raised; and, most importantly, the enactment of a state income tax made it possible to increase state aid substantially. In a hard-fought statewide referendum in November 1972, school groups and their coalition allies resoundingly defeated a proposal to repeal the new income tax.

Oklahoma: Annual Tax Levies

Levy elections are as old as the state. Oklahoma's constitution of 1907 was the first to contain an overall property tax limit:[23] "the total taxes for all purposes ad valorem basis shall not exceed in any taxable year 15 mills on the dollar." Subsequent amendments have raised the standard school tax rate to 35 mills for operating and a few more for the building fund.

School boards are authorized to levy 20 mills without a plebiscite, and none fail to use all that authority. The constitution authorizes the voting of two additional one-year levies, a "local support" levy and an "emergency" levy, not to exceed 10 and 5 mills respectively. Levies may also be voted for a building fund, and in 1973, 567 of the 642 school districts did so.[24]

Results of levy elections are unreported, but the assistant state superintendent for finance estimates that, since 1960, annual passage rates have been in the range of 92-97 percent—surely the highest passage rate in the nation.[25] The extraordinary liberality of Oklahoma voters may be related to a legal provision, enacted two generations after the constitution, which allocates a large portion of state support money for "Incentive Aid," which is apportioned by the number of mills of local property tax in excess of 20 mills up to 35 mills. Ergo, a vote for a local tax rate of less than 35 mills is a vote to forfeit some "Incentive Aid."

The rare defeats of emergency aid and support levies occur in two circumstances; usually, "when the school administrator has not informed the electors that the Incentive Aid of a district will be reduced if these mills are not levied;[26] and occasionally, because of a local "school fight," like that in Oklahoma City in 1970, when a court mandated plan for racial integration of the schools nearly resulted in defeat of three levies and stimulated forty-five thousand votes in contrast to the previous record of nine thousand.[27] Several participants voted on only two of the levies, because they could not "present an ad valorem tax receipt." The letter of the antiquated constitution's property tax limitation was being honored as its intent was being utterly negated. The tax receipt no longer is required.

Oklahoma seems to have remedied the paramount disadvantages of the tax election system. By a little ingenuity, the schools have achieved a degree of revenue stability, and at an enviable level. It also appears that Oklahoma now has the forms of direct democracy without its substance.

Oregon: Annual Budget Elections

An extraordinary amount of school policy voting occurs in Oregon. Annually there are elections on the budgets of both the local districts and the countywide intermediate districts. There also are frequent referenda on community college budgets, bond issues, special tax levies for serial bonds, and—a unique Oregon institution—changes requested by school boards in the district's "tax base."

Most of the district and county referenda are held concurrently with the school board elections in May. Although electoral approval of the district budget is not a legal imperative, it is a financial necessity for all but a handful of districts. Consequently, elections are repeated until the budget is ratified—in 1972, the electorate in one district voted on the school budget on May 1, July 10, August 7, September 11, and October 5. Approval of the 350 district budgets required 504 elections in 1970 but only 420 elections in 1972.[28]

Most school boards trim the budget slightly for a repeat effort. In the sixty local districts which voted more than once during 1972, forty-two budgets were trimmed before passage, sixteen were passed at the original figure, and two were passed at a slightly higher amount.

Voting characteristically is light at school special budget elections, usually attracting 25-30 percent of the registered voters. A few districts have higher participation rates and some repeats generate more interest, e.g., the fifth election mentioned above attracted 47 percent of the electorate.[29]

The Oregon system is similar to the systems in New York and New Jersey, with several exceptions. Oregon has no alternative provisions for tax levy authorization when school budgets are not ratified by the electorate; and budget elections occur in all districts, including Portland, which was obliged to shorten the 1971-1972 school year after requests for a budget increase were defeated overwhelmingly three times.

The Oregon law has a superficial resemblance to Colorado's electoral approval being required for budget increases in excess of 6 percent, but the two systems are profoundly different and Colorado has few referenda. The difference is that the base of the Colorado limitation sans referendum is the budget of the preceding year, whereas Oregon's limitation derives from the historical "tax base" of each county and school district. The actual "tax base" of each unit of local government is the figure computed by annual increments not in excess of 6 percent from the dollar amount of the budget in 1916, the year of the property tax limitation amendment of the state constitution. To the extent that a local unit in some years did not hike the budget by 6 percent, its current official tax base is less than 6 percent compounded from 1916. For a local unit established since 1916, the computation begins with its initial budget.

The historical tax base of nearly all districts, local and intermediate, is ridiculously inadequate. In many instances it is one-sixth or less of the

Table 2-19
Oregon School Financial Elections, 1972

Type	Districts	Elections	Passed	Pct. P.
Budget elections				
Local districts	322	420	321	76
Intermed. districts	27	28	17	61
Community colleges	9	14	9	64
Special tax levies*	26	31	11	36
Bond issues	33	42	15	36
Tax base changes	14	16	1	6
Total	431	551	374	68

*For serial bonds
Data source: Oregon Department of Education, *Financial Statistics*.

Table 2-20
Oregon School Budget Elections

	1970	1971	1972
Local districts			
No elections	16	na	17
Held elections	350	331	322
1 election	222	242	262
2 elections	70	53	29
3 elections	29	29	22
4 elections	10	8	7
5 elections	3	—	1
Number of elections	504	464	420
Intermediate districts (counties)			
Held elections	27	26	27
Successful elections	14	15	17
Number of elections	32	28	28
Community colleges			
Held elections	9*	9	9
Successful elections	9*	9	9
Number of elections	16*	18	14
Summary			
Districts held elections	386	366	358
Number of elections	552	510	462
Passage rates-local districts			
Passed with 1 election	63%	73%	81%
Successful/total elections	70%	71%	76%

*Estimate.
Data source: Oregon Department of Education, *Financial Statistics*.

current school budget, e.g., the base of Coos district 9 in 1972 was $739,398, but the budget approved by the electorate was $7,576,634.

Any district may establish a new tax base by voting a specific amount at a special election, although this rarely occurs. Eleven local districts and three community colleges conducted tax-base-change elections during 1972, but all, except one community college, were unsuccessful. One may presume that refusals of tax-base-change proposals usually are intended to be votes against "more taxes." If so, that evidently is another instance of fiscal illusions and self-deception, since Oregon expenditures for public schools, despite use of the historical tax base, are slightly higher than those in adjacent states.[30] The practical effect of refusing to change the tax base is retention of direct democracy.

The importance of the referendum system in Oregon is augmented by that state's strong reliance on the property tax, which supplies 68 percent of public school revenue.[31] The 1916 constitutional amendment had the same unanticipated consequences as those in Michigan and Ohio. It did not produce a firm tax ceiling with occasional referenda affording flexibility. Instead it altered the policy-making process, transferring final responsibility for school budgeting to the electorate. In some respects it is *sui generis* and constitutes participatory democracy at the maximum.

Washington: Annual Levies and Supramajority

The voters of Washington considered five hundred referenda in 1970, four hundred seventy-four in 1972. As in Oregon, the levy elections are the product of a tax limitation law enacted in 1932 and inserted into the constitution in 1944.[32] In both states, as in Michigan and Ohio, the constitutional freeze was accomplished by popular initiative, and that single exercise of direct democracy unwittingly begat direct democracy as the method for the fiscal policy-making of schools.

The overall rate limitation of 40 mills is substantially higher than the figures in other states with an overall tax limitation, but schools in Washington are no less dependent on voted millage and they confront the highest voting hurdles. In other states the schools are assigned most of the "within" millage, but Washington schools got only 12 of the 40 mills when assessment ratios were 25 percent or less. When a 50 percent ratio was established officially (but not fully observed), the legal maximum for schools was adjusted accordingly to 6 mills. The effective legal maximum for schools is therefore 3 mills or less of market value, depending on local assessment practice, a rate that is inadequate for most districts even though Washington schools derive only 40 percent of their revenue from local sources.[33] Most districts depend on extramillage, and "special levies" has become a misnomer. The constitutional provision has created the same anomaly as elsewhere: The legal tax rate limit is 6 mills, but 14 mills must be levied to qualify for state equalization grants.[34]

The requirements for passage of special levies are stringent, to say the least. Authorizations are for only one year, and schools may schedule only one repeat election. Passage requires a 60 percent affirmative vote at an election in which the number of voters is at least 40 percent of the number in the preceding regular election. That unique participation standard disqualified twenty-one proposals which received a 60 percent affirmative vote in 1970 and twenty-one in 1971 but none in 1972.[35] Was that because of greater interest in 1972, the scheduling of more levies and bonds concurrently with regular elections, or because of a lower turnout at the preceding regular election? This suggests that scheduling may be even more of a strategic decision in Washington than elsewhere. The 40 percent requirement is particularly critical for Seattle, which had to conduct repeat elections in 1970 and 1971 to pass its usual thirty to forty million dollars operating levy. The larger the community, the more difficult it is to get people to vote on school measures.

Special elections are expensive. A League of Women Voters publication reports that the costs of special elections average a dollar per voter, which may eat up as much as a tenth of the extramillage, and that during the 1956-1966 decade, the election expense of the Seattle school district exceeded a million dollars.[36] Participatory democracy is not free.

Quantitatively, 1972 was a golden year for Washington schools—two hundred million dollars of extramillage was voted; but from another standpoint it was a disaster. Success was achieved in only 77 percent of the voting districts, compared with 89 percent success the previous year, and 25 percent of the operating levies were two-time losers; the increased amount for operating levies resulted in the shrinkage of building-fund levies to the vanishing point; and there were over a hundred repeat elections as compared to seventy in the two previous years. Evidently most districts did well in 1972, but also more districts were in trouble.

The rising number of unsuccessful districts appears to be the inevitable concomitant of increasing reliance on special levies. This is principally a city problem in Washington—all but twenty of the eighty-six districts without special levies in 1968-1969 had less than a thousand pupils.[37] To cope with the hazard of levy defeat, districts are adopting a minimax strategy, segmenting the levy with the hope that part of the package will pass. A 1973 statistical bulletin from the office of the superintendent of public instruction warns that if the governor and legislature "fail to come to grips with the school district finance problem," it is possible that the volume of levies submitted will increase and the success rate of recent years may decline "drastically."[38]

Perhaps in no state has the tax levy system been the subject of as much controversy. It appears to be a perennial issue. During the 1960s, school forces made four futile efforts to amend the constitution. "The public

Table 2-21
Washington School Levy Elections

	1970	1971	1972
Operating levies			
Passed first election	216	208	175
Failed	73	94	118
Passed second election	31	43	36
Failed	39	25	73
Total	359	370	402
Districts			
Submitted levies	261	262	259
Passed some levies	231	233	199
Amount ($million)			
Passed	175	172	200
Failed	19	23	44
Failed twice	15	18	27
Building fund levies			
Passed	21	14	7
Failed	15	11	10
Amount passed ($million)	7	1	.5
Bond issues	105	48	55
Total referenda	500	443	474

Data source: Superintendent of Public Instruction.

displays a strong attachment for the system, perceiving it as a valuable means of controlling school boards,'' says an observer.[39]

The most recent effort was the Temporary Levy Study Commission, a blue ribbon body with ample funds for research. Its reports in 1971, two tomes of a thousand pages, are curious displays of how to avoid grasping the nettle. The opening pages sound the schoolmen's tocsin:

The common school system of Washington State is in trouble financially and politically. Costs state-wide are far surpassing the state government's guaranteed expenditure level, and even as the need for special levies increases, voter support seems to grow more precarious.

Widespread dependence on the special levy does not, however, attest to any popularity for it among educators, or among voters, for that matter. The special levy is one of the most unreliable and unstable possible sources of school funding. . . . Even when levies are passed, the affected communities pay a cost in educator and layman energies diverted to the levy from other concerns, and the levy campaigns are often conducted in an atmosphere of such extraneous vagaries that even the weather may affect an election outcome. Few other governmental budgets could survive such testing.[40]

The commission's few recommendations, principally to adjust and augment state support, said little about special levies. It "recognized the likelihood of continued reliance on special levies at the local level for the next few years.''[41] Evidently the Special Levy Commission viewed the system as untouchable, and therefore proposed to mitigate its impact by more state support.

West Virginia: Five-Year Levies and Supramajority

Tax levy elections in West Virginia are a by-product of a unique tax limitation scheme written into the constitution in 1932: overall maximum rates, ranging from 5 to 20 mills, for four classes or property; and allocation of the tax between classes of local governments, the schools being assigned slightly less than half (see Table 2-22). County school boards may, for example, levy—without referendum—4.59 mills on farms and owner-occupied residences and 9.18 mills on most other property.

This is one of the most ingenious, inflexible, and stringent tax limitation schemes ever devised. The ceiling is exceptionally low—probably closer to 10 than 15 mills since most property is in Class II, the school district share is smaller than in most states, and the requirements for voting extramillage are formidable. Provisions for voting "additional" millage were not established until 1958. "Additional" millage requires a 60 percent affirmative vote, authorizations may not exceed five years, and additional millage may not exceed 100 percent of the constitutional rates. The latter restriction is unusual and highly significant. Few states limit the amount of millage that may be voted, and such limits appear to be inconsequential except in North Dakota and West Virginia. Currently (1972-1973), thirty-two of the forty-five school districts are levying the maximum additional millage.[42]

If any property tax limitation scheme could be effective, this is it, and the pattern of prevailing rates indicates that it exerts restraint on taxes and school budgets. The constitutional rates prevail in eleven districts; thirty-two have doubled rates by voting the maximum additional millage; only twelve districts have intermediate rates. Even with full-value assessment

Table 2-22
Maximum Property-Tax Rates (mills) Prescribed by West Virginia Constitution

Class		Overall	Schools
I	Intangibles and agricultural personalty	5	2.295
II	Farms and owner-occupied residences	10	4.59
III	Other property in rural areas	15	9.18
IV	Other property in municipalities	20	9.18

Data source: *Public School Finance Programs, 1971-72*, p. 363.

and generous state support and federal aid, austerity appears to be the norm for West Virginia schools.

Election statistics are unavailable. Certainly the volume is modest, perhaps only a dozen in some years. But levy elections manifestly are important for West Virginia schools, since half of the operating millage of most districts is dependent on them. A "prime problem" of the system, says a state official, is the supramajority vote; most levies would pass with a simple majority rule.[43] Nonetheless, the passage rate should be extraordinarily high, since few elections involve rate increases, and most future elections will be concerned only with renewals. Elections to initiate additional millage, however, may generate acute and protracted controversy, as in Randolph County, which voted six times before passing a new levy in 1968. Following the fifth election, sanctions were imposed by the National Education Association for inadequate support of the schools, and prior to the sixth one the entire faculty threatened to resign. Evidently the threat was credible.[44]

Other States

The Alabama constitution prescribes a maximum tax rate of 12½ mills, but numerous school districts have been authorized by particular amendments to levy additional amounts (usually 5 mills) by referendum. The Alabama practice of enacting special legislation by constitutional amendment produces an unique mode of school tax election. The special levy is legitimated if a majority of the votes in the specific school district are favorable to the amendment. If not, "subsequent elections may be held at intervals of not less than one year."[45] Since most authorizations are permanent, referenda are not frequent, although a third of the school systems have special levies.

Table 2-23
Arkansas School Levy Elections

	1970	1971	1972
Renewed at same rate	291	324	302
Voted increased rate	57	36	52
Rejected increased rate	26	20	16
Voted decreased rate	—	1	2
Total	374	381	372

Data source: Arkansas Department of Education.

All school taxes in Arkansas are voted at the annual school election in March. The ballot states the number of mills proposed for operating expense and the number for debt service. There are no repeat or special elections. If the vote on the total millage proposed is negative, the existing levy continues another year.[46] This system appears to achieve popular participation in policy making and control with a minimum of commotion and revenue instability.

Operating levies in excess of 10 mills in Florida require voter approval, and may not exceed two years duration. Levies for longer periods are authorized simultaneously with bond issues.[47] No records are kept of operating levy elections, but the number of fiscal referenda is small —according to a newspaper report, there were twenty-one in 1967 of which fifteen were approved.[48] Bond referenda are more significant than operating levies. During the period 1964-1968, only one bond issue failed; subsequently 40 percent have failed. "A number of our school districts have had bond issues defeated which required them to go on double sessions or use portable facilities," a state official reports.[49]

Georgia school districts may vote to exceed the constitutional limit of 20 mills. An authorization remains in effect until repealed or superceded by another referendum. Only ten of the one hundred eighty-eight districts have voted extramillage, and in 1973 only six were levying more than 20 mills.[50] The low frequency is a result of the relatively high official ceiling, market-value assessment (at least officially), and the small proportion of school revenue derived from the property tax—only 30 percent.[51]

Until 1973, referenda were required for operating levies above 30 mills in Idaho. Thirty-two districts had voted extramillage in 1972-1973; fifty-three had the statutory maximum of 30 mills; and thirty districts had lower rates. General fund levies are limited to one year. The 1973 legislature reduced the maximum levy authority of school districts without an election to 27 mills. Building fund levies also require referenda. They may total 15 mills, need a two-thirds majority, and are for periods up to ten years. Two-thirds of the districts currently have building fund levies.[52]

A Kansas school district may budget or expend for operating expense no more than 105 percent of the amount budgeted per pupil in the preceding year, unless more is authorized by the board of tax appeals or a referendum. There are no records, but the department of education states that about a dozen budget referenda occur annually and approximately half of the proposals are approved.[53]

Levy elections are new in Minnesota, first authorized by a 1971 law. A levy authorization remains in force until repealed by another referendum, which may be called by petition as well as by the school board. The system has not caught on, although a levy of 30 mills is required for the state foundation grant.[54] During the first eighteen months, only five small districts held elections and three proposals failed.[55] According to a state official, "School officials seem disposed to refuse to use the referendum on the assumption it will fail anyway."[56] Instead they have sought special consideration for their districts from the legislature. That is a plausible tactical choice in view of the legislature's record of generosity and the absence of any local tradition of voting for taxes. Only 30 percent of school operating revenue is raised locally.

Mississippi school districts may levy 3 mills by referendum in addition to the 25 mills statutory limit. The authorization remains in effect unless repealed by another referendum or by petition of a majority of the electors. No statistics are available, but apparently most of the districts have proposed extramillage and most proposals have been successful. A state official states that there is no dissatisfaction with the system, but many districts would like to hike the legal limit to 30 mills.[57] A backdoor referendum may occur on building levies, which may be levied without referendum unless the proposal is "adequately opposed by petition of the electorate."[58]

Montana's six hundred and seventy school districts hold numerous levy elections, because extramillage authorizations are for only one year. The ballot states both the amount to be raised by additional taxation and the number of mills. Most districts have voted levies, which account for about a fifth of the revenue of Montana schools. The dependence of the schools on the voters is related to assessment practices. The state foundation program requires local levies of 25 mills in elementary districts and 15 mills in high school districts. Boards may levy up to 125 percent of the foundation program amount without a referendum. Why should more be needed? Residential and agricultural property is taxed at 30 percent of assessed value, and the customary assessment ratio is 40 percent. Hence 40 mills amounts to only 5 mills on true value. Levy elections occur concurrently with school board elections in April. If a proposal is defeated, there usually is time for only one repeat effort. School boards are advised by the Montana Education Association not to reduce a repeat proposal lest that engender a credibility gap.[59]

School budget elections are held annually with school board elections in February in the smaller communities of New Jersey. Such type II districts are those township, town, and borough school districts which have not opted to be under the law for city (type I) districts. In February 1973, the budgets were defeated in one hundred sixty-nine of the five hundred thirty-three type II districts. When a budget is defeated, the school board certifies to the county board of taxation the amount "necessary to provide a thorough and efficient system of public schools."[60]

Only two districts of South Dakota are using their authority to vote extramillage. Three legal provisions contribute to the nonuse of extramillage. The taxing authority of school boards sans referendum is unusually large—40 mills on nonagricultural property; a 60 percent assessment ratio; and the fact that extramillage requires a 75 percent majority.[61]

Twenty-eight mills must be levied by Utah school districts in order to secure maximum benefit for the state equalization program. Up to 10 additional mills may be levied if the electorate chooses to institute the "state-supported leeway" program, as have twelve of the forty districts. Voted authorizations may be modified or terminated only by another referendum.[62]

Schools in Wyoming make scant use of their authority to vote extramillage—only nine districts in 1971 and only two in 1972. Referenda also are required to establish a building fund.[63]

Types of Referenda Systems

The preceding inventory discloses three distinct types of school referenda; each originated in different historical eras and apparently for different purposes. The budget elections of New York and New Jersey are elements of the traditional school meeting, an institution that also continues in rural New England and some townships of the Midwest.[64] Some districts conduct budget and school board elections at the annual meeting; others have an election day. These are instances of referenda which originated as deliberate choices of direct democracy. Oregon, however, acquired the institution quite inadvertently, although now it is the most extensive practitioner. The systems of Delaware and Arkansas also appear to be instances of intentional direct democracy. *All* school taxes are voted by the people and, as in New York and New Jersey, there are no legal restrictions on the amount of budgets and tax rates.

The most recent type is the budget limitation system of Colorado and Kansas, where referenda are required for budget increments greater than 5 or 6 percent. Manifestly the purpose is inhibition of spending and taxing rather than participatory democracy, and popular participation will be infrequent except in a period of rapid inflation. The purposes are similar to those of the tax levy systems, but the method is more flexible and reasonable. It does not contemplate a flat ceiling on taxes, merely some insurance against extravagance. The earlier method of a legal maximum tax rate could be characterized as a meat axe tactic; this might be called a modern, enlightened method of expenditure control. It appears to be the referendum system most satisfactory for school officials: Rarely will they be obliged to wage campaigns; they can make modest increases in budgets and tax rates; and there is no revenue instability. Although Oregon originated the device, its sponsors erred by tying it to the year 1916; consequently it metamorphosed into the annual budget election system.

Arkansas has a unique system, in form a tax levy type, but more similar in nature to budget elections. Actually the school budget is voted each year, although the ballot question is the tax rate rather than the budget amount. If the principal interest of New York voters is the tax rate, the systems are essentially the same. Both achieve popular participation and stability of school revenue, but an Arkansas school board does not have the option of raising the tax rate without the voters' approval.

Tax levy elections are the modal type of school referenda, existing to some extent in twenty-two states. Excepting the recent Minnesota case, they owe their existence to property tax limitation laws, and definitely were not intentional choices of plebiscitary democracy. Although a few of the systems antedate the First World War, this institution is largely a legacy of the Great Depression, when a wave of tax delinquency furnished ammunition for "tax relief" agitation. It is anomalous that those depression-era expedients survive forty years later even though the referendum adjustment valve has nullified the purpose of those laws. Their survival is the joint result of embalming them in state constitutions, inertia, the unpopularity of the property tax and the illusion that the laws are significant inhibitors, and possibly because direct democracy has come to be attractive to some communities and some people, either as intrinsically gratifying or as a control device. Turnout rates suggest, however, that school referenda are not valued highly by a majority of the populace.

The tax levy systems fall readily into two classes: the twelve indefinite-period levy systems and the ten term-levy systems, counting California and Ohio in the latter class. Clearly, this is the most consequential of the interstate variations. The volume of referenda in the indefinite-period systems is a minor fraction of that in the term levy states. Thus, Illinois has far more districts than Ohio and Michigan, but less than a third as many elections. The volume is small in all but two of the indefinite-period states and great in all but two of the term levy states.

For school officials, the indefinite system is much preferable. There are few occasions to go "begging" and less energy and time are consumed by campaigns. Revenue is more stable and, above all, there is no danger of losing a renewal. Loss of a new levy request may be painful, but loss of a renewal can be catastrophic.

Another conspicuous variation is that while most states permit each school district electorate to tax itself as much as it pleases, a dozen states prescribe maximum amounts of extramillage. Some of the parameters are so high that they are irrelevant, e.g., 38 mills in Louisiana and Utah, 40 in Illinois, and 50 in Michigan. The others also appear to be of inconsequential effect except in North Dakota and West Virginia, where numerous districts are at the legal ceilings.

In seven states, the "economy" objective of legal tax limitation is being realized in an appreciable degree because of supramajority voting rules: 60 percent in Washington, West Virginia, and for increases of more than a fourth of the legal rate in North Dakota; two-thirds for building funds in Idaho and Kentucky and for operating levies above 37½ mills in Missouri;

and 75 percent for any extramillage in South Dakota. The record confirms that the supramajority hurdle has a potent effect in Washington, West Virginia, and North Dakota, and is the source of intense dissatisfaction by education groups. A few levies lose in Washington because of the forty percent turnout rule, but that requirement is not an antimajoritarian device; nor was the former 55 percent majority rule for special elections in Ohio.

Thus, a few states practice local popular sovereignty with the system rigged against the schools by supramajority rules or by limits on the amount the local sovereigns may "buy"; whereas New York and New Jersey restrict popular sovereignty in the other direction by permitting a school board that has the temerity to adopt the budget it prefers even after it has been rejected twice by the sovereigns. The foundation and equalization program laws of several states also restrict popular sovereignty by exerting a potent influence on decisions, notably in Oklahoma. West Virginia appears to occupy one pole, with the greatest obstacles to choosing expenditures, and Oklahoma is at the other, with its Incentive Aid program which makes the local sovereigns almost rubber stamps.

There has been relatively little change in the state systems since the depression. Levy referenda were discontinued by North Carolina[65] and begun by Utah in 1967 and Minnesota in 1971. Colorado switched from the levy system to the 6 percent increment system, and Missouri to indefinite-period levies. Michigan, in 1948, facilitated passage of levies by switching to simple majority voting and facilitated bond issues by authorizing levies of twenty years. Ohio also has assisted the schools by repealing the 55 percent rule for special and primary elections, by authorizing indefinite-period levies, and by raising the extramillage requirement of its foundation program.

Perhaps the most extensive changes have been the inclusion in state grant formulas of local share or local effort requirements which "encourage" communities to vote extramillage.[66] Unlike California, Ohio, or Oklahoma, the Michigan law does not "dictate" extramillage, 7 mills suffices to qualify, *but* the grant formula specifies that the local share of the foundation program is the yield of 20 mills based (significantly) on state equalized valuation.[67] The Oklahoma Incentive Aid is maximum encouragement. Realistically, it has established a statewide school tax rate of 35 mills, and makes the annual levy elections sheer ritual. Oklahoma schools are assured 35 mills regularly, while the cherished political symbols remain undisturbed—the constitution still reads 15 mills, and taxes are voted by the people.

A political scientist will notice some intriguing phenomena in the school referenda systems. They abound with illustrations of the significance of myths and political symbols. The Oklahoma referenda exhibit the distinction between manifest and latent functions. The manifest function is providing revenue for the schools, but the voting continues even though only ritualistic because of the latent functions. One observes how frequently reality diverges from appearances. Compare the tax rate provision of the state constitution of any state with a current tax duplicate. The Oregon law appears to be identical to the budget limitation laws of Colorado and Kansas, but the reality is annual budget elections. It is surprising that rock-ribbed Ohio is an enthusiast of direct democracy, while it appears natural for Oklahoma, the cradle of populism, to have the greatest volume of school referenda—about two thousand annually. But a brief inspection of the statutes reveals that most of the Sooner referenda are peculiar, and more authentic direct legislation occurs in Ohio.

The school referenda systems are laden with reminders of the importance for political systems of historical accidents, phenomena scarcely ever mentioned in textbooks.[68] Because of a drafting *faux pas*, the Oregon tax limitation scheme metamorphosed into a different system. In contrast to its Ohio and Michigan neighbors, Indiana has no constitutional tax limitation and hence no school referenda, because its constitution can not be amended by popular initiative, which in turn is because the progressive constitution drafted by the Indiana legislature in 1913 was ruled invalid by the courts,[69] whereas the progressive movement wrought new constitutions replete with I & R in Ohio and Michigan. If the depression may be called an accident, then most of the tax limitation laws were accidental and so was the way their referenda provisions subsequently evolved. Indeed, school districts became the one important arena of direct democracy in America by a huge accident. No matter how the state systems are counted—as twenty-seven, or forty-seven including the bond election states, or as seventy-four—only a handful originated as intentional choices of popular government. Since most were incidental devices of expenditure control schemes which have been largely abortive, if school referenda now are regarded as intrinsically good, this is a large scale instance of goal displacement.

Notes

1. $2.95 was the median rate for K-12 districts in 1969.

2. Richard F. Carter and William G. Savard, *Influence of Voter Turnout on School Bond and Tax Elections* (Washington: U.S. Office of Education, 1961), p. 12.

3. Colorado Department of Education, "A Review of Colorado's Public School Foundation Act" (1972), p. 7.

4. Roger C. Mowrey, letter of April 25, 1973.

5. *Public School Finance Programs, 1971-72* (Washington: U.S. Office of Education), p. 128.

6. Joe M. Aspin, director of finance, Kentucky Department of Education, letter of April 10, 1973.

7. Most are operating levies; in most years the number of bond issues is less than ten. The bond board's records do not distinguish them, and the department of education has no records.

8. *Cipriano* v. *City of Houma*, 395 U.S. 701 (1969).

9. Michigan acquired direct democracy locally in 1933 by the happenstance of a rarely used direct democracy provision in the state constitution: The Fifteen-Mills limitation was initiated by petition. Subsequently city officialdom in league with schoolmen used the same provision to divert 78 percent of the yield of the state sales tax, the "Diversion Amendment" of 1946. That direct democracy foray also spawned unforeseen deleterious results, a decade of financial stringency in the state government and attendant acrimonious politics.

10. Denzel C. Cline, *Pay the Piper* (Bureau of Governmental Research, Michigan State College, 1953), pp. 20-21.

11. That relic of 1933 also was retained in the 1962 constitution, but it has been rendered a nullity by recent Supreme Court decisions.

12. *Report of the Governor's Commission on Educational Reform* (September 20, 1969), p. 10.

13. Proposal C lost by 1,816,178 to 1,325,130 and Proposal D by 2,097,949 to 962,556.

14. United Press International dispatch, Akron *Beacon Journal*, July 10, 1970, p. C3.

15. Akron *Beacon Journal*, November 10, 1971, p. G3.

16. Marvin Shamberger, director of research, Missouri State Teachers Association, letter of May 13, 1973.

17. "State Limits in the City School Districts," (New York: State Education Department, December 1970).

18. Details for 711 elections are contained in Lloyd B. Omdahl et al., *Nine Years of School Bond and Mill Levy Elections in North Dakota*, Special Report No. 24 (Bureau of Governmental Affairs, University of North Dakota, January 1971).

19. Ibid., p. 39.

20. Ibid., p. 3.

21. *State Constitutional and Statutory Restrictions on Local Taxing Powers* (Washington: Advisory Commission on Intergovernmental Relations, 1962), p. 70. Hereafter cited as ACIR, *State Tax Limitations*.

22. The support of Ohio schools during the 1950s was generous only as measured by the approval rate of levies and bonds.

23. ACIR, *State Tax Limitations*, p. 28.

24. Letter of Assistant Superintendent Cecil E. Folks, June 19, 1973.

25. Letter of Cecil Folks, April 3, 1973.

26. Ibid., letter of June 19, 1973.

27. Associated Press dispatch in *The Blade*, Toledo, Ohio, January 28, 1970, p. 3.

28. All figures are from the annual "Summary of Financial Elections," compiled by the Oregon Department of Education.

29. The Oregon tables list the number of registered voters in each school district as well as the yeas and nays.

30. Cf. U.S. Office of Education, *Digest of Educational Statistics, 1971.*

31. *Public School Finance Programs, 1971-72*, p. 270.

32. ACIR, *State Tax Limitations*, p. 30.

33. (Washington) Temporary Special Levy Study Commission, *Summary Report and Research Reports* (March 1971), p. 9. Hereafter cited as Levy Commission *Report*. The schools also receive 2 mills collected by the state government.

34. *Public School Finance Programs, 1971-72*, p. 351.

35. Data from the annual statistical bulletins of the Superintendent of Public Instruction, No. 163-70 (December 1, 1970), No. 4-72 (January 7, 1972), and No. 5-73 (January 8, 1973).

36. "The 40%/60% Voting Requirement," *Facts and Issues* (No. EL-5, July 1966).

37. Levy Commission, *Report*, p. 10.

38. Bulletin No. 5-73, p. 2.

39. Professor James Best, University of Washington.

40. Levy Commission, *Report*, pp. 7-8.

41. Ibid., p. 45.

42. Data supplied by West Virginia Department of Education.

43. Assistant Superintendent of Education Aaron Rapking, Jr., letter of April 9, 1973.

44. *Federal Times*, December 18, 1968, p. 22.

45. The language of most of the thirty-five amendments.

46. Frank M. Cannady, research supervisor, Arkansas Department of Education, letter of April 2, 1973.

47. Ray Bazzell, Florida Department of Education, letter of April 4, 1973.

48. *The Blade*, Toledo, Ohio, April 24, 1968, p. 44.

49. Bazzell letter.

50. O. H. Joiner, associate superintendent, Georgia Department of Education, letter of April 10, 1973.

51. *Public School Finance Programs, 1971-72*, p. 85.

52. Ibid., p. 89; Idaho Superintendent of Public Instruction, "Tabulation of Tax Levies, 1972-1973."

53. Dale M. Dennis, director of school finance, Kansas Department of Education, letter of April 9, 1973.

54. *Public School Finance Programs, 1971-72*, p. 174.

55. S. Walter Harvey, director of research, Minnesota Department of Education, letter of June 13, 1973.

56. Harvey letter.

57. Ruby M. Thompson, supervisor of finance, Mississippi Department of Education, letter of April 11, 1973.

58. *Public School Finance Programs, 1971-72*, p. 174.

59. Ibid., p. 188; and information supplied by the Montana Education Association.

60. *New Jersey Statutes Annotated*, sec. 18:7-82.

61. Gale D. Schlueter, director of statistical services, South Dakota Department of Public Instruction, letter of April 9, 1973.

62. *Utah Code*, sec. 53-7-24; *Public School Finance Programs, 1971-72*, p. 325.

63. Mark A. Peterson, Wyoming Taxpayers Association, letter of June 19, 1973.

64. Some school meeting communities are rural only in the eyes of the law, e.g., villages and densely populated areas on the fringe of cities. The senior author participated in school meetings in such a community in Lansing Township, Michigan.

65. Prior to 1967, North Carolina school districts could supplement the state appropriation, which supplies the basic operating budget, only by referendum; but since discontinuance of the referendum requirement, a referendum would only be a device for pressuring the county commissioners. A. C. Davis, controller, North Carolina State Board of Education, letter of April 12, 1973.

66. In debate at the 1973 session of the Ohio legislature of the proposal to raise the millage qualification to twenty-four mills, opponents said it would require a hundred districts to raise their taxes.

67. *Public School Finance Programs, 1971-72*, p. 163.

68. The lacuna is a result of trained incapacity in the political science guild. Now that political science has matured (professedly) by abandoning descriptive studies in order to get on with the "important work" of developing explanatory theory, direct observation of the "nuts and bolts" of governments and politics is unrespectable research. The fashionable activity is "state policy research," which is in hot pursuit of some presumed determinants of public policies in the fifty commonwealths by correlating state expenditures for welfare, miles of highway, teacher salaries—*any* "output" that is handy in the *Statistical Abstract* with *any* other tables therein, which thereby are ipso facto "inputs" and "explanatory variables." The mountain of supersophisticated correlations and factor analyses seemed to have proved beyond the shadow of a doubt that income is a potent explanatory variable and that the correlation is positive, i.e., that rich states spend more for public schools, welfare, etc. than do poor states.

The policy research enthusiasts will not learn why Michigan expenditures for schools catipulted c. 1950 (that "unexplained variance" of only 70 percent); indeed they will never know it occurred nor the impact of the diversion amendment and the aforementioned modifications in 1948 of the referendum system. If they are ever told that some states have school referenda and others do not, they will never find the explanation by indiscriminately plugging figures of Census Bureau publications into canned computer programs. Explanation of some of the most significant interstate policy differences requires some actual knowledge of state and local history and politics, which has been woefully lacking in state policy research journal articles. There have been significant and valid findings, but some of the announced profundities long were common knowledge among public finance practitioners.

69. *Ellingham* v. *Dye*, 178 Ind. 336 (1913).

3

The Decisions of the People: Voting Rates, Approval Rates, and Determinants

This chapter treats several related subjects: voting rates and the factors that influence turnout; approval rates of bond proposals by number and amounts; and the approval rates of operating levies. Numerous factors that may affect approval rates are examined, especially the effect of supramajority requirements for approval of bonds. The chapter concludes with an investigation of the relationship of outcomes to turnout rates.

Suffrage Restrictions

One of the factors contributing to the generally low voting rate in school elections through 1970 was that in fourteen states only "taxpayers" could vote.[1] The effect of that archaic suffrage restriction varied tremendously among communities and states, being less in those states where the spouses of taxpayers could vote. In one of the recent Supreme Court cases, 60 percent of the registered voters of the Louisiana city were ineligible to vote on fiscal questions.[2] Obviously the effect was almost negligible in some places that boast of being a "community of homeowners" where taxpayers' spouses could vote. Naturally there are no statistics on how many nontaxpayers would have voted if legally eligible, but the influence of this disfranchisement can be gauged by reference to the proportions of renters and homeowners that vote in school levy elections. Thus, data available from election surveys of twenty communities in four states show that homeowners and their spouses ranged from 54 percent of the persons voting—in one sample, to more than 80 percent—in three samples.[3]

The taxpayers only era was ended on June 29, 1970 by a Supreme Court decision.[4] The familiar rationale for this anachronism, i.e., that only taxpayers have a stake in bond elections, was rejected by the Court on two counts. First, all residents of a community are affected "substantially" as consumers by bond questions relative to the provision of public facilities. And second, the exclusion rests on the fallacy that only "taxpayers" pay taxes. So-called nontaxpayers actually pay property taxes indirectly by rent cheques and purchases of other goods and services, since a large portion of property tax revenue is from assessments of commercial property and landlords and commercial firms shift the burden.[5]

Table 3-1
Voting Rates and Results of School Levy Elections in Cuyahoga County, 1960

	May Primary		November General	
	Yes	No	Yes	No
Bedford	2,085	2,318	6,849	3,173
Cleveland	64,831	71,189	210,977	77,237
Cleveland	59,685	75,864	206,713	77,732
Garfield Hts.	2,436	3,927	10,428	5,428
Parma	8,925	10,764	29,957	15,970
Rocky River	1,863	2,615	6,018	4,025

Data source: Archives of the Ohio Secretary of State.

Voting Rates

Three generalizations may be made about the turnout for school referenda: the voting rate usually is rather low; there are tremendous differences, from less than 10 percent in some elections to over 90 percent in others; and amazing fluctuations may occur in the the same community. Data on the subject are meager; only three states issue voting rate statistics.[6] Those disclose that there are substantial interstate differences—distinct degrees of "low." The rate for budget elections in New York was 20 percent in 1971 and only 12 percent in 1970. The median rate in California levy elections is consistently 40 percent. The median rate for Oregon budget elections during 1972-1973 was 32 percent.[7] The mean rate of a national sample during the period 1948-1959 was 36 percent, and exceeded 50 percent in less than a fifth of the elections.[8] However, school election voting is not low everywhere. Although never measured, the average voting rate in Ohio can be estimated as between 60 and 70 percent.[9]

The voting on the Lane County, Oregon community college levy during 1972 illustrates the gyrations that can occur in a community. The turnout on June 23 was 62 percent, only 12 percent for the repeat election on July 18, and 18 percent for the third round on August 29.[10] Lane County is not unique; observe the contrasts in the five Ohio cities of Table 3-1.

What factors influence voting rates? Little is known, because there has been so little investigation. One would expect it to be related to community characteristics and traditions, the substantive importance of the issue, and the amount of opposition and community conflict. Surely that is true, but the evidence is only fragmentary. Occasionally there is a convergence of voting stimuli as at Bowling Green, Ohio in November 1966. In that college town which prided itself on passing school proposals, the addition to the district of a rural area suddenly triggered intense and well organized opposition. There were elements of both rural-urban conflict and town and gown. Aggressive campaigns were waged by both sides, and the concurrence of four tax levies added up to a wad of money in the eyes of numerous taxpayers. The result was more voter interest in the referenda than the offices, and a turnout of 83 percent.

A national survey of voting rates during the period 1948-1959, sponsored by the United States Office of Education, found correlations between turnout rate and the three characteristics of school districts listed in Table 3-2.[11] The differences are modest, but each pattern is logical. One would expect some correlation of voting rate with the proportion of school revenue derived from the local property tax. Nor is it surprising to find that the voting rate is lower in high-school districts than in elementary-school districts, and highest in K-12 districts—the more grades, the larger the proportion of parents in the electorate.

Trichotomizing the national sample by size of school enrollment[12] revealed a rather strong negative correlation of district size and voting rate in bond elections, as one would expect. The findings for tax elections contradict logic, our observations of elections in Ohio, and other scattered data. These findings may be erroneous because of the sampling, which was adequate for bond elections but unsatisfactory for tax elections. Fortunately the Oregon statistics permit an investigation. Grouping the districts into seven class sizes, measured by the number of registered voters, reveals a sharp, monotonic association between district size and voting rate.

Although nonpecuniary issues are undoubtedly the primary concern in some school elections, they are difficult to quantify. It is, therefore, exceedingly difficult to measure their impact on voter turnout. However, evidence of a correlation between turnout and the monetary importance of elections is available from the aforementioned higher turnout in districts that are above the median in reliance on the property tax; the Oregon tax base change elections; and data on the size of bond issues in the national sample (see Table 3-4). Evidently there is considerable economic motivation and rationality in bond elections.

Oregon's tax base change elections, which occur concurrently with regular elections, provide additional evidence that voting rate is related to the monetary significance of referenda. In 1972, the voting rate on tax proposals averaged 60 percent at the primary and 75 percent in November. Few voters ignored that ballot, and evidently many went to the polls in May expressly because of the tax issue. Oregon's tax base elections are *sui generis* in more than one respect.

The Office of Education study cross-tabulated turnout and a host of variables in search of determinants, but overlooked the paramount one: the importance of the concurrent election, if any. Observe the contrasts of the

Table 3-2

Voting Rate by District Characteristics National Sample, 1948-1959*

By Type of School		By Proportion of Revenue from Local Sources	
Secondary only	26.8%	Districts below median	30.8%
Elementary only	29.2	Districts above median	34.5
Elem. and Sec.	34.3		
By Size of District**	Bond	Tax	Both
Large	30.0%	34.5%	31.1%
Medium	33.5	33.2	33.3
Small	39.3	33.5	37.2

*2630 elections in 583 districts.

**Trichotomizing the distribution measured by enrollment.

Data source: Carter and Savard, *Influences of Voter Turnout,* pp. 17-18.

Table 3-3

Voting Rate by Size of School District, Oregon Local Budget Elections, 1972

Registered Voters in District	Elections Held	Voting Rate over 30%		Mean
		Elections	Percent	
Below 1000	190	133	70	39%
1000-1999	71	36	51	32
2000-4999	68	27	40	29
5000-9999	58	14	24	26
10000-14999	10	2	20	25
15000-49999	17	4	24	25
50000 & over	6	0	0	22
All districts	420	216	52	33

Data source: Oregon Department of Education.

Table 3-4

Turnout Rate by Amount of Bond Issue, National Sample, 1948-1959

Amount of Bond Issue	District Size		
	Small	Medium	Large
Lowest quartile*	29.9%	22.7%	25.0%
Second quartile	41.4	32.9	26.4
Third quartile	46.4	35.1	30.0
Highest quartile	38.5	37.9	35.8
N elections	(396)	(610)	(585)

*Quartiles are within each district size group.

Data source: Carter and Savard, *Influence of Voter Turnout,* p. 16.

turnouts of the Cuyahoga County cities in May and November, Table 3-1, and those of Portland budget elections in 1971 and the tax base change referendum coincident with the 1972 primary, Table 3-19. The pattern is unmistakable. With rare exceptions, turnout is low for referenda scheduled as special elections or at school meetings. It is higher for those on school board election day—the practice in several states. It is likely to be somewhat higher for those concurrent with primary elections, and it is maximal for those at presidential elections. This explains why New York and Ohio are at the poles of the turnout continuum. Budget elections in New York are held at the school meeting or a school election the following Wednesday; whereas most school referenda in Ohio occur at general elections. (Ohio has one each year.)

Low participation in school referenda scheduled separately or at school board elections may be disconcerting, but it is hardly mysterious. Primary, municipal, and county elections normally attract only a minor fraction of the electorate, often as little as 30 percent. The concern to "keep the schools out of politics," which has led to separate elections for school boards exacts its price in low participation. In terms of democratic values, 33 percent participation (Oregon) appears to be a steep price when 60 or 80 percent could be had by using general elections. Also it seems to be an unnecessary cost. Regular elections are used in Ohio by choice of the respective school boards, and there are no visible untoward effects.

No one really knows how much turnout is affected by get-out-the-vote campaigns of school groups, but it is our impression that campaigns usually have more effect on who votes than on the number of votes. Indubitably some campaigns do boost turnout substantially. One of the most successful was the 1959 campaign in Detroit, which raised the vote total to 306,000 compared to 238,000 in the preceding levy election,[13] but the turnout rate was still only 44 percent. Tallies of three successive Portland elections in 1971 suggest that strenuous campaigning preceded the third effort, yet the turnout was advanced to only 30 percent.[14] It obviously takes a general election, particularly in a metropolis, to produce a high voter turnout.

The evidence is clear that in metropolises high turnout is usually advantageous for school proposals, sometimes tremendously so, but that is difficult to achieve. School officials are caught on the horns of a dilemma. If the proposal is scheduled at a special or school board election, voting will be very light; if it is scheduled with a general election, a large fraction of the voters will ignore the proposition ballot, as did 27 percent of the Detroit voters in 1966 and 32 percent in 1968 (see Table 3-17).

Trends: Volume and Approval Rates

Comprehensive data are available for school bond referenda since

1961-1962, published by the United States Office of Education. There are no comparable nationwide data for tax levy referenda, but we have secured data for over several years for a few states, which suffice to delineate trends.

The trends of bond elections, presented in Fig. 3-1 and Table 3-5, are not obscure—up and down and leveling off. They are not, however, of equal dimensions and timing. There has been less change in the dollars than in the election statistics. The annual number of elections has declined from two thousand to only slightly more than a thousand, but there has been less fluctuation in the value of the bonds considered. School boards continue to request more than three billion dollars annually, as the decrease in the number of proposals has been largely offset by the increase in their size. The average proposal in 1962 was $1.3 million; it was $2.7 million in 1972.

The sharp decline in the amount proposed by school boards between 1969 and 1972 can be accounted for by stabilizing school enrollments and increasing voter resistance since 1968. Measured in dollars, the approval rate skidded from nearly 80 percent in 1965 to 41 percent in 1971. When nearly four billion dollars was requested in 1969, the approval rate plummeted, and school officials have since been obliged to temper their aspirations and scale down the amount requested. The approval rate edged up in 1972, at a dollar volume slightly more than that of a decade ago, but of course it bought substantially less bricks and mortar because of inflation.

It would be a mistake, however, to ascribe the decline exclusively to "taxpayer resistance." Each September from 1950 through 1968, facilities had to be provided for a million more children than the previous year, but the increase slowed to seven hundred thousand in 1969 and only three hundred thousand in 1970.[15] The postwar baby-boom tide had ended and the era of expansion was over. Hence the post 1969 shrinkage in the amount proposed has an objective basis. Enrollment stability affected not only the volume but also the character of bond proposals; the portion for expanded facilities has been shrinking. Surely it is easier to "sell" to the electorate bond proposals for additional classrooms to handle expanding enrollments than proposals for maintenance, renovation, and replacement construction. During the expansive 1950s, the approval rate was over 80 percent.[16] That change in the character of school construction projects may be the principal cause of the recent slump in approval rate. "Taxpayer resistance" may be as much a function of the nature of the construction proposed as of price tags.

Comprehensive data on bond elections of each year since 1962 are presented in Appendix Table B-1. Appendix Table B-2 furnishes a state-by-state summary of bond elections for the decade 1962-1971. In absolute terms, California is found to be in a class by itself; it conducted a tenth of the elections during that decade, and authorized more than three billion

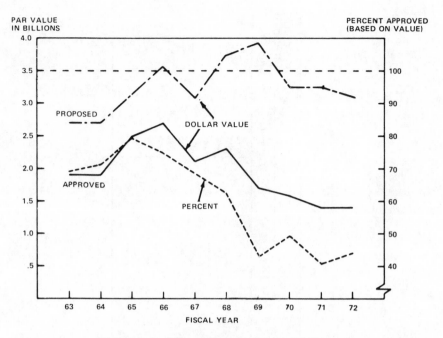

Figure 3-1. School Bonds Approval Rates

dollars—a sixth of the amount for the entire nation. The electorates of five other populous states also authorized more than a billion dollars. New York ranks sixth in absolute amount, because bonds of the state's largest school systems are not subject to referendum. Pennsylvania is absent from Table 3-6, because it has very few referenda.

When amounts approved are standardized as per capitas, amazing interstate differences appear. The per capita amounts approved during the decade ranged from $41 in West Virginia to nearly five hundred in Alaska. Some high-expenditure states are to be found in all regions of the country except the South, which indicates that income (or wealth) is a major influence. Voter attitudes are also important. For example, Nebraska expenditures were substantially greater than those of any of the six adjacent states except Colorado. Similarly, Minnesota and Michigan expenditures were substantially higher than those of the other states in the Great Lakes region. Other influences were operative in some states. Geography and rapid population growth in conjunction with high income account for the extraordinary expenditures of Alaska and Nevada. Population growth also contributed to higher expenditures in Texas and California than in the other western states except Nevada. A wave of school consolidation may have augmented expenditures in some states.

Table 3-5
Number and Outcomes of School Bond Elections, 1962-1972

Fiscal Year	Elections Held	Issues Approved	Percent of Issues Approved	Value (million) Proposed	Value (million) Approved	Percent of Value Approved
1962	1,432	1,034	72.4	$1,849	$1,273	68.9
1963	2,048	1,482	72.4	2,659	1,851	69.6
1964	2,071	1,501	72.5	2,672	1,900	71.1
1965	2,041	1,525	74.7	3,129	2,485	79.4
1966	1,745	1,265	72.5	3,560	2,652	74.5
1967	1,625	1,082	66.6	3,063	2,119	69.2
1968	1,750	1,183	67.6	3,740	2,338	62.5
1969	1,341	762	56.8	3,913	1,707	43.6
1970	1,216	647	53.2	3,285	1,627	49.5
1971	1,086	507	46.7	3,337	1,381	41.4
1972	1,153	542	47.0	3,102	1,365	44.0

Data source: U.S. Office of Education, "Bond Sales for Public School Purposes," various issues.

Table 3-6
Value of School Bonds Approved, 1962-1971

Amount (million)		Amount per Capita	
California	$ 3,157	Alaska	$497
Texas	2,105	Nevada	253
Michigan	1,554	Minnesota	202
Ohio	1,234	Texas	188
Illinois	1,172	Michigan	175
New York	1,004	Vermont	163
Subtotal	10,226	California	158
Other		Colorado	158
states	9,108	Nebraska	156
Total	19,334	Rhode Island	153

Surprisingly, approval rate is not a reliable indicator of the generosity of the voters. The expenditures of some states with high approval rates were quite low, e.g., Louisiana and Arizona. Only three of the top ten states in per capita amounts authorized were among the top ten for election success. Two high-expenditure states, Minnesota and Michigan, had low approval rates. Either the proposals are exceptionally large in those states or there are numerous repeats and the school boards get the money by persistance. In Michigan it is the latter; there are numerous repeat elections.

It seems reasonable to expect tax levy election trends to match those of bonds. The absolute amounts of tax levies approved necessarily have not diminished. But the trend for approval of tax rate increases is similar to the trends observed for bond elections. Nationwide, there was a rather steady decline of the approval rate during the 1960s, which halted in 1970. This is demonstrated by the only available state time series graphed in Figure 3-2. The irregularities in the trend line of each state are caused principally by fluctuations from year to year in the volume of requests. (Observe the correspondence of volume and percentage approved in the California, Michigan, and North Dakota tables in Chapter 2.)

The varied location of the state graphs in Figure 3-2 is a function of different tax levy systems, which produce different proportions of new and renewal levies. Illinois is lowest on chart, because it has an indefinite levy system. The proximity of the Ohio, North Dakota, and Michigan graphs shows that the proportion of renewals is approximately the same in those short-term levy systems. The best yardstick for interstate comparisons is the approval rate of new levies, which in the 1970s was slightly above 40 percent in Michigan and Ohio and 30 percent in Illinois.

The approval rate of new levies also is the best trend measure. Unfortunately, Ohio is the only state with the records. Observe the amazing correspondence of the Ohio new-levies approval rate and that of bonds nationwide during 1967-1972.

Table 3-7
School Bond Approval Rates, Decade 1962-1971

| | High Approval Rates | | Low Approval Rates | |
State	Percent Approved	Amt. per Capita	State	Percent Approved	Amt. Per Capita
Connecticut	92.6	$146	Kansas	61.5	$ 71
Louisiana	92.5	104	Minnesota	60.5	202
New Mexico	91.0	141	California	58.0	158
Utah	89.5	137	Michigan	58.0	175
Nevada	88.9	253	Wisconsin	56.7	105*
Pennsylvania	88.9	26*	South Dakota	56.3	76
South Carolina	88.9	11*	Iowa	55.4	106
Rhode Island	87.4	153	North Dakota	54.1	83
Alaska	86.2	497	Ohio	53.1	116
Arizona	85.4	97	West Virginia	41.0	41

*No referenda for bonds issued by some school systems.

Data source: From Appendix Table B-1.

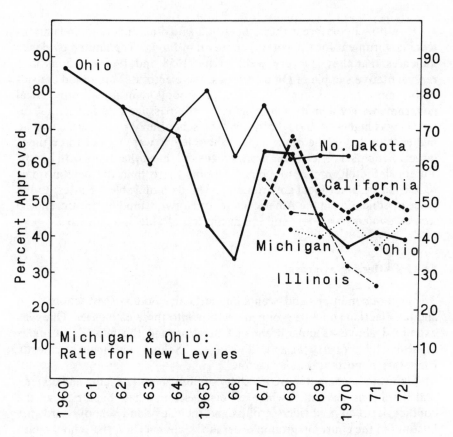

Figure 3-2. Approval Rates of School Tax Levies

Table 3-8
Relative Success of Schools and Other Local Governments Sample of Eleven Ohio Counties

	No. Approved		Pct. Approved	
	1958	1968	1958	1968
Bonds				
Schools	60	36	69	77
Other units	22	14	56	54
Op. Levies				
Schools	97	145	87	73
Other units	74	107	64	79

Data source: James Ginocchio, "Local Tax and Bond Referenda in Ohio," pp. 28, 33.

How do schools fare in the competition with other functions and units of local government for the voters' approval of funds? The limited evidence indicates that they do very well. In the 1958 and 1968 elections in a representative sample of Ohio counties, the electorates approved considerably more bond issues and levies for schools than for all other local governments combined; and in general, the passage rate for school requests was higher. Although, by 1968 the school-levy passage rate was no higher than that of the other units, school levies were two or three times larger. Schools have been far more successful than other units with bonds. Voters definitely prefer to "buy" schools more than the capital items requested by other local governments. The data of Table 3-8 attest to the place of education in the American creed. Notwithstanding the aforenoted trends, evidently schools still are at the top of voter preferences.

Factors Affecting Approval

The host of conditions and events that influence outcomes of school bond and tax elections may be grouped usefully into three categories. One was examined above—secular trends of taxation and the public's attitudes regarding the property tax and "high taxes." School enrollment manifestly is another important secular factor.

Opposite in character are a variety of idiosyncratic events and ephemeral conditions, several of which are discussed in other chapters, e.g., the conflict between civil rights groups and the Cleveland school board; the hostility to the court integration order at Oklahoma City; the school board decentralization controversy in Detroit and the coincident "busing" court order; disagreements over the location of new school buildings or their appurtenances; dissatisfaction with specific school policies or teachers or administrators; rural-urban antagonism or that between old-timers and newcomers; the existence of a reservoir of alienation, either temporary or accumulated. The impact of this class of variables on school elections defies standardization and generalization. The influence of some specific temporary condition on a particular election occasionally can be measured with some success, as we will illustrate; but about all that can really be said is that school elections are subject to the hazards of a melange of local and ephemeral events and conditions, as school officials well know.

School elections are not, however, entirely kaleidoscopic. In the third class of variables are those which are more than local and occasional, whose impact is somewhat lawful, which are susceptible to measurement, and for which there are available data. There has been some previous research on two variables: voter turnout and supramajority voting requirements. Others which merit notice are: size of bond and tax proposals;

frequency, timing, and ballot bunching; prevailing tax rates; the wealth of districts; and the provisions of state grant laws.

One nonephemeral variable, the taxpayer voting qualification, has been interred by the Supreme Court, a decision that diminished the color of American federalism more than one might suspect. Spouses were "taxpayers" in some states but not in others. Three states had interesting literal applications of Calhoun's venerable concurrent majorities theory. Passage of both bonds and tax levies in Louisiana required concurrent majorities of the individual taxpayers and the assessed valuation. Wyoming and Nevada permitted the propertyless to vote on bonds, but required concurrent majorities of the voters and the taxpayers.

A common belief among veteran local officials is that a coincidence of several expenditure proposals may imperil all of them; and in some communities officials engage in consultation and clearance arrangements to avoid "bunching."[17] Is this just folklore? Not entirely. The aforementioned Bowling Green election with three operating levies and a bond issue cum levy was a clear test. Only the picayune levy for "retarded children" could win on that overloaded ballot. (Who could vote against retarded children?) However, within a year the large school levy and the county home bond issue were presented singly and passed.

The one levy at Bowling Green that failed when repeated illustrates another consideration: the size of the clientele of a program is important. Penta County vocational school's problem was not mysterious. Spread over five countries; its clientele was too thin. It was not "our school" for the bulk of the voters, and the intensive campaign could not overcome that handicap.

One would assume that approval rate is related to the frequency of going to the well for two reasons: voter psychology, and proposals should have greater merit if school officials exercise more self-restraint. Thus, the approval rate of California levies in 1968 was phenomenally high with about half the normal volume of proposals. In North Dakota, the highest approval rate was in 1965 with seventy proposals; and when one hundred ten levies were requested the following year, the approval rate slid twenty percentage points. Also, we have observed that some of the states with the highest approval rates for bonds have few referenda. Wirt and Kirst computed the correlation of approval rates and frequency of bond elections during the 1960s. For the set of states requiring supramajorities, the coefficient was $-.30$, but only $-.16$ for those requiring only a simple majority.[18]

Sufficient time series data are available for measuring the approval-rate/frequency correlation for tax levy elections in three states. The coefficient is $-.30$ in California, $-.23$ in North Dakota, but nil in Ohio, where the secular decline was so great as to extinguish any association of approval rate and volume. A correlation coefficient of $-.30$ is not negligible, but in statistical terms it explains only a tenth of the variation.[19] Indubitably frequency of requests is an important factor within a community and statewide in years of a large fluctuation in volume, but overall and in the long run, frequency is less influential than casual observation might suggest.

In numerous instances the amount requested is a critical factor; indeed all fiscal referenda could be considered as a game in which officials are obliged to predict how much the voters will "buy." However, the data on this point present a mixed picture; there are striking inconsistencies. Here it is appropriate to distinguish three species of school referenda: bond issues, tax levies, and budget elections.

The most distinct linkage of amount requested and voter decisions occurs in Oregon budget elections. School boards often trim the amount of defeated budgets in order to get them ratified. In 1972, the budgets of sixty districts were rejected by the voters one or more times. On the second round, thirty-five boards proposed smaller amounts, but twenty-five stuck to the initial figure, and thirteen succeeded. When the one hundred fifty-seven repeat elections were over, thirty-five of the budgets had been reduced.

Repeat elections appear to be a bargaining process. For example, the initial budget of Lane District 69 was defeated badly in May and again in July. The board then pared its request by $23 thousand (a 2 percent reduction), but that was defeated by the same overwhelming margin. For the fourth effort, the board trimmed another $18 thousand, which also lost, although not so badly. Apparently the board regarded the third figure as rock bottom; it proposed the same amount for the fifth election in October. The budget carried by a comfortable margin, as the crisis—October—and no doubt a vigorous campaign drew a record turnout. The statistics show clearly that the decisive factor was turnout, but surely the calendar and fatigue also were significant factors.

The bearing of size on success of tax levies is confusing. When *all* levies are considered, the correlation of approval rate with size appears to contradict logic: In Michigan in 1972, the approval rate of levies of less than 5 mills was 58 percent, but 84 percent for those above 10 mills, and even for those over 20 mills! The same is true for Ohio. The anomaly results from putting new levies and renewals in the same bag. Renewals are large, usually in the 10-20 mills range, and they pass routinely in Ohio and sooner or later in Michigan; but not so for the smaller new levies, which are identified on the ballot as "new" or "additional." Size consequently is pertinent only to new levies.

The records of California, Michigan, and Ohio provide sufficient data for analysis here. Although new levies and renewals are not distinguished, the California Department of Education tabulates the "size of tax in-

Table 3-9
Budget Bargaining in Oregon Lane District 69, 1972

Election Date	Proposed Budget	Votes Yes	Votes No
May 1	$1,172,717	333	814
July 10	1,172,717	309	719
Aug. 7	1,139,612	280	590
Sept. 11	1,121,388	570	734
Oct. 5	1,121,388	1082	709
Previous budgets			
1971-72	1,022,899		
1970-71	958,502		

Data source: Oregon Department of Education.

Table 3-10
Approval Rate by Levy Size, Michigan, 1972

	All Levies		Pct. Won		Additions		Pct. Won
Mills	Total	Won		Mills	Total	Won	
Below 5	197	113	58	Below 2	82	51	62
5-9	148	112	67	2.0-2.9	37	14	38
10-14	122	103	85	3.0-3.9	34	12	35
15-19	70	58	83	4.0-4.9	16	5	31
20 & up	11	9	82	5.0-5.9	23	4	17
				6.0-6.9	7	0	0
				7.0-10	8	6	75

Data source: Michigan Educational Association.

crease.'' Levies with no increase are renewals; a fact obviously known to California voters, since the approval rate is 98 percent.

The effect of size on approval rate is different in each of these states. The response of California voters to size is displayed in Table 2-2. Size definitely is important; there is a distinct negative correlation, but only in the range between four and eight mills. Very large levies are as successful as those of eight or ten mills, and those of four mills do as well as smaller ones.

Currently size has more influence on levy success in Michigan than in California. The correlation is equally consistent and the approval range is much greater, from a 62 percent approval rate for new levies of less than 2 mills to zero for those of 6 mills in 1972. More than half of the successful proposals were less than 2 mills, whereas two-thirds of the successful ones in California are greater than 4 mills (which may be about equivalent to two

Table 3-11
Approval Rate by Levy Size, Ohio New Levies 1972*

Mills	Total	Won	Percentage
Below 2	45	14	31
2.0-2.9	37	16	43
3.0-3.9	29	6	21
4.0-4.9	19	9	47
5.0-5.9	21	11	52
6.0-10	13	8	61

*Elections of May 2 and Nov. 7.
Data source: Ohio Educational Assn.

in Michigan). Another conspicuous difference is that at the upper end of the size distribution, the approval rate levels off in California but bounces back in Michigan.

Levy size is less consequential for Ohio voters. When the 1972 elections are tabulated by one-mill intervals, it can be seen that size is not an important determinant of approval rate in Ohio. Proposals in the 3-mills interval were the least successful in 1972, and very large levies were the most successful. We are chary of post hoc speculation, and we will not hazard an "explanation" of these interstate contrasts. One commonality, however, should not be overlooked. All three states evidently contain communities with a great tolerance of school taxes. Some very high rate increases pass in California, and they are the most successful category in Ohio and Michigan.

There are numerous reasons why the association of bond size and approval rate might be slight. Often controversy about bond issues concerns substantive issues, such as the need for replacement of buildings; the location of new ones; revision of attendance districts, design, or facilities. Not infrequently a defeated bond proposal subsequently passes in a modified form and even with a higher price tag. (See Chapter 5 for some examples.) Also, size is a relative matter; it is a function of the object of the proposed expenditure. Four hundred thousand dollars is a picayune bond issue, but it may not have that appearance to a voter when it is designated for a swimming pool. (Pools are itemized separately in Michigan and usually defeated.) Size also is a function of the size of the jurisdiction; a $5 million issue is hardly the same size in Middletown and Megalopolis.

Nationwide data are unavailable, but information about the amount of each election is available for California, Ohio, and Michigan—more than a third of all school bond elections occur in these states. Evidently the importance of size varies considerably with the times. In fiscal 1969, size seemed to be of little concern to Californians, but in 1972 the prospects were bleak for any proposal larger than half a million dollars.

Table 3-12
Approval Rate by Size of Bond Issue

Bond Amount Mil. $	Number of Elections				Percent Approved			
	California 1969*	California 1972*	Mich. 1972	Ohio 1972	California 1969*	California 1972*	Mich. 1972	Ohio 1972
0-49	62	20	26	18	47	50	43	50
.5-.9	36	25	8	18	36	20	87	39
1-1.9	27	20	21	43	30	15	24	30
2-2.9	22	6	26	27	36	33	23	30
3-4.9	24	13	24	16	33	15	8	13
5-9.9	27	11	12	7	33	18	8	0
10-19	18	3	4	4	28	0	50	25
20 up	3	4	2	3	33	0	0	100
Unknown	—	—	8	—	—	—	50	—
All	221	102	131	136	37	23	29	32

*Fiscal years.

Table 3-13

Bond Approval Rate by Size per School Enrollment, Ohio, 1967 (percent passed)

Type of District	Size of Issue/ADM*		
	$50	$50-100	$100 up
City	80	100	100
Rural	76	60	50
Statewide	76	73	60

*ADM = Average Daily Membership.
Data source: Byron Marlowe, "Voting Behavior."

In the years when large cities pass bond issues, there may be considerable variation between approval rate measured by amount and approval rate measured by elections. Thus in 1972, the approval rate in Ohio was 32 percent of the elections, but 48 percent of the amount, as the electorates of Cincinnati, Toledo, and Columbus approved large issues.

The best way to measure bond size is as a ratio of the amount to the school system enrollment. One analysis using that yardstick in Ohio disclosed that relative size has less influence on voter approval in cities than in rural areas and small towns. There was a sharp negative association of approval rate and bond size per average daily enrollment outside the cities—only. "Voters in urban and rural areas have very different perceptions about what are proper amounts."[20]

The economic conditions within a community should have some effect on decisions in the voting booth. In exploring this premise, one investigator found that high local tax rates did not result in greater resistance to new levies and bonds.

In nearly every year the highest rates of voter approval of new issues occur in districts which have tax rates at both extremes of the existing property tax scale. Districts with average tax millage consistently have the most difficulty passing new issues. In the case of bond issues, the opposite of the common sense assumption is true—voter approval tends to increase with increased total millage.[21]

Another aspect of a community's economic condition is its wealth, particularly the assessed valuation per schoolchild. Tax proposals should be more successful in those districts with the most taxable wealth. In Ohio that hypothesis is half true; there is an association of approval rate and assessed valuation in city districts, but not significantly so in rural ones. This fact and the fact that levies pass even in districts with very high tax rates may reflect the influence of educational standards, particularly those mandated by statute.

Table 3-14

Approval Rate by Assessed Valuation per Pupil, Ohio New Levies, 1966 (percent passed)

Type of District	$10,000 or less	$10- to $20,000	$20,000 or more
City	50	52	62
Rural	51	53	54
Statewide	51	53	56

Data source: Byron Marlowe, "Voting Behavior."

Table 3-15

Effect of the Supramajority Rule in California

School Year	Percent Approved		Pct. Majority Vote	
	Elections	Amounts	Elections	Amounts
1966-67	40	29	81	82
1967-68	45	39	92	86

Data source: Henry W. Magnuson, "Results and Trends in California School District Bond Elections, 1954-1959," p.7.

Supramajority Voting Requirements

Passage of school proposals requires supramajority votes in fifteen states. Bonds require a 55 percent majority in Nebraska; 60 percent in Iowa, Mississippi, Oklahoma, New York,[22] South Dakota, Washington, and West Virginia; and a two-thirds majority in California,[23] Idaho, Kentucky, Massachusetts, Missouri, New Hampshire, and North Dakota. Supramajority requirements are embedded in state constitutions and apply to all local governments. Most are about a century old, legacies of the internal improvements and municipal-corruption scandals of the nineteenth century. Subsequently the practice has been extended by seven states to some or all tax levy elections. Although these requirements were adopted without reference to schools—in fact some antedate the public school system—their principal effect today is on schools.

The supramajority hurdles have tripped a large number of school bond proposals, particularly in California. In school years 1967 and 1968, for example, 40 and 45 percent of the proposals in California were approved, but 80 and 90 percent would have been without the two-thirds rule. When measured in dollars, the effect of the rule was even greater.

Supramajority restraints have been especially critical for repeat elections. During the period 1954-1959, seventy-seven California proposals were defeated at repeat elections; but only six of these polled less than 50 percent of the votes.[24] The two-thirds rule explains the enormous volume of bond elections in California. Elections are repeated and repeated, as in Berkeley where five unsuccessful attempts over twenty years preceded the passage of a school bond issue in 1948. Four elections in the period 1959-1961 failed, one polling 66.27 percent but not 66.67 percent.[25]

A study of the operation of the two-thirds rule drew these conclusions:

First, the very high rates of simple majority approval suggest that the local councils and boards submitting the proposals have been remarkably in tune with their electorates. Second, it is the two-thirds requirement that is responsible for almost all of the defeats—and for the *appearance* of discord. Although the requirement makes it seem so, the local councils and voters are not out of step.

Third, the effect of the requirement is not incidental, limited, or of minor consequence. Instead, its influence is both substantial and strongly repressive. Finally, the citizen and taxpayer suffers a twofold injury, especially in an era of rising costs and interest rates. First, he is denied the use of needed facilities, which the community wishes constructed, until a crisis enables a two-thirds majority to be mustered. Costs go up while he waits. The ironic result is that communities are forced not only to do without necessary capital facilities, often for long periods of time, but also to pay substantially higher prices when construction finally takes place.[26]

How many bonds and levies are thwarted by supramajority requirements in unknown. Data are available for one other state, North Dakota, where a 60 percent rule defeats a lot of bonds and levies. The effect of West Virginia's two-thirds rule was illustrated in the facts of the recent Supreme Court case challenging its constitutionality. The plaintiffs stated that Roane County schools "had not been basically improved since 1946 and fell below the state average both in classrooms and facilities." The suit was brought after five bond and levy elections in every one of which the affirmative vote had been above 50 percent. Significantly, *amicus curiae* briefs supporting the plaintiffs were filed by the Missouri State Teachers Association, the Seattle School District, the National School Boards Association, the Association of School Administrators, and the National Education Association.[27]

The Supreme Court opinions in the legislative apportionment cases, and a case overturning the Georgia county-unit election system,[28] furnished education groups with the argument that supramajority requirements are analogous to malapportionment of legislatures and hence also incompatible with the "equal protection of the laws" principle of the Constitution.[29] The Court had reasoned that malapportionments are discriminatory, because they "dilute" and "devalue" the votes of people in underrepresented constituencies.

The concept of "we the people" under the Constitution visualizes no preferred class of voters but equality among those who meet the basic qualifications. The idea that every voter is equal to every other voter in his State, when he casts his ballot . . . underlies many of our decisions. . . . The conception of political equality . . . can mean only one thing—one person, one vote.[30]

It is argued that if malapportionment is an unconstitutional discrimination because it devalues the votes of some people, then supramajority requirements also are unconstitutional, because "No" votes are given more weight than "Yes" votes.

When stripped to its essentials, the two-thirds requirement has the following results: (1) In effect, it confers *two* votes on every qualified citizen who, for whatever reason, opposes capital financing measures submitted by his locally elected governing body; (2) It gives *one* vote to each person who supports the proposals of his local government. This result seems doubly ironic. It means that the clear will of the community—expressed *both* by (1) a majority of an equally apportioned local legislature, *and* by (2) a majority of the voters participating in a bond referendum—can nevertheless be thwarted by a minority of the electorate. Thus the two-to-one advantage to the "no" vote contradicts the concept of voting equality.[31]

That argument acquired additional strength in 1969 when the Supreme Court struck down the Louisiana and New York taxpayer suffrage rules as unconstitutional discrimination, deeming the alleged state interests to be insufficient to justify "fencing out" nontaxpayers in elections which distinctly affected them. The principle of political equality in voting was reaffirmed and applied explicitly to referenda.[32]

Challenges occurred simultaneously in three states and were successful initially. In 1969, supramajority rules were held invalid by the state courts of California, Idaho, and West Virginia.[33] The latter one became the test case, as it was appealed to the Supreme Court, which disagreed with the state judges and sustained the supramajority requirement. From 1962 through 1969, the Court ruled in favor of political equality in voting; on June 7, 1971, it ruled in favor of one of the most blatant forms of political inequality. That *volte face* is one of the most striking instances of how abruptly the "higher law" occasionally can change when some changes occur in the personnel of the Court.[34]

Chief Justice Burger's opinion was not a model of scholarship and logic. It included such chestnuts as: "Wisely or not, the people of the State of West Virginia have long ago resolved to remove from a simple majority vote certain decisions as to what indebtedness may be incurred and what taxes their children will bear." With a little thought instead of resort to stale cliches, the Chief might have been able to figure out that most of the debt would be paid by those voting rather than by their children. With a little knowledge of public finance he might have realized that bonds not only are a standard practice, but are the only way most school districts can buy buildings. And he might have considered the fact that saving the children from debt is also saving them from having better quality schools. This decision saved them doubly, from having better buildings and a more adequate operating budget, since an operating levy also had lost because of the supramajority rule. The deference to the "resolve of the people long ago" is, as Jefferson said even longer ago, rule of the present generation by the dead hand of the past. Apparently the Chief was oblivious of the beautiful inconsistency of justifying a law because it prevents one generation from foisting debt on the next one, when that very law is the policy choice of "the people" of 1872. Nor did the Chief take notice that this is an instance of triple minority rule. A minority of the voters prevailed over the majority and over the school board elected by majority vote, and this minority rule system continues because supramajority votes are required for amending state constitutions.

There are two ways to deal with inconvenient precedents, explain them away or simply ignore them. Justice Burger did both. He did not explain why the one man-one vote principle bars dilution of the vote by the indirect path of malapportionment, but does not bar this direct, unblinkable devaluation, and one more extreme than several of the apportionment cases.[35] Instead he elected to refute the challengers' reliance on the Georgia county unit and the Louisiana bond cases. "The defect of those cases," he explained, "lay in a dilution of voting power because of group characteristics—geographic location and property ownership;" whereas the West Virginia constitution singles out "no discrete and identifiable minority" for special treatment. Since "there is no independently identifiable group or category that favors bonded indebtedness over other forms of financing," no sector of the population is "fenced out." By that logic, the challengers lacked two requisite characteristics; they were not a minority and not black or nontaxpayers or redheads. The Constitution protects minority rights but not the rights of a majority! Even the facts used in that specious reasoning were fallacious. After five elections in which the Yes votes were in the 52 to 55 percent range, palpably there were distinct groups in Roane County. Phrasing the ballot question as being a choice between issuing bonds or "other forms of financing" was preposterous for a case from Roane County—and many other school districts as well.

Perhaps the challengers were handicapped in getting the Court to face the fundamental issue—minority rule—by being obliged to latch their argument to the Equal Protection clause, since that was the peg used by the Court in the precedents. The issue would be more appropriate for the Due Process clause. The question should have been: is this system of minority rule due process of law? In any event the Chief engaged in little thought about that question. The minority rule matter was treated cavalierly, as though of little moment, by reference to the few supramajority provisions in the Constitution—Senate votes on treaties and impeachment (of dubious pertinence) and the Bill of Rights (as irrelevant as ironical), and by the profundity that "there is nothing in the language of the Constitution, our history, or our cases that requires that majority rule prevail on every issue." That was a shocking misrepresentation of the issue before the Court. The appellees were not asking that "majority rule prevail on every issue," only that the system be not rigged to prevent majority rule. A local judge in Idaho displayed more understanding of both facts and the issue:

There is no question that the one-third two-thirds requirement gives the one in the one-third class two votes as [compared] to the one in the two-thirds class . . . . By virtue of debasing the vote of the one who is voting Yes as against the one who is voting No, the minority can prevent an educational system, recreation, roads or anything else that requires the municipality to be indebted.[36]

The Supreme Court appointments subsequently assure that the supramajority rules will continue for the foreseeable future. Hence it is appropriate to assess their effects. Indubitably they have profound impact in numerous communities, including some outside California and West Virginia, but their overall effect on the volume of school bonds is less than the California or North Dakota election statistics suggest. Wirt and Kirst compared the passage rate (for the period 1961-1969) of the supramajority states in each region with the simple majority states, and found them identical, except in the West.[37] We have gauged it by a different way in Table 3-16, which indicates that the difference is not in the West; it is in California. During the litigation period California was temporarily in the simple majority set, and in two of those three years the passage rate of that set was lower than the rate of the supramajority states. For prior years, if California data are deleted, the passage rate of that set was never below that of the simple majority states.

The impact of supramajority rules varies considerably among the fifteen states. The supramajority requirement is irrelevant in Kentucky where nearly all issues are exempt from referenda by being classified as revenue bonds. Possibly it is inapplicable to most of the bond referenda in New York. It has not handicapped the schools of New Hampshire and Massachusetts, where four-fifths of the proposals of the last decade were approved. Nebraska's 55 percent rule is a low hurdle. The difference between three-fifths and two-thirds appears to be important. The only supramajority states that had approval rates in excess of 75 percent were two New England states and Oklahoma and Washington—two of the 60 percent rule states. Bonds in Washington, as well as tax levies, are subject to the 40 percent turnout rule, which in some years necessitates several repeat elections.[38]

Table 3-16
School Bond Approval Rate by Voting Requirements (percent approved)

	1966	1967	1968	1969	1970	1971	1972
Supramajority states	69.1	65.2	67.1	54.4	51.7	52.5	49.4
Simple majority states	74.3	67.2	67.6	57.8	53.7	45.4	46.1
Supra. less California	74.3	68.5	70.1	61.3	—	—	—

Data source: Appendix Table B-1.

Evidently the minority rule system has had its greatest impact in California and West Virginia. In the mountain state that is reflected in the 40 percent approval rate and an investment of only $41 per capita during the last decade. West Virginia schools have faced enormous obstacles: emigration, low income, and the two-thirds rule. In California there have been many defeats and repeats, with very few large issues approved recently. The overall effect in dollars, however, is less clear. Despite the low approval rate, the $156 per capita during the last decade placed California in seventh place among the referenda states, and far above Ohio, another industrial state with comparable income. But, particularly in light of her population explosion, it is impossible to determine how much the two-thirds rule has curtailed California's expenditures.

Supramajority rules seriously handicap passage of operating levies in Missouri and West Virginia. In North Dakota and Washington their principal effects appear to be delay and repeat elections, which of course deny schools revenue for that long. With respect to bonds, the foremost effects are delay and repeated elections, rather than curtailment of school construction. Of course, delay may be mighty consequential for a community. And repeat elections may make some contribution to the volume of community conflict. Allen Clem has characterized the supramajority rules as "change-resisters" and "spend-stoppers."[39] Evidently, overall and in the long run, they have not been very effective with respect to expenditures for school construction.

The Elastic Electorate: Turnout Effect

Participation fluctuates in the elections of all jurisdictions, but nothing matches the elasticity of the school election electorate. For the national sample of the Office of Education study, the mean voting rate was 36 percent with a standard deviation of 26 percent; i.e., the rate was either above 60 percent or below 10 percent in more than a third of the elections in that period. The knowledge that much smaller turnout differences have significant effects on presidential and state elections has stimulated much speculation and a few investigations of what effect turnout has on the outcomes of referenda. Plausible chains of logic have been spun out in both directions, and proponents have marshalled some hard data that support each of the contradictory hypotheses.

The most popular turnout-effect hypothesis is that there is an inverse relationship between turnout and success of referenda proposals, particularly school proposals (the locus of most of the research). Exponents of the negative relationship hypothesis say or imply that the effect is quite substantial. The reasoning is straightforward from the incontrovertible premise that low turnout is the norm. Since two-thirds or more of the populace "stay home," it is a plausible inference that the participants are those people with an uncommon interest in the schools, which should be parents, teachers, other school employees and their relatives, and perhaps some suppliers. The habitual voters also include some middle-class civic activists whose civic pride and norms include that of unswerving "support for our schools." Thus the defacto school electorate has two elements, a hard core of loyalists and a fluctuating proportion of other "disinterested" persons. To the extent that this analysis is factually correct, it follows that low turnout is propitious for school measures. Then, as the turnout rate rises, the passage rate declines as the composition of the electorate is modified by increments of voters who are not hard-core loyalists. A large turnout of course may mobilize more loyalists, but there is less margin for expansion; there is far more elasticity to the other component.

There are two distinct reasons why high turnout may have an adverse effect on the success of school measures. High turnout not only diminishes the proportion of the electorate that perceives direct benefits, but also is likely to "bring in more lower-income and less well-educated groups which are more likely than other groups to oppose increases in local government costs," as Tom Flinn has noted.[40]

Prima facie evidence of the validity of this hypothesis abounds. The PTA furnishes the troops of every school election. School officials, who themselves belong to the community's elite, routinely solicit support from elite associates and "explain" the "need" for the tax levy or the bond project to the rotary clubs. A "citizens committee" of local notables is often fabricated; and school elections are regular projects for the League of Women Voters. There also is a formidable amount of statistical evidence which appears to confirm the hypothesis: The California data on tax levy elections (Table 2-4) and the massive national sample in the Office of Education study of "The Influence of Turnout" reveal the same pattern of negative correlation.

In both bond and tax elections, in all district sizes, there was greater turnout at elections where issues were defeated. The relationship of turnout to outcome was greatest for bond elections in large districts and for tax elections in small districts.

Regularly, more elections succeeded than failed when turnout was low. The point where success turned to failure varied from bond to tax elections, and from large to small districts. There were more failures than successes in: (a) large districts, when the turnout reached 30 percent at bond elections and 27 percent at tax elections; (b) medium sized districts, when turnout reached 25 percent at bond elections and 17 percent at tax elections; (c) small districts, when turnout reached 23 percent at bond elections and 14 percent at tax elections.

However, failure was not a consistent consequence of higher turnout. In large districts, when turnout for bond and tax elections reached 63 and 53 percent, respectively, the elections succeeded as frequently as they failed. Large district bond elections actually profited from greater turnout. But in medium and small districts, although the greatest impact of turnout on failure was in the middle range of turnout, failure continued to be a frequent concomitant of greater turnout in the higher ranges of turnout.[41]

An alternative hypothesis to explain the observed negative correlation between turnout and outcome has been spawned by the discovery by social scientists of political alienation and the alienated voter.[42] Observations that fluoridation proposals have fared better in low than in high turnouts,[43] and some case studies of alienation using school elections data, have generated the negative voting theory and the alienated-voter model for referenda.[44] The hypothesis is that turnout fluctuations are a function of the amount of participation by alienates, and that referenda proposals pass with low turnout but are defeated by high turnout when numerous alienates appear. The foundation of this hypothesis is the community-structure theory that communities are composed of two politically significant groups: civic leaders and other persons who are satisfied with the existing regime, and a mass of mostly lower-status citizens only loosely attached to the community and possessing latent feelings of dissatisfaction. The first group are community activists, presumably supportive of referenda proposals and comprising the core of voters for local elections. The other group is portrayed as fluctuating between apathy and opposition to the community leadership. Ergo, the electorate of most referenda is composed principally of the first group, which facilitates passage of proposals, but occasionally turnout is large because numerous alienates have been attracted to the arena to give vent to their feelings by protest voting.

Political alienation has been prominent in studies of fluoridation referenda, and has been observed in open housing and metropolitan government plebiscites,[45] and in most of the case studies of school referenda. It was responsible for at least three of the defeats of the cases treated in Chapter 8 and contributed to three others, all of which were high-turnout elections. These few cases, in which political alienation was extraordinarily great and undeniably influenced the balloting, do not, however—for several reasons—justify the conclusion that turnout rates and outcomes in school elections are principally a function of alienation. Flinn's observation about the change in the class composition of the electorate that accompanies turnout rate is a more plausible *general* explanation of the negative association of turnout and outcomes. Also, if 60 percent of school proposals are defeated, is alienation rampant in that many communities of the nation? Consider the Ohio data in Table 3-1. Does the amount of alienation fluctuate wildly between May and November? And how can that hypothesis (or the older one) explain the high-turnout victories in November? A study of referenda during two decades in "Littletown" found alienation to be an important factor in only one of the several defeats; the other defeats were attributable to vocal, organized opposition or lack of civic club support. The common characteristic of the high-turnout elections was publicity rather than alienation.[46]

The hypothesis of a negative association between turnout and success has acquired such wide currency in political science literature that it has acquired almost the status of a law, e.g., "there is a fairly well established relation between the size of the vote and the probability of a favorable vote."[47] If it is a law, surely it is a disconcerting one for school teachers, who are obliged to teach that voting is the preeminent civic obligation and that election turnout is an index of the health of a democratic polity. That dilemma, however, may not have occurred to many school people, because apparently the more prevalent view among school officials is that the turnout-success relationship is positive rather than negative. Articles appear in school journals on how to "Promote School Levies" and "Bring Out the Vote."[48] A sample of Ohio officials were unanimously of the opinion that the larger the vote, the better the chance of passage.[49] Their scheduling decisions reflect that conviction; they prefer a general election day, preferably a presidential one.

The reasoning that the turnout-outcomes relationship is more likely to be positive is based on quite different factual premises. The assertion that a low-turnout election attracts only the core of school loyalists is denied. When the turnout is less than 30 percent, said a Grand Rapids official, "they fall into two categories: (1) the confirmed 'no' voter protesting not the issue but the property tax, and (2) the 'yes' voter who always supports educational issues."[50]

The other counter factual premises are stated in Roberta Sigel's explanation of why in Detroit "a modest change in turnout will benefit the levy; it will nearly guarantee a lop-sided victory." That is because of the co-existence of two factors: (1) a large reservoir of potential pro-voters among large segments of the population which have a tradition of non-voting, who are only intermittent voters, principally women, Negroes, and apartment dwellers; and (2) a solid core of opponents who are regular voters. The anti-millage voters are predominantly people with no children in school and parents of parochial school children. They are white, working class, residents of single dwellings, with moderate or low incomes. "There is in the Detroit population a segment whose resistance to increased school taxes is unwavering. The hard rock of opposition will show up in substantially the same numbers from election to election."[51] The postulate is that most of the intermittent voters are not antitaxers, but instead have a favorable attitude toward expenditures for schools, absorbed from the American ethos. Hence a large turnout in Detroit will "bury" the durable and regularly voting hard rock of opposition.

The factual components of the scenario for positive turnout-outcomes relationship are particularly apropos to metropolises, because of large black populations. Gross data analysis of voting in Chicago,[52] Cleveland, and Detroit confirms that blacks are far more supportive of school expenditures than whites. At school elections in Cleveland during the 1960s, the mean Yes vote was 83 percent in black wards to 55 percent in white wards.[53] The Detroit data confirm that blacks also are the intermittent voters, and when the referendum is scheduled concurrently with an important election, an astounding proportion may not use the proposition ballot.[54]

The voting in Cleveland and its suburbs, Table 3-1, is an amazing demonstration of a positive turnout-outcomes relationship. That is not exclusively a Cleveland area phenomenon. The relationship also is positive in Portland, Detroit, Grand Rapids, and generally for school districts in Ohio. The average approval rate of school proposals at special elections in Ohio for the decade of the 1960s was thirty-five percent, distinctly greater for those at primary elections, still more for those at off-year general elections, and eighty percent at presidential elections—a perfect correspondence with turnout.[55]

Clearly, the hypothesis of a negative turnout-outcome relationship has considerably less validity than its reputation; the glamour of the alienated voter theory and the gargantuan scale of the Office of Education study's sample may account for its uncritical acceptance. The alienation theory is a foundation of sand. To infer a general negative relationship from the thimble-full of alienated voter case studies, as some sociologists have, requires a string of dubious assumptions: that the less participatory, "unintegrated" people in a community are reservoirs of latent alienation (inactive = alienation); that high turnout is only a function of more voting by alienates; and that the increment to the electorate in high turnout is preponderantly negativistic voters. Stone found that those assumptions did not hold for "Littletown." Sigel found that the proportion of negativist voting is very high in low-turnout elections in Detroit, which also is true of Cuyahoga County cities, large and small. High turnouts at referenda in

Table 3-17
Race and School Referenda Voting in Areas of Detroit, November 1966 and 1968*

Percent Black	Turnout		Support		Blank Votes	
	1966	1968	1966	1968	1966	1968
Below 25	65%	81%	44%	27%	14%	13%
25-75	61	89	33	32	32	35
Over 75	60	78	74	58	42	48

*Sampled areas were school attendance districts.
Data source: Frederick M. Wirt and Michael Kirst, *The Political Web of American Schools*, p. 103.

Table 3-18
Association of Turnout and Outcomes in Grand Rapids

Election Date	Building Levy		Operating Levies	
	Votes Cast	Pct. Yes	Votes Cast	Pct. Yes
April 1966	31,832	44.1	24,498	52.4
Feb. 1967	33,060	48.2		
June 1967	20,960	41.8	22,760	43.5

Data source: Memo, Grand Rapids Public Schools.

every instance were caused by publicity and/or concurrence with important elections, rather than by a revolt of the alienates; and in every instance, the intermittent voters in the aggregate were far more favorable toward the levies or bonds than the voters at low-turnout elections.

The investigators in the Office of Education study measured the covariation of turnout and outcomes. Their mistake, and that of the numerous writers who have since repeated "there is a fairly well established relation," was to forget that correlation ≠ causation. The negative causal relationship, undoubtedly to be found under *some* conditions, could be entirely "spurious correlation." In fact, this may be the most widely accepted instance of spurious correlation in recent social science.

For ascertaining causation, three methods are superior to the one used in the Office of Education study. One is measurement of turnout-outcome covariation for the school districts of individual states, as we have done for California and Ohio—with contrasting results. Another method is to measure covariation over time within the same community, as the cases of Tables 3-1, 3-9, 3-18, and 3-19, all of which display a moderate to strong positive relationship, as do measurements for longer time spans in Detroit and Cleveland. These are direct measurements of the effects of *actual turnout changes*, which avoid the pitfall of spurious correlation. The best method of all is measurement of repeated elections on the identical issue, as in Tables 3-1, 3-9, and 3-18. Unfortunately such data exist for only a few cases outside Ohio and Oregon. One in an unidentified suburb, "Robindale," with a positive turnout-outcome relationship, is treated in the next chapter.

The issue was essentially the same in the Portland election series —raising taxes. Three budget elections during 1971 failed to secure approval of an increment outside the tax base. Then the school board tried to beard the lion by proposing a new tax base, which would permit larger budgets without annual referenda. That was a bold strategy, in view of the near perfect record of Oregon voters of rejecting such proposals, but the Portland board had nothing to lose. The long shot also failed, but with the high turnout generated by the primary election, that radical proposal did better than the previous budgets.[56] As in Detroit and elsewhere, a small change may affect the outcome slightly either way, but a turnout leap is likely to be quite beneficial for school proposals.

Oregon, with an abundance of repeat elections and voter registration figures for school districts, provides a laboratory for testing the turnout-outcome hypothesis. Examination of those repeat elections during 1972 with unrevised budgets discloses numerous instances of both positive and negative turnout-outcome relationships. Sharp turnout increases coincided with victory for the repeat elections in several districts, but there were also coincidences of higher turnout and defeat by wider margins than the first time, and some budgets passed with lower turnout. There were more instances of a positive than of a negative turnout-outcome relationship.

The Oregon data indicate that: (1) Turnout rate is important; it usually exerts some effect. Of the thirty-four turnout changes, only once was the voting ratio unchanged. (2) The conventional wisdom of a "well established" negative turnout-outcome relationship is false. There is no turnout-outcome law; the relationship tends to be positive in some communities and negative in others. (3) The frequency of positive relationships appears to exceed that of negative relationships, although not greatly in Oregon. It may be noted that this Oregon sample provides favorable conditions for the negative relationship to operate. The property tax is exceptionally important in Oregon, the source of more than two-thirds of school revenue. The data are for the current era of "taxpayer resistance," and the consistent defeat of tax base change proposals attests to the tax consciousness of Oregonians. Most of the districts are numerically small communities; there is not a single large city among the cases of Table 3-20.

If the conventional wisdom is false, what can be said about the impact of

Table 3-19
Association of Turnout and Outcomes in Portland

| Election | Votes Cast | | | 37 Pct. Yes |
	Yes	No	Total	
Budget				
May 3, 1971	22,677	40,404	63,081	35.9
June 10	23,660	35,251	58,911	40.2
Sept. 28	26,290	45,072	71,362	36.8
Tax base change				
May 23, 1972	68,105	80,639	148,744	45.8

Data source: Oregon Department of Education.

Table 3-20
Turnout and Outcomes in Oregon Repeat Elections with the Same Budget, 1972

	Number of Elections		
Increased turnout—budget passed	15		
Increased turnout—budget defeated by a larger margin			7
Increased turnout—closer defeat	3		
Increased turnout—same ratio		1	
No change in turnout or ratio		2	
Decreased turnout—budget passed			6
Decreased turnout—closer defeat			1
Decreased turnout—worse defeat	2		
Summary			
Positive T-O relationship	19		
Negative T-O relationship			14
Same turnout or no effect		3	

Data source: Oregon Department of Education.

turnout? Some generalizations have been advanced by two investigators who discovered that the general notions about referenda may be incorrect. Arnold Spinner developed an incremental turnout theory with these elements:

(1) There is a stability in any school district in the voting behavior of the electorate in school referenda. (2) This stable pattern usually passes the referenda. (3) Due to the nature of the politics of education, the first upswing of votes upsetting this stability will result in referendum defeat. (4) The vast majority of this first increase will represent No voters, probably all the No voters in the district. (5) When the same tax is finally passed through subsequent resubmissions, the total vote will increase even further. This increase will almost totally be represented by Yes voters.[57]

Spinner found that New York budget elections fitted his nest of hypotheses.

On the basis of "Littletown," Clarence Stone proposed a comprehensive explanation of referendum voting that is a revision of the alienated-voter theory.

(1) Most citizens are little concerned with local government, but several factors draw local elites into involvement. (2) A low-turnout referendum is likely to consist preponderantly of voters who are active in civic affairs, whose counsel and support has been solicited, which contributes to the high frequency of adoptions in low turnouts. (3) A high-turnout referendum necessarily involves those who are usually inactive and who often are poorly informed. For these inactivists the political scene is highly unstructured; consequently their attitudes are malleable and their voting preferences are volatile. (4) Therefore high turnouts are less predictable and, although less likely to yield a favorable result, may yield anything from crushing defeat to comfortable victory for proposals.[58]

Although Stone's frame of reference is not school elections, there is considerable congruence in these two chains of reasoning. Both investigators perceive that the usual community situation is a stable pattern of referenda voting in which most measures are approved at low-turnout elections—a nice fit with the finding of the Office of Education study that most school proposals are successful at low-turnout elections. Stone explains that the success of measures at the customary low-turnout referenda is facilitated by the fact that the participants are "preponderantly" civic activists (which is not always true).

From this point the paths diverge, and we have three contradictory hypotheses about high-turnout referenda. The Office of Education study says that the greater the turnout, the lower the probability of approval, except in large school districts. Spinner says that defeats are most likely at intermediate-level turnout, because of an influx of antitaxers; but that when turnout gets high, the antitaxers are usually outnumbered. And Stone says that the outcomes of high turnouts are unpredictable, because the attitudes of the political inactivists are malleable and their voting preferences are volatile. A fourth writer, Tom Flinn, attributes the negative correlation of the Office of Education study, not to alienation nor malleable attitudes, but to the lower enthusiasm for taxes on the part of lower-status people.

Spinner's theory has the singular merit of some validation by actual examination of the results of turnout change. The Office of Education study relied on inference from the correlation pattern. There is no evidence that the measures which passed at low-turnout elections would have failed with large turnouts, or vice versa. Spinner's findings also correspond rather well with the direct measurements of turnout change which we have gleaned. His theory, however, suffers from its limited applicability to those few states with annual budget elections. Bond and tax levy elections are more sporadic, and his scenario of three elections with turnout increments rarely occurs.

There is abundant evidence for all of Stone's postulates, but one of them may not be applicable to school referenda: The superficiality and randomness of the political opinions of the masses has been well documented, but do their attitudes regarding expenditures for public schools or paying property taxes fit the same mold? His theory is at variance with much of the data we have assembled: In numerous communities, school referenda fare badly at low-turnout elections and in many others the outcome of a high turnout definitely is not unpredictable.

We suggest a different explanation of the turnout-outcome relationship, which the evidence shows to be positive in some communities and negative in others: Whether it is strong or weak is a function of the extent that modification of the composition of the defacto electorate accompanies turnout variation. The direction of the relationship depends on the characteristics of a given community's electorate, specifically the extent to which that electorate's composition at low- and high-turnout levels corresponds to the characteristics postulated by the rationale for the negative relationship, *a la* Stone, or the positive relationship, *a la* Sigel, or the three-levels pattern *a la* Spinner.

The prevalent assumption, notably in alienation literature, that the conditions postulated by the negative relationship rationale are universal has been taken for granted. The preceding data demonstrate that in numerous communities a low-turnout electorate is not skewed to facilitate passage of school measures. Instead the truncated electorate is skewed by an inordinate proportion of retirees and other persons opposed to taxation, who for that very reason are suspicious and critical of local officialdom and elites backing the expenditure proposals. In such a community, a high-turnout election produces a more representative electorate which is likely to endorse a previously defeated measure—often by a landslide. The conditions postulated by the positive relationship rationale are maximal in metropolises, and we have seen no election statistics indicative of a negative relationship there. Furthermore, the positive relationship occurs elsewhere, even in rural Oregon, and the weight of the evidence from direct measurements indicates that positive relationships are the more frequent. Admittedly, that evidence is from too few states and communities to warrant any dogmatism.[59]

We conclude with that disconcerting caveat *ceteris paribus*. All things frequently are not equal in school referenda, where so many wild cards—"idiosyncratic variables"—can nullify any of the more or less lawful variables, including the turnout-outcome relationship of a community.

Notes

1. Only taxpayers could vote on bond issues in Arizona, Alaska, Colorado, Florida, Idaho, Louisiana, Michigan, Montana, New Mexico, New York, Oklahoma, Rhode Island, Texas, and Washington; on some operating levies in Michigan and Oklahoma; and on all levies in Louisiana.

2. *Cipriano* v. *City of Houma*, 395 U.S. 701 (1969).

3. The cities are listed in Table 8-8.

4. *City of Phoenix* v. *Kolodziewski*, 399 U.S. 204 (1970). This decision was presaged by two cases which were not definitive because their questions were too narrow: The above-cited *Cipriano* v. *Houma* case concerned a city revenue bond election rather than general or full-faith and credit bonds: The other case challenged the qualifications for voting in the noncity school districts of New York, the ones with school meetings and budget elections, for which the franchise extended to parents of public schoolchildren and persons "who own or lease taxable real property." Since renters could vote, who was excluded? Plaintiff Kramer was a bachelor residing with his parents. *Kramer* v. *Union Free District*, 395 U.S. 621 (1969).

5. Technically the exclusion of nontaxpayers from tax levy elections remains undecided, but the reasoning of the opinion in the bond case is so clearly applicable that Louisiana and Oklahoma have discontinued it, and surely Michigan as well.

6. Turnouts necessarily are computed in Washington in order to comply with the 40 percent rule, but the published tabulations do not report them, only indicating those levies that lost because of the 40 percent rule.

7. Computed by the authors from Oregon statistical tables.

8. Richard F. Carter and William G. Savard, *Influence of Voter Turnout on School Bond and Tax Elections* (Washington: U.S. Office of Education, 1961). We have estimated the proportion of referenda with turnouts above 50 percent from their frequency distribution graphs, pp. 26-31.

9. Most Ohio referenda occur at general elections, which have turnouts of 70 to 80 percent, and most of the remainder at primaries, which run about 30 percent.

10. Oregon Department of Education, "Summary of Budget Elections."

11. Carter and Savard, op. cit., pp. 15-19.

12. Carter and Savard tabulated turnout by district size for the nine Census regions. Their tabulation showed "small" districts as having the highest voting rates in only four regions. However, the sampling of tax elections was not entirely satisfactory. The distribution by size was

trichotomized before being segregated into regions, which could foul the results. That also could easily occur by combining states into regions; combining four states with straight negative correlations might produce a different pattern. And since there are such tremendous interstate differences in the form and incidence of tax elections, region is an inappropriate category.

13. Roberta S. Sigel, "Election with an Issue: Voting Behavior of a Metropolitan Community in a School Fiscal Election" (unpublished study, 1960).

14. The Portland voting figures are in Table 3-20.

15. Annual public school enrollments have been (x1000):

| 1950 | 25,111 | 1960 | 36,087 | 1968 | 44,742 | 1970 | 46,531 |
| 1955 | 30,045 | 1965 | 42,280 | 1969 | 45,843 | 1971 | 46,822 |

Statistical Abstract of the United States, 1972, p. 118.

16. Carter and Savard, op. cit., p. 10.

17. Interviews with local officials in Ohio by James S. Ginocchio, "Local Tax and Bond Referenda in Ohio" (thesis, Bowling Green State University, 1970), p. 60. Another example of the concern about bunching was the dismay of Eugene, Oregon officials when the school board scheduled a bond issue and a serial levy renewal without prior consultation. City and county officials were planning four levies for the primary election a few weeks later. The perturbed city fathers urged better coordination in the future. Robert E. Agger, "Community Influence on School Policy," in Alan Rosenthal, Ed., *Governing Education* (Garden City, N.Y.: Doubleday, 1969), p. 70.

18. Frederick M. Wirt and Michael Kirst, *The Political Web of American Schools* (Boston: Little, Brown, 1972), p. 142.

19. The measure of the influence of one variable on another is the coefficient of determination, which is equal to the square of the Pearson coefficient of correlation. Thus when $r = 0.30$, only 9 percent of the behavior of the dependent variable is "explained."

20. Byron Marlowe, "Voting Behavior in School Bond and Tax Elections in Ohio, 1946-1969," p. 7. This chapter draws extensively on that unpublished study by the research director of the Ohio Education Association.

21. Marlowe, op. cit., p. 8.

22. A 60 percent majority is required in New York only for a bond issue in excess of 10 percent of full property valuation.

23. The supramajority provision in California was suspended in 1969 by a decision of the California Supreme Court holding it unconstitutional, but

that decision probably was nullified by the 1971 decision of the U.S. Supreme Court sustaining a similar provision of the West Virginia constitution.

24. Henry W. Magnuson, "Results and Trends in California School District Bond Elections, 1954-1959" (California Department of Education, 1960), p. 7.

25. Stanley Scott and Randy Hamilton, "Extraordinary Voting Requirements v. Equal Representation: A Constitutional Challenge," in *Emerging Issues in Public Policy: Research Reports and Essays, 1966-1972* (Berkeley: Institute of Govermental Studies, University of California, 1973) 97-102. See pp. 100-101.

26. Ibid.

27. *Gordon* v. *Lance*, 403 U.S. 1 (1971). Briefs supporting the supramajority rule were filed by the California Taxpayers Association, the city of San Francisco, and the attorney general of Washington.

28. *Gray* v. *Sanders*, 372 U.S. 368 (1963); *Westberry* v. *Sanders*, 376 U.S. 1 (1964); *Reynolds* v. *Sims*, 377 U.S. 533 (1964), and companion cases.

29. "No State shall . . . deprive any person of the equal protection of the laws . . . ," a clause of the Fourteenth Amendment (1868) of the Constitution.

30. *Gray* v. *Sanders*.

31. Scott and Hamilton, op. cit.

32. The *Cipriano* and *Kramer* cases cited in footnote 4.

33. *Lance* v. *Board of Education*, 153 W.Va. 559, 170 S.E. 783; *Shannon* v. *Larez*, 87 Cal. 871, 471 P.2d 519; *Bogart* v. *Pocotello*, unreported opinion of an Idaho trial court.

34. This was one of the first effects of the appointments of Justices Burger and Blackmun.

35. Justice Harlan recognized the inconsistency of this opinion with the precedents and concurred by reference to his dissent in the Gray case.

36. Quoted in Scott and Hamilton, op. cit.

37. Wirt and Kirst, op. cit., p. 144.

38. Fourteen bond proposals in Washington in 1970 secured 60 percent majorities but failed because of the 40 percent turnout rule, but only two in 1971 and two in 1972. Half of those measures were rescheduled and passed.

39. Allen Clem, "Money and Schools: Campaign Strategy in School Bond Elections" (Governmental Research Bureau, University of South Dakota, No. 16, February 1964), p. 1.

40. Tom Flinn, *Analyzing Decision-Making Systems: Local Government and Politics* (Glenview, Illinois: Scott, Foresman & Co., 1970), p. 100.

41. Carter and Savard, op. cit., pp. 114-117.

42. Murray B. Levin, *The Alienated Voter* (New York: Holt, Rinehart, and Winston, 1960).

43. Thomas Plaut, "Analysis of Voting Behavior in a Fluoridation Referendum," *Public Opinion Quarterly* 23 (1959-1960): 213-222; William Gamson, "The Fluoridation Dialogue," *Public Opinion Quarterly* 25 (1961): 526-537. A subsequent and more comprehensive study states that alienation has been considerably less important in fluoridation referenda than the previous case studies implied. Robert L. Crain, Elihu Katz, and Donald B. Rosenthal, *The Politics of Community Conflict: The Fluoridation Decision* (Indianapolis: Bobbs-Merrill, 1969).

44. Clarence N. Stone, "Local Referendums: An Alternative to the Alienated-Voter Model" *Public Opinion Quarterly* 29 (1965): 213-222; Maurice Pinard, "Structural Attachments and Political Support in Urban Politics: The Case of Fluoridation Referendums," *American Journal of Sociology* 61 (1963): 513-516.

45. Howard D. Hamilton, "Voting Behavior in Open Housing Referenda," *Social Science Quarterly* 51 (1970): 715-729; E. L. Dill and J. L. Ridley, "Status, Anomie, Political Alienation and Political Participation," *American Journal of Sociology* 68 (1962): 205-213.

46. Stone, op. cit.

47. Norman Boskoff and Harmon Zeigler, *Voting Patterns in a Local Election* (Philadelphia: Lippincott, 1964), p. 71.

48. Noland C. Kearney and John H. Harrington, "Bring Out the Vote," *School Executive* 76 (1957): 76; George S. Martin, "P.T.A. Promotes School Levies," *Nation's Schools* 46 (1950): 53; Dewayne E. Lamka, "Thorough Selling Job," *American School Board Journal* 134 (1957): 50.

49. Ginocchio, op. cit., p. 59.

50. Milton Miller, director of planning, Grand Rapids Public Schools, unpublished memorandum, June 1967.

51. Sigel, op. cit., ch. 4.

52. In James Q. Wilson and Edward C. Banfield, "Public Regardingness as a Value Premise in Voting Behavior," *American Political Science Review* 58 (1964): 883.

53. Louis S. Masotti, "Patterns of White and Nonwhite School Referenda Participation and Support: Cleveland 1960-1964," in Marilyn Gittell, Ed., *Educating an Urban Population* (Beverly Hills, Calif.: Sage, 1967), pp. 253, 255.

54. Wirt and Kirst, op. cit., p. 103, from data provided by Norman Drachler, Research Department, Detroit Public Schools.

55. Ginocchio, op. cit., p. 51.

56. Oregon guarantees high participation for tax base change referenda by requiring them to be concurrent with primary or general elections.

57. Arnold Spinner, *The Effects of the Extent of Voter Participation upon Election Outcomes in School Budget Elections in New York State, 1957-1966* (unpublished dissertation, New York University, 1967). Quoted in Lawrence Iannacconne and Frank W. Lutz, *Politics, Power and Policy: The Governing of School Districts* (Columbus: Charles Merrill, 1970), p. 208.

58. Stone, op. cit., pp. 220-221.

59. The authors of a sophisticated campaign handbook for schoolmen note that turnout is important for outcome. They discount the importance of alienation, and say that the evidence on the direction of the turnout-outcome relationship is "inconclusive." Michael Y. Nunnery and Ralph B. Kimbrough, *Politics, Power, Polls, and School Elections* (Berkeley: McCutchan, 1971), pp. 9, 49, 121. A positive relationship was observed in a vote on whether to establish kindergarten in Eugene, Oregon schools. A post-election survey disclosed that the proposal was favored by considerably more nonvoters than the voters, and turnout appeared to have been responsible for the proposal's defeat. Agger, op. cit., pp. 76-77.

4

School Levy Elections: Strategies and Campaigns

Our emphasis here is on the activities that precede a campaign, and which are likely to have more influence on election results than the overt campaigning. Our concern is with all the politics of school referenda, not merely the more visible public aspects. What are the devices and strategies for building community support for schools, for preparing the way for a levy or bond proposal, and for fashioning a specific ballot proposition? How may the character of a community's power structure relate to the strategies selected and the modus operandi? What strategies are used for repeat and critical elections? Of course campaigning is not unimportant, so from (considerable) direct observation and an assortment of obscure sources, we have assembled some information about campaign organization and techniques. Much of the content is applicable to both levy and bond elections, but the latter have some distinctive elements which are reserved to the next chapter.

Schoolmen as Politicians

"A day does not go by in which I don't spend at least five minutes working on an upcoming bond or levy issue," remarked a school superintendent in a large city; another "explained the voting patterns of the various sections of the city in such detail, it reminded me of a political science class."[1] As election day approaches, the office "looks like a campaign headquarters," as the staff works feverishly supplying information to campaign speakers and news media and literature to the small army of volunteer campaign workers, while school principals mobilize the teachers and the PTA.

Tax and bond issues compel schoolmen to be politicians, in fact on a larger scale than most local politicians. Supposedly aloof from "politics," the school superintendent actually is the biggest politician of many communities. Politicking is an inescapable component of his job; and it can be the foremost and most critical one. The days may be numbered for the superintendent who is a loser. The importance of the political role is openly acknowledged in some communities, and a few superintendents are renowned for their political acumen.[2]

Schoolmen are trapped in the same role conflict as city managers. Both offices originated for the express purpose of establishing a chief executive who should be a superlative professional and completely insulated from "politics," but the realities of their jobs demand that they "exert leadership," i.e., be politicians. Folklore also prescribes that school board seats are not for politicians, but when a fiscal proposal goes to the ballot, board members have no choice but to step forward and "carry the ball."

How should school officials handle the uncomfortable role contradiction? A familiar coping strategy is to disclaim the political role and to avoid the politician image by an aloof and neutral stance toward all community politics, confining attention and talk exclusively to school business, and pretending that school elections are "nonpolitical." Recently, however, there has been some doubt about the wisdom of that traditional coping strategy. In fact, some school administration literature denounces it as a myth and a dysfunctional myth as well, and ascribe to it responsibility for the high frequency of school proposal defeats.

Strategy and Community Power

The waves of community power studies and voting research, along with the advent of the celebrated campaign techniques of the "new politics," have furnished ammunition for the thesis that schoolmen should be eager politicians. Nunnery and Kimbrough urge schoolmen to learn the lessons of voting behavior, and become sophisticated in the techniques of campaign politics, using polling and mass media methods (prudently).[3] But that is not enough; they also should employ the insights of community power analysis in order to perceive the nature of that invisible web of influence, the "power structure" of the community. The major thesis of these true believers in community power theory is that the magic key for school referenda success is a thorough knowledge of the intricacies of the community's network of influentials and its norms and *weltanschauung*, and the ability of schoolmen to co-opt the "power structure" on behalf of school policies and objectives. The minor premise is that such knowledge can be acquired only by manifold participation in community affairs, and that the power structure can be co-opted dependably only by the schoolmen who have acquired standing therein. That does not oblige schoolmen to be Machiavellians or to exploit the local influentials, Nunnery and Kimbrough say reassuringly; it merely entails "leadership" and enlightening the community elite about the "needs" of the schools. If the premises be granted, the thesis is incontrovertible, although some schoolmen may find that the boundary between manipulation and leadership and enlightenment is less obvious and more troublesome than Nunnery and Kimbrough imply.[4]

Nunnery and Kimbrough advise more than the co-option of community elites that has long been a routine strategy of school elections. (The "citizens committee" proclaiming the virtue of the proposal is a fixture of virtually every controverted election and frequently of noncontroversial ones as well.) The *sine qua non* of electoral success, they say, is an astute tailoring of political strategies by reference to the characteristics of the local power structure.

School officials should not plan elections in ignorance of the dynamics of the power structure. The behavior of the structure will greatly influence the outcome of elections. Election campaigns do not deal with an amorphous mass of citizens who are equal in their ability to make ideas acceptable. Except for the minority of school districts going through periods of disorganization or development, the district in which schoolmen will be exercising leadership will be a highly structured, complex power system, with hierarchies (or a hierarchy) of leadership.[5]

Some of the influentials in the hierarchies, they say, hold "enormous power resources to influence elections," and can "mold the opinions of voters concerning the acceptability of educational proposals." Below them is an odd assortment of power-wielders, grassroots leaders, elected officials, and organization activists whose importance should not be discounted. They should be cultivated, because their influence in neighborhoods on elections may be substantial; and, while not policy makers, they may influence the thinking of the men at the top. Running a school system without knowing who the influentials are is "irresponsible leadership."

Schoolmen also need detailed knowledge of the communications network and all the organizations, both formal and informal—the subsystems of the community political system. Channels are required for effective communication to the influentials and the organizations, in the parlance of political science, "access."

Two other elements of the power structure are cited as critical for strategy: (1) the dominant civic beliefs of the community's influentials and (2) their norms—i.e., all the expectations about leader behavior, and such specifics as, do some influentials expect private consultation and their acquiescence before any school proposal is announced publicly. "Many proposals have failed" because some norms were violated. Schoolmen should not only learn the norms and beliefs, and design election campaigns that influence opinion leaders, they also should influence elite beliefs.

The process of developing norms about community living (and education) is of critical importance to educators planning long-range developments. School leaders must be a part of this dynamic process. Rather than attempting to insulate themselves from the dynamics of power, educators must be represented in the daily discussions of "what kind of town do we want." By exercising their power in this process, they can establish baseline concepts in the interest of quality schools that will support a series of successful school elections for years to come."[6]

Employing the favorite categories of community power research, Nunnery and Kimbrough suggest strategies appropriate for open and closed political systems, a monopolistic type of power structure, a "democratic pluralist" one, competitive elite systems, and multigroup noncompetitive structures. The last category refers to a system characterized by elite consensus on basic community policy but with rival groups striving for economic advantage. A stable power structure is viewed as a necessity; consequently in a transitional community with a "mushy" political system, a "significant part of the strategy of school elections is to build a stable power structure."[7]

The election strategy appropriate to the closed political system of a monopolistic power structure is not a subtle question. "Winning an election over the opposition of an active power structure with a high degree of closure is very difficult." The starting point necessarily is an effort to convince the coterie of influentials. If the reply is *nyet*, what are schoolmen to do? They can postpone elections and try to persuade the influentials by such devices as: revise the proposal to the satisfaction of the influentials, organize studies of school needs with key influentials participating, attempt to organize latent centers of power, bring pressure from outside sources, or bargain by offering a *quid pro quo*. The other possibility is the most hazardous: an effort to defeat the local power structure by trying to mobilize latent groups and running a grassroots campaign.

Competitive elite systems are, by definition, characterized by struggle between power blocs with divergent views about the kind of community desired. "Citizen engagement in policy making is neither widespread nor functional," and organized interest groups are less instruments of citizen participation than captives of informal power blocs. Here, a paramount strategy of schoolmen must be "building agreement and seeking compromise." The emphasis should be on those that maximize cooperative planning, with efforts to enlist participation by the key influentials of competing blocs. If interelite conflict happens to be about the kind of schools desired, schoolmen may face a Hobson's choice and be obliged to make alignments. In that event, school elections "are the means by which regime conflict is resolved."

Since in a pluralistic power structure there is a constellation of power centers with largely different sets of influentials for each policy area, the first task of educators is to identify those influentials interested in schools and most sympathetic to school proposals. Some grassroots campaigning is necessary for school elections in any type of power structure, but, pluralistic systems afford the optimal conditions for the grassroots strategy. Indeed it is a logical requisite by the usual definition of pluralism as a polycentric *and* open political system with a high rate of popular participation.[8]

Precampaign Activity

School election campaigns, themselves episodes of but a few months, are frequently the culmination of years of extensive planning, research, palaver, and exertion by school officials and their staffs. The lead time of bond proposals necessarily is usually long, and it may be substantial for operating levies (except renewals). It takes time to formulate proposals that are feasible, technically and politically; it may take considerably more time to prepare their way to the ballot. There is a consensus among schoolmen that precampaign activities are indispensable and exceedingly important. The assorted activities may be grouped under three somewhat sequential categories: building community support for its schools, laying the groundwork for an election, and formulating proposals and making the decision "to go."

The paramount "variable" for school elections is a community's prevailing attitude about expenditures for schools. That there are profound differences between communities is indubitable, but just how much school officials can affect the level of "community support" is less certain. Nunnery and Kimbrough are confident that community support can be changed by schoolmen who, employing their advice about community power analysis and co-option of elites, exert vigorous and sustained "political leadership."[9]

There is some empirical basis for the thesis that the level of community support is elastic. A study of school districts in four states found little consistent relationship between school fiscal policies and such socioeconomic factors as income, unemployment, density of population, and age of population. The data indicated that the kind of political system is an important determinant of educational policies and that the quality of education is related to the character of the political system—its openness to new ideas and leadership—and to the ability of educators to influence the political system.[10]

Modifications of school programs to fit the preferences of the citizenry was the road to high-level community support posted by a group of university consultants for a school board after a series of election losses. The vote tallies, they hypothesized, are "one of several indexes of the level of a continuing relationship which exists between the people of the community and their schools. When most school policies and procedures are acceptable to a majority of the people, that relationship is high and support at the polls is a commonplace."[11]

Certainly schoolmen cannot ascertain the preferences of "a majority of the people" merely by talking to the influentials of the local power structure. Communication only with the elite subjects schoolmen to "unrepresentative and biased reflections from the people." The need is for a base of accurate knowledge about the total community served, for "representative information *from* the people, as a means of clearing up misinformation, reducing tensions, and orienting school programs."[12] But the post-World War II trends of urbanization; population mobility; and, above all, consolidation—which has reduced the number of local districts from the 115,000 in 1940 to only 16,500—have left board members and administrators few opportunities to know citizens or to talk to them directly and informally, while most citizens have no convenient way to communicate *to* the schools. The need is for two-way communication. Hence, communication channels *from* the people must be deliberately contrived to provide, in the fashionable jargon, better feedback. Therefore, the familiar advisory committees and other elite consultative devices should be supplemented by *the* way to secure "representative" information: community opinion surveys.

This technique proved to be very useful to the schools of one gold-coast suburb, where an opinion poll disclosed a paucity of citizen information, voluminous misinformation, and some distinct preferences. The poll results were used in formulating the millage and bond proposals and for the election campaign, which dealt with the information deficit and misperceptions and "sold" the proposals as the means to the revealed preferences of "the people." Both measures carried comfortably, ending a losing streak. Thus, community support level can be changed, and reorientation of school programs in accord with the communicated desires of the community is one way to do it.

The advocates of two-way communication acknowledge that their prescription is not a panacea. Community support changes may be wrought by such "natural" phenomena as major political events, economic changes, or modifications in the social composition and organization of the community. "Although the importance of contrived change is not to be denied or overlooked, there is evidence to indicate that such change is small in comparison with natural change."[13]

A study of school-community relations by Professors Richard Carter and John Sutthoff of Stanford University advances the thesis that community support is principally a function of "understanding." Their study disclosed that communities with greater understanding among their leaders have better records in financial elections and that "successful support is dependent on a state of understanding between schools and community."[14] They define understanding as a common perception of the situation. Observers may disagree about what should be done in a situation, but given a common perception of the situation, there is a basis for development and progress.

Communication is the magic key to understanding, according to conventional wisdom. When schools encounter formidable resistance to proposals, the usual reflex is a greater volume of information output through public reports, press releases, public meetings, etc. Carter and Sutthoff reject the naive view that all failures of social interaction are attributable to deficiencies in communication. "Little is to be gained from a simple effort to increase the information outputs of schools," they say. "We must know what to communicate—that is, what is important to the needed understanding."[15] They do not venture to prescribe what information is needed, but they offer some methodological advice.

"The greater understanding must come first among leaders of school and community." Understanding among voters may not follow automatically, but it is even less likely that it can be obtained directly, apart from leaders. Understanding requires effective communication, and community leaders are in the best position to communicate.[16]

Carter and Sutthoff emphasize the importance of effective mediating agencies. Particularly in large districts, some agencies must inform the community about the schools and, equally important, the schools about the community. Some individuals—teachers, principals, community leaders—perform that role, but the most important mediating agencies are the school board, local mass media, parent organizations, citizens committees, and opposition groups. The school board has the explicit legal responsibility to perform that service, but it may default or be ineffective, as demonstrated by the creation of ad hoc citizens committees to fill the role.[17]

What factors are important in school-community relations? Carter and Sutthoff asked (by mail survey) board members, superintendents, civic officials, and mass media executives in four hundred school districts. They were told that the "factors that help" most often are:

Characteristics of students: programs, achievement, athletics, and pride in school

Communication between school and community: open houses; parent-teacher conferences; parent-teacher relations; PTA and parent clubs; PTA campaigning; mass media coverage of schools; relations with civic institutions; and informal contacts.

Administrator characteristics: professional qualifications; relations with parents; and values, beliefs, and goals.

Staff characteristics: quality of teachers and relations with students.

Services by the schools: availability of school facilities; and special services such as health, transportation, and a retarded-children program.

They were told that the "factors that hurt" most frequently are:

Stable political opposition: unorganized chronic critics; organized critical groups; voter turnout; and the conservative nature of voters.

The communicatory activity of that opposition: use of mass media, bulletins, and public meetings; and the quality of opposition techniques.

Criticisms of education nationally.

Property assessment procedures.

Students quitting school before graduation.

The responses reflected some differences between large and small districts. Informants in large districts assigned more importance to services and the role of mediating agencies. Labor unions, chambers of commerce, and large taxpayers usually are more important factors in large districts. Informants in small districts attached more importance to staff and administrator capabilities, and assigned foremost importance to the administrator, who is valued for his professional and personal attributes but who also may be a source of difficulty in school-community relations.[18]

Laying the Groundwork

Most bond elections and some levy proposals require careful and extensive planning and preparation over a period of one or two years or longer. Cautious school officials will develop the proposal carefully, study previous election results, assess the opinions of community influentials, perhaps conduct a community opinion poil, examine the following of school leaders, select the election date carefully, and insure that all legal requirements are met.

Any proposal presumably is an outgrowth of recommendations from some data base—a comprehensive school survey, a building survey, a curriculum study, or a management survey. Preparation of the data base usually involves some citizen advisory committees and perhaps outside consultants. (An expert is someone away from home.) Data collection and analysis are performed by the school staff and consultants. The advisory committees review the data, perhaps inspect buildings and equipment, and participate in the formulation of recommendations.

Use of a citizens study committee has important advantages: it is a medium for two-way communication, for "input" of community values and opinions; it should improve the quality of judgments and decisions; it is a handy device for increasing citizen "understanding" of school "needs"; the proposal is invested with legitimacy ("the people" were consulted) and the endorsement of a prestigious citizens committee; and committee members are likely to be enthusiastic campaigners for their own proposal. A successful citizens study committee is a ready-made campaign organization. Numerous observers have pointed out that citizen participation is among the most effective means of increasing citizen concern and understanding. The first step of a recent successful bond election in San Diego, for example, was the appointment of a citizens review committee comprising one hundred fifty representatives of school neighborhoods and twenty business and civic leaders. After three meetings to review the data regarding capital facilities and needs, the group endorsed the superintendent's proposal.[19]

Nunnery and Kimbrough recommend using "at least" four opinion polls: before deciding whether to hold an election, another near the midpoint of the campaign, a third one in the final days of the campaign, and one immediately afterward for post mortem analysis. The "predecision poll" should be designed to determine the voters' overall opinions about the schools, their notions of the needs, the extent of knowledge and misinformation, and their sources of information about schools. There are a variety of possible uses for poll data: as an aid in making a decision about holding an election, identifying and responding to the interests and concerns of the several "publics," selection of communication techniques, identifying areas of potential support and opposition, identifying the kind of information that should be communicated to the voters, and identifying steps that might be quickly and reasonably undertaken to create a more favorable climate among the voters.[20]

Another major preparatory step is consultation with community influentials to ascertain their views and solicit their support prior to making the decision to call an election or at least before announcing it. The process may be quite informal and invisible, but it surely occurs to some extent before most bond proposals and major tax levies, and in many communities it may be one which school officials dare not overlook. The actors probably would call this activity "touching bases" and "sounding out" the views of important people or securing the advice of community leaders renowned for their good judgment and civic spirit. A social scientist would call it the process of co-opting the community elite or securing clearance from the local power structure. Chapter 5 contains an illustration of this phase of laying the groundwork.

Formulating the Proposal

"We realized that the voters would never approve a 4 mills levy, although we felt that was the amount we needed, so we decided on 3.75 mills," said the superintendent.[21] Formulating a proposal is not merely a technical matter of budgetary statistics or building blueprints. Frequently it entails a balancing of the aspirations of school officials, the financial "need," against hunches or an educated guess about what amount has a good prospect of approval by the electorate. As Wirt and Kirst say, schoolmen are obliged "to anticipate the public's acceptable limits," and "when schoolmen are defeated on the referendum they urge, their anticipatory wisdom was poor."[22]

For anticipating what amount is feasible, school officials must rely on their experience; straws in the wind; and, perhaps considerably, their intuition. Consultation with local elites may be the principal systematic method; occasionally advisory committees are used. The most ambitious method is a predecision poll, a device which was used successfully in Birmingham, Michigan.

We felt it necessary to determine the level of community support as accurately as possible in order to formulate an appropriate millage proposal. Our objective was to put a millage proposal before the people which would merit maximum support rather than to blindly place on the ballot an issue which would either: (1) request too much, regardless of the need, and thereby lose, or (2) request much less than the community desired and was willing to support. Accurate knowledge about the kind of school program the community would support was of crucial importance. Shaping a millage proposal eventually reflects the elements of *what for* and *how much*.[23]

The Birmingham poll results revealed some programs and policies that were wanted and also the existence of a reservoir of latent support —another utility of polling. The prospects for passage of a large operating levy were good if the proposal reflected the desires of the community and if the latent support could be activated. "What for" is of even greater significance for bond proposals. The absolute dollar amount may be considerably less important to most citizens than what buildings? where? with what design and facilities? (This is illustrated in the next chapter.)

In states with short-term levies and frequent renewals, the amount occasionally involves use of the combination-levy strategy. If the expiring levy is already a substantial one, the school board may try to augment its revenue by proposing a renewal at a higher rate, what might be called an incremental strategy. That was done deliberately by the Detroit board in 1959. Instead of offering the voters a new levy and a 4½ mills renewal, a 7½ mills combination was proposed. That, says Roberta Sigel, was "a calculated gamble. If the renewal and addition had been separated into two propositions, the results might have been quite different. Probably most voters primarily wanted to renew the old levy, rather than to self-impose 3 more mills, but they were not permitted that choice."[24]

Apparently the combination strategy is used most frequently in Michigan. During the period July-September 1972, about as many combinations as simple additions were proposed (see Table 2-12), and the combinations were twice as successful. Combinations also have been very successful in Ohio and were numerous during the 1960s, but have been infrequent subsequently.[25] Apparently the response to taxpayer resistance has been more use of combinations in Michigan and less in Ohio.

If a school district has some voted levies in force, another strategy may be possible: a partial offset of a new levy by reduction of another. Thus, a 5 mills operating levy increase in Birmingham was made more palatable by a 2.4 mills reduction of the building levy.[26]

Officials are advised by Nunnery and Kimbrough to "select the election date carefully," but they do not say how. The evidence suggests that "there is no 'best' month (although October is more frequently associated with success), and taxpaying months, holiday seasons, and summer months (when school is not in session) are frequently associated with failure."[27] If officials are aware of any turnout-outcome relationship, that may be a consideration, as it definitely is in Ohio where 90 percent of school proposals are scheduled concurrently with regular elections and two-thirds at general elections in order to secure high turnout and avoid election expense. In states with annual school elections that is the usual date, either by statutory mandate, as in Arkansas, New York, and New Jersey, or by custom as in Michigan, Montana, and Oregon. A few practical considerations may be pertinent. The date must allow time for an adequate campaign.[28] Coincidence of school proposals with others, or at least overloaded ballots, should be avoided. Occasionally a special election is chosen, usually for bond issues, in order to have the ballot alone and the undivided attention of the electorate. Scheduling of repeats is subject to statutory restrictions in a few states, e.g., only one is permitted in Washington, and only two within the same calendar year in Ohio. In some states, repeat scheduling is constrained by the date of the fiscal year, which requires prompt repeats of budget election in New York and Oregon and allows time usually for only one repeat in Montana. Financial necessity often allows school boards precious little chance to "select the election date carefully."

The participation of citizen advisory bodies in formulating proposals may be extensive and decisive or may have only a token or window dressing role. It appears to be largely a function of the gravity of the situation and the need of school officials for allies. We have observed some large levy and bond campaigns without an ad hoc advisory committee, but if the situation is critical, as in the Detroit election described below, a citizens committee will have a prominent role.

Preparing for an Election in Birmingham

Birmingham, Michigan, an affluent Detroit suburb of fifty thousand, during 1960-62 provides an excellent example of precampaign strategies.

The shock of its first tax levy defeat stimulated two years of frenetic activity which achieved the simultaneous approval by a comfortable majority, 62 percent Yes, of an 11 mills operating levy and a $5 million building program, and concluded with a large-scale postelection survey by the consultants who had done a predecision study of school-community relations. Birmingham officialdom did a remarkably comprehensive job of cultivating community support, preparing the groundwork, and fashioning the proposals, using nearly the entire repertoire of precampaign activities. There were two polls, two outside consulting organizations, several citizens study and consultative committees, plus a community planning conference; the local elites were effectively co-opted. A grassroots style campaign paid off handsomely in modifying attitudes of the populace.

The levy defeat in March was partially recouped by passage of a smaller levy in June, but the school board believed that more millage was imperative and, also, was contemplating two major building projects. Consequently, numerous studies were launched in rapid order. A citizens curriculum study committee, with research provided by the school staff, was constituted to propose "improvements." Another committee was established to study salaries and to make recommendations apropos obtaining and retaining better teachers. A university group was engaged to do a building study, and another to investigate school-community relations. A novelty was a four-day community planning conference.

The superintendent of schools held a community educational conference on April 4-7 in order to place the needs of the District before the citizens. During day and evening sessions several hundred representative citizens heard: (1) the Board of Education discuss its written goals, (2) preliminary reports of the Citizens Curriculum committees and salary committees, (3) preliminary reports by outside professional building survey and community survey consultants,(4) panels of outside and local professionals and speakers discuss new developments in education.[29]

All sessions included "stimulating discussion," and were reported extensively in the press and the district's newsletter. Following the conference, the staff began compiling the "needs of the district" for the next five years, a step in formulating an election proposal to be considered by the school board.

The community relations study entailed an ambitious poll using two samples, one of registered voters and one of adult residents, in order to discover any differences among people who register and vote in school elections, who register but don't vote, and who don't register. Considerable time and care were devoted to formulating the forty-five minute interview schedule. General areas in which information was thought desirable were identified at a meeting of the consultants with the board, the administrative staff, the Citizens Curriculum Committee, and the local press. As per that canon of survey research which is honored more in the breech than the observance, the instrument was pretested. The findings of the survey by professional interviewers over eight weeks were publicized in a series of newspaper articles.

Inclusion of a local school administrator on the consultant team facilitated study design and logistics, and also expedited feedback, so that immediate use could be made of the research data in curriculum planning, building planning, public relations, and the election campaign. The survey finding that the populace wanted "good teachers" was implemented promptly by greater staffing effort, creation of the citizens salary committee, and development of a new "competitive" salary schedule. The desires of respondents for foreign language in elementary schools and more stress on the "3Rs" were granted instantly. But the suggestions for expanded services were not, because the system already furnished those services about which a newspaper reporter was encouraged to write a feature series. Numerous respondents thought taxes were higher than in neighboring communities or too high; that prompted the collection of comparative data regionally and nationally on tax rates and salaries, which became a major focus of campaign "information." Because a third of the sample thought that school funds were not always spent wisely, an "open door information policy" was instituted, reporting financial decisions and data in press releases, a newsletter, and annual reports. Only a fifth of the populace thought the schools had insufficient funds. "These results indicated an obligation to interpret the community's high level of educational aspirations, coupled with the consequent required level of financial support"—a pay-the-piper theme. The previous building program was the major source of dissatisfaction; in fact only 40 percent of the respondents would vote "tomorrow to raise taxes for building needs." Building use policies were liberalized, a staff study was initiated to determine whether building costs could be cut without impairing effectiveness, other building programs were visited, a citizens consultative committee was established, and the board's *planning* program was heavily publicized.

Several of the survey findings were directly pertinent to the decisions made in developing the ballot propositions and the strategies employed in the election campaign. The survey showed a high degree of public confidence in the school board and staff. It revealed a reservoir of latent support largely untapped in previous low turnout elections, and it identified the categorical groups that should be the targets of registration and vote-dogging activity. It indicated that the recommendations of the curriculum studies were in tune with public preferences. It made possible the aforementioned changes, which were fully publicized. It disclosed areas of lack of information and misinformation, which were dealt with before and during the campaign. It gave direction to the campaign propaganda, which reinforced emphases built into the election proposals. The survey also revealed the magnitude of the "communications problem": the number of people who felt inadequately informed, the reluctance of supportive groups to register and vote, the discrepancy between the prevailing financial support level and the community's aspirations, and the need to focus communication on such intangibles as curriculum needs and a better quality professional staff. The survey indicated that an operating levy that was packaged as fulfilling community preferences would likely pass, if latent support could be mobilized, but that more resourcefulness would be required to sell more buildings. Hence, the aforementioned steps were taken to improve the school board's image as thrifty planners who consulted both the experts and the community, and a campaign theme tied buildings to the overarching goal of a better educational program.

The studies of the citizens committees and the professional building survey indicated the need for a $5 million building program and eventually 11 more mills for operating. The board opted for only 5 mills immediately, with more envisioned within three years, which was announced to the public by a five-year budget projection. A large citizens advisory committee considered both short- and long-term needs and the acceptability of both proposals. Upon its endorsement, the building proposal and an 11 mills combination levy were scheduled for an election in November, one month before the expiration of a 6 mills levy.[30]

The postelection survey demonstrated that the election result was not exclusively because of the success of a vigorous grass-roots campaign, with seven hundred fifty block workers, in mobilizing latent support. The diligent precampaign activities in conjunction with the campaign achieved substantial changes in public attitudes. Possibly Birmingham was rather an ideal situation for achieving "contrived" change in the level of community support.

Campaigns

School referenda campaigns are similar in form and content, but they vary tremendously in scale. An operating levy renewal may be such a perfunctory affair that the campaign consists of little more than announcements at PTA meetings and a press release reminding voters, particularly parents, that a renewal levy will be on the ballot at the forthcoming election. Conversely, a building levy, a bond issue, or a large new operating levy may entail a substantial campaign. Repeat elections not infrequently are intense affairs.

Normally the campaigns are relatively inexpensive. School boards are barred by statute from dipping into the treasury and they must rely on donations and volunteers. Usually there is an abundance of volunteers; PTAs, individuals, and business firms donate services as well as a little

Table 4-1
Attitude Changes in Birmingham

Question	Attitude	1961	1962
How well are school funds used?	Wisely	63%	75%
Are the people kept adequately informed about school affairs?	Yes	58	75
What is your opinion about the costs of the new schools?	Cost too much	38	31
During the past year or two, school building policies have:	Improved	—	43
	Not changed	—	11
	Degenerated	—	6
	No opinion	—	40

Source: R. Smith *et al., Community Organization and Support for Public Schools,* pp. 65-67.

cash; and they frequently pay for newspaper advertising and printing bills. Supplying the wherewithal is a standard chore of the ad hoc citizens committee. A recent study reports that the cash budget of campaigns in large districts of Ohio rarely exceeds $30 thousand.[31] There are occasional exceptions; e.g., it was estimated that the Detroit campaign described below cost $100 thousand dollars.[32] That, however, was only 15¢ per voter and 33¢ per vote cast. Few political parties or candidates could match the low unit cost and the efficiency ratio of school election campaigns.

A school superintendent has a marvelous ready-made campaign machine, one that any politician would envy: the teachers and other school employees; the PTA; frequently the league of women voters; and even the school children, who carry campaign leaflets to that most important segment of the electorate, their parents. Furthermore, this machine is geographically comprehensive, with several workers in every neighborhood. Schoolmen have other advantages not enjoyed by politicians. Their propaganda—in discreet form—is disseminated by churches and other organizations. They have ready access as speakers to the clubs, the ready-made audiences, and they need spend little or nothing for media advertising since the media generously publish so much of their "information" as feature articles or front-page news. Often the superintendent has another advantage; he may elect to take a prominent role or to remain in the background and let the school board members and others "carry the ball." Occasionally a citizens committee takes full responsibility for the campaign.

Citizen Campaign Committee

A standard feature of any substantial campaign is a Citizens Action Com-

mittee or a Citizens for Better Schools group, organized to provide resources and prestigious endorsements and to assist in enlightening the
electorate. These groups may be little more than a letterhead and the
nominal purchaser of advertising, the official sponsor of advertising as
required by law or custom. Or they may be actively involved, raising
money and services, giving speeches, and "talking it up" informally.
Occasionally these concerned citizens participate in strategy planning and
prove to be energetic canvassers.

This device for co-opting the community elite provides prestige and
some degree of legitimacy for the proposal. The committee members are
likely to be valuable sources of advice and intelligence because of their
familiarity with community norms and the currents of public opinion. They
are organization members and thereby are in numerous communications
networks, which enables them not only to hear but also to purvey information readily. Many of them are local opinion leaders, and although community influentials are not the only opinion leaders,[33] they may be the most
influential ones. As speakers, they are articulate and have access to audiences. They can provide an assortment of other resources, both tangible
and intangible: the necessary cash and services such as free space for a
headquarters, free printing and other advertising and public relations resources. If a grass-roots campaign organization is wanted, they are capable
of creating it. A school referendum is not won merely by cultivating the
local notables, but they can open up resources to educators for carrying the
campaign to "the people." Furthermore, use of citizens committees contributes to the ongoing objective of nourishing community support for
schools, since participation always is the most effective way of generating
enthusiasm and loyalty.

There may be an important invisible payoff from cultivating the elite
and fabricating a large campaign committee of local notables. To the extent
that the power structure is successfully co-opted, the opposition is reduced
in size and denied leadership. Even if some influentials are not persuaded to
support the proposal, they may agree not to oppose it; few will be eager to
oppose publicly a proposal endorsed by many of their peers. This may be an
explanation of why visible organized opposition occurs infrequently; the
leadership is preempted.[34]

Perhaps the most valuable function of the citizens committee is that it
clothes the goals of schoolmen with at least some appearance of legitimacy.
What could be more disastrous for an election proposal than for it to have
the appearance of being an effort by school personnel to benefit themselves, of being a struggle between "the school people" and "the taxpayers"? Necessarily, schoolmen always portray the election proposal as a
measure to improve or maintain the quality of education and as benefitting
the children—even if the direct purpose of a levy is to raise salaries.

Conversely, the opposition argues that it will benefit only school personnel or exploit the taxpayers for wasteful capital expenditures. The school board is an official legitimizer, but because of its dual role, it is not a neutral and disinterested legitimizer. The use of citizen committees in the gestation stage and for campaigning augments the legitimacy of the ballot proposition by making it a proposal from "the people."

Apropos is the currently fashionable systems theory definition of a political system as a set of conversion processes by which government organs—the authoritative allocators of values—convert "demands and supports" from the environment into "outputs," i.e., public policies and programs. School referenda are anomalous; the systemic roles are transposed. The demands are made by the officials rather than segments of the citizenry, and the citizens become the decision makers. Wirt and Kirst suggest alternative perspectives about the nature of school referenda, two alternative models of school policies. The referendum may be conceptualized as "a local conversion mechanism for citizens directly to control the conversion process within a school system," or as "a device for schoolmen to reach directly into the environment for support of their decisions."[35] They imply that the latter model may approach reality more frequently than the former. We would not disagree; however, the decisions schoolmen place on the ballot are not necessarily only their "demands". It is inaccurate to say that school referenda are merely and exclusively schoolmen making demands on the taxpayers. There is no lack of individuals and groups urging school boards to add services and facilities, or to expand, upgrade, and enrich programs.[36] A demand, however, reaches the ballot only via a school board decision; that is, in the form of a demand by the schoolmen. Consequently, there is a built-in legitimacy problem. Schoolmen must convince voters that the demands are not exclusively their own and that the ballot proposition confers benefits on others, as the Birmingham board did so skillfully. Citizen committees are devices for transforming the schoolmen's demands into demands by others, by "the people". Even though the citizens committee has been manufactured by schoolmen, this is not necessarily a hoax. The members of the fabricated committee may be quite sincere demanders.

Campaign Organization

Communicating with the voters may require a formidable organization. A public relations veteran with experience in school elections advises that the campaign be built around a citizens committee, whose chairman is not a schoolman, not even a board member. The first half of a typical campaign of six or eight weeks, he says, should concentrate on recruitment, organization, and planning. He suggests four major operational committees: publicity and promotion, contacts with special groups, finance, and get-out-the-vote.[37] A somewhat similar model was used successfully by a suburban Wilmington, Delaware school district.[38]

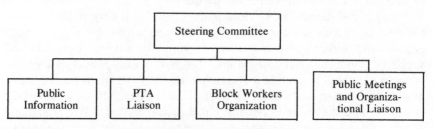

Structure of Wilmington Campaign Organization

There is a consensus among the pros that the canvassing organization is the most critical unit, "the real key to success." The formula of one educational consultant is, for every ten homes one well-trained canvasser equipped with handbooks that cover in question-and-answer form almost any concern of the budget-conscious electorate. Voters who are ignorant of the issues, he says, vote No. "To pass an issue today, you simply must have an all-out campaign of public education; you must take the issues to the voters right in their living rooms."[39] Canvassers should also be equipped with registration, voting, and ballot information, and be aware of which categorical groups merit the most attention and effort, e.g., new residents, young voters, and parents.

Perhaps few campaign organizations fully achieve Englehardt's formula for comprehensive or saturation canvassing, but some approach it. A campaign in San Diego mobilized five thousand volunteers, with a semi-autonomous committee in each of the one hundred fifty school communities. "Each of the school-based committees set its own financial goals, means of raising money, and methods of voter contact. Communication among the school-based groups was facilitated by a newsletter. A speakers' bureau was formed and endorsements were secured from over 100 organized groups."[40] An even larger canvassing army was recruited for a campaign in Toledo, which began with a city-wide gathering at sixty schools for a closed-circuit TV kick-off program, after which ten thousand volunteers dispersed, each with a bundle of literature and a list of ten names for interviewing.[41] Routinely, literature is distributed to parents via schoolchildren and sometimes children engage in canvassing, but that has to be done with discretion to avert charges of exploitation. It may be acceptable for them to distribute notices of public meetings, election day, and facts that appear in the public prints but outright propaganda may be forbidden by local mores.

Two of the most important tasks of canvassers are registration and getting out the vote—the right votes that is. In Toledo, the registration drive focussed on parents. The registration co-directors were school principals who operated through the other principals and the PTAs to reach nonregistered parents.[42] Unless the referendum is concurrent with a general election, registration and vote-dogging activity can be more rewarding for school issues than for ordinary elections. Possibly this is a phase of campaigning that is frequently fumbled. It requires the middle-class, political-novice volunteers to emulate the grubby activities of a ward heeler. Badgering and shanghaiing people to register and vote is an unseemly business, incongruous with the elevated rhetoric of school campaigns, and requires repeated follow-ups, bulldog persistence, and some outright brass. It is time-consuming; the initial canvass must collect the names of all adults in the district, which must be checked against the registration rolls at the county building.

Occasionally one sees some hard-data evidence of the significance of canvassing. A survey of a budget election and a proposal to establish kindergarten in Eugene, Oregon, indicated that the measures lost not because they were minority viewpoints in the community but because the campaign failed to deliver the potential votes.[43] The registration and vote drives certainly contributed to reversing the tide in Birmingham, where, in the second election, the propositions carried in all but two precincts—one which lacked a block organization and one with a disproportion of retirees.[44] In numerous, perhaps most, school referenda there may be less opportunity for a campaign to affect the results by switching votes, because of the stability of attitudes, than by effective mobilization of votes.

A few *faux pas* get reported. Some publicity gimmicks, such as picketing and other demonstrations by eager schoolchildren, turn out to be counterproductive. A Columbus, Ohio board of education stimulated teacher support for a tax levy by distributing a list of the improvements it would bring; but, when the promised improvements failed to appear a few months afterward, a credibility gap developed and the teachers threatened a strike.[45] Then there was the blooper by a teacher canvassing in an area where the educational level was low, who tried to achieve rapport by using the language of the people. "That man who came down here to talk to us talked so bad and seemed so stupid," one parent explained, "that we figured if he was educated, we didn't want our kids to have none of it."[46]

Campaign Themes and Literature

In large communities there may be quite an assortment of campaign literature, ranging from ponderous, fact-saturated handbooks for speakers and canvassers to single-sheet flyers. Much of it is crude do-it-yourself mimeographed material; some is attractive, slick copy that reflects the arts of a public relations firm. Occasionally—rarely—it is aimed effectively at readers on-the-run and displays originality as an attention-catcher—e.g., a recent Detroit cartoon booklet "This is an Irate Taxpayer," published by "The Leprechaun Search Committee;" more typical is the latest Detroit "Basics for Speaker," a formidable opus with this table of contents:[47]

1. Eight (or Nine) Points for Every Speech
2. Introduction to These Basics for Speakers
3. Some Millage Facts You Will Want to Talk About
4. Why the Millage Campaign Must Succeed
5. Building and Making Your Speeches
6. Handling the Question Period
7. Sample Speeches
8. Regional and Central Contact Persons

A prominent characteristic of much of the literature is the quantity of argumentation, facts and figures. Although campaign materials do add emotional appeals to the facts and logic, particularly in repeat elections, school people continue to defy the propaganda maxims of advertising and public relations. They cling to the assumptions that voters are thirsting for solid information and that voting decisions are made by ratiocination. The political pros would scoff at much of the literature as naive. (The authors respect that naivete.)

Standard equipment for canvassers and speakers is a long list of "Questions and Answers." Many are idiosyncratic items pertinent to the specific proposal and environment, but others are of quite general application.

Q: How can we "sell" the retired or the family with no students in school?
A: 1. Good schools protect the value of his home.
A: 2. Taxpayers had to pay to support schools when they were in school.
A: 3. A community that is a good place to live must have good schools.
A: 4. The retired voters also could be reminded of the support they receive by laws passed and paid for by the younger generations such as social security, medicare, and double dependent deduction for those over 65. A homestead exemption for the retired also will be voted on Nov. 3.
Q: If we vote "no" won't we put pressure on the legislature to do something?
A: It would not help us now and the students would be penalized. The best way to affect legislation is to contact them directly. They can and have interpreted defeat of local levies as a simple statement by the voter that he is opposed to additional taxes at all levels.
Q: Aren't the new industries and new homes in Twinsburg bringing in additional tax revenues to the schools?

A: Yes, but the additional revenue has not kept up with increasing costs. There is a lag between the time the new industry goes up and the time it is on the tax duplicate . It may take two or even three years before new construction is on the tax duplicate in its entirety.

Q: How can we be sure the school budget is reasonable and accurate?

A: The greatest safeguard is the County Budget Commission, which carefully reviews and must approve the budget before it is placed in effect.

Q: What will happen if the 6.72 mil levy fails to pass?

A: It will be placed on the Ballot again in December. If the levy does not pass, schools may be forced to close.[48]

Much of the campaign pitch necessarily is situational: the specific reasons why more operating millage or a construction project is "needed" and the things the proposal is designed to furnish.

The money to be derived will just about cover the anticipated deficit for 1968, allow the board to provide for the annual increase in salaries due to increments, and set aside $10,000 for student growth.[49]

The 5.5 mills is earmarked for salaries of teachers and nonteaching employees. "I'm optimistic," superintendent Poling said. "I think the people realize that our salary schedule is low. If the levy fails, we just won't be able to put in any type of competitive salary schedule.[50]"

The 2.9 mill addition would provide enough to wipe out the deficit. Passage would also permit the system to reinstate educational television, replacement of textbooks, enlarging the number of books in school libraries, replace aging buses, and resume maintenance programs for existing structures.[51]

One of the most frequent bits of campaign advice scattered thoughout educational administration journals is simplicity.

Confine the campaign to those three or four main points. Most voters don't want to know as much as the administrator of the school board and couldn't remember it all if they wanted to hear it.[52]

Too much school bond literature is about as readable and inviting as a weather bureau report. Graphs, charts, tables —these hold little interest for the bridge devotee, the factory worker, the housewife, or many professional people. Keep the language simple and to the point. Pitch it to the man on the street. Never use the word "needs"; use "opportunities" instead, and remember that the public has little idea of what the term "mill" means. It is best not used.[53]

Three other tips: highlight support, emphasize objectives, and focus on the children. Endorsements by organizations and prominent individuals should be trumpeted. Voting is influenced tremendously by affiliations and reference groups; it is more of a social than an individual act.[54] The objectives of the proposal—the payoff for the community—should be stressed: ". . . show what is in it for each sector of the community, if possible. If it is a bond proposal, stress how the location of new schools and improvements will better serve children."[55] Tie it to educational programs:

Always focus on the benefits for children, even if this requires some circumlocution. This last point is illustrated by an account of two bond elections in the same community. The brochure of the unsuccessful campaign displayed a picture of the contemplated new building with a caption giving its name, location, and capacity. The brochure of the second and successful campaign pictured winsome children with the caption "Our Children and Our High School Needs."[56]

How to deal with the sticky matter of costs? One recommendation is to allocate one segment of a brochure for cold turkey, where the cost is laid out in a straightforward manner. Then don't mention cost again; play up educational services to children and play down educational costs.[57] One school administrator learned that lesson by experience. "Throughout the bond campaign we talked buildings and dollars. When we stopped to listen to the voters, we heard them talking children and learning. That's what we should have been saying all along."[58]

Another approach is to express the bill in terms of the cost to a family or a household. Aggregate cost may be awesome, and besides the voter qua taxpayer is more interested in the cost to him. Thus a construction proposal might be illuminated by: "If your last year's taxes were $300, your *yearly* costs for these school bonds (principal and interest) will be $16; your total *weekly* cost for our children will be 31¢."[59] That technique has been used to express salary increases to be provided by a levy: "This is a proposal to raise salaries 60¢ an hour or $4.25 a day." The superintendent thought that more discreet than "$775 more a year"; besides, "many of our residents are familiar with union procedures which deal with the hourly rate."[60]

One of the interesting aspects of school referenda is the rich variety of media used to disseminate the message. Schoolchildren carry leaflets home; the school newspaper issues a parent's edition. The local newspaper carries a sudden flood of letters to the editor and display advertisements purchased by various groups—businessmen, parents, the PTA, and assorted ad hoc committees. In addition to radio and television spot announcements, there may be automobile bumper stickers, billboards, window cards, bus cards, and "VOTE" tags. Literature is distributed on main street, door-to-door, and at PTA meetings, football games, and other public events. There may be any manner of publicity stunts, such as picketing by mothers or children, some of which are ingenious: In San Diego, an ad was placed on milk bottle caps; and in East Canton, the superintendent and board president operated a "Superintendent's Office—Sidewalk Branch." Some campaigns have movies, "A Crowded Day at Evanston High." The Birmingham campaign had a fifty-unit slide show. Usually there is some direct mail, four times in the Birmingham campaign.

Several polls have reported speakers' bureaus and newspapers to be the foremost source of information for voters. In most communities, the newspaper is generous with news items and feature stories, and frequently lends editorial support as well. The speakers' bureau may comprise members of the citizens committee and school board, and perhaps the superintendent and staff people. Some consultants advise schoolmen to remain in the rear and let the "citizens" do the talking, but some do not heed that advice; e.g., Toledo superintendent Dick is an indefatigable orator, who makes one hundred fifty speeches in a campaign. Occasionally a combination of professionals and laymen is used, as the three-member teams in Birmingham, where a citizen described the ballot propositions, a professional discussed personnel and curriculum needs, and board members fielded the questions.

Some campaigns use the small group technique by organizing tea parties, etc. The Sylvania, Ohio, "Small Group Discussion" program for example, used two hundred discussion leaders, each equipped with a preliminary training period and a kit of audio-visual aids and literature. For any questions that stumped a volunteer there was a "hot line" to the school office manned by school board members. By augmenting the usual speeches to community organizations with small-group meetings, "we are taking the campaign directly to the voters," the superintendent said.[61]

Strategy in Repeat and Critical Elections

Critical elections stimulate additional measures. Although some repeats may not be viewed as critical, they always raise the questions: Why did it fail? What new or additional strategy can be used for the repeat try? "Adjustments," say Wirt and Kirst, "will vary depending on the size of the defeat; a narrow loss is worth another referenda effort while a large defeat requires considerably rearrangement of the school policies which the referenda funds were to support."[62]

Preparation for a repeat is likely to involve one or more well-publicized studies of the school system by professional consultants and/or local committees. In Bowling Green, Ohio, the large Citizens Committee to Study School Operations and Finance took its mandate seriously; its subcommittees scrutinized facilities, special service, high school curriculum and budget, and elementary curriculum and budget. Since a factor in the previous levy defeat was the merger with a large rural district, representation was allocated judiciously and the chairman was a prominent farmer. Having proffered advice generously, the committee endorsed a new levy, which passed, with the committee operating as a campaign organization.[63]

Should the repeat request be scaled down? It frequently is, but the Montana Education Association advises boards to stick to the original figure, on the grounds that a reduction erodes a board's credibility. Voters may infer that the first proposal was not carefully derived or was "padded"; and if boards develop a pattern of trimming the request, the electorate could adopt a complementary pattern of rejecting initial requests.[64] The Oregon statistics show that boards usually try the same budget twice before trimming it. In Michigan repeat proposals are usually trimmed, even repeats of renewals. For bond proposals, the blueprints are usually altered for a second try.

One strategy apparently is not efficacious for repeats: the *quiet* strategy. The school board in "Midwest County" tried a quiet election, to avoid arousing opposition; but it was the antitax people who came to the low-turnout annual school election. The levy lost again, by a small margin, at a second election. On the third effort, victory was achieved by a vigorous campaign which boosted the turnout by 70 percent and carried the measure even though the newspaper editorialized against the resubmission.

That case illustrates the hazards of repeat levy elections. They may embitter the opposition and escalate conflict. School authorities are vulnerable to the charge that they are disregarding the "will of the people" and that repeat elections lack legitimacy and constitute harassment.

This month . . . voters twice turned down a request to raise the school tax. . . . But will they settle the matter? Not at all. The school board's strategy is to harass the voters. This unjustified tactic of calling repeated elections is an expensive form of pressuring. The legislature should outlaw it.[65]

A prominent strategy of repeat tax elections , one that occurs with disconcerting frequency in Ohio, is a hint or a firm announcement that defeat of a levy will necessitate reductions in school programs. "I am sure that if the levy is defeated for a fifth time," one superintendent said, "consideration will have to be given to cuts in spite of the fact that my philosophy is opposed to cuts."[66] The board may announce a list of cuts *if*: band and orchestra, busing within the city limits or for secondary school students, educational TV, possibly school lunches, and perhaps even athletics! A variation is to discontinue some services a few months before another election. This is a desperation strategy and a hazardous one. It inevitably triggers controversy between devotees of each program and may end up pitting teachers defending the "educational program" against irate parents, band boosters, and athletic fans. If cuts precede an election, they evoke the cry of "political blackmail." If they are announced beforehand, there will also be the cry of "wolf." "They are bluffing; they wouldn't dare eliminate football."

This strategy is a grievous tactical error, according to the campaign pundits. If the levy carries, it may be a Pyrrhic victory. If the levy fails, the officials may have to eat a lot of crow; they may be unable to carry out the announced cuts. To this advice, some school boards might retort that they confront a fact, not a theory.

Occasionally boards make the ultimate "threat" by playing their last card, an announcement of a temporary suspension of operation.

The Elmwood Board of Education will meet in special session Tuesday night at 8 in the high school gymnasium with the expressed purpose of closing the Elmwood schools if the levy fails to pass in the November election.

Carl Oman, superintendent, said today the board has decided to close the schools on November 15 if the levy fails. "Actually they don't have a choice in the matter. We will have to scrape to meet payrolls until November 15," Mr. Oman said.

We want as many people in the school Tuesday night as we can get to hear the board's report and to ask questions. The board will adopt a resolution to close the schools should the levy fail.[67]

This announcement that Elmwood has a full-blown school crisis will produce a packed house for a school board meeting that will not be dull. It also will evoke shouts from antitaxers that the legislature "should pass a law against school closings."

The Opposition

There is a curious peculiarity about school tax and bond elections. Often they have a striking resemblance to elections in the Soviet Union; there is only one visible campaign organization. A visible counter-campaign is exceptional in levy elections, although perhaps not on bond issues. Probably covert opposition is considerably more frequent than we are aware, with some self-selected leaders operating informally without literature or advertising, using only oral communication. The infrequency of a visible counter campaign appears to be the product of three factors: the strength of the standing consensus that public schools should be financed more or less adequately or generously; the symbolic appeal of education and children; and the success of schoolmen in co-opting community elites, thereby depriving any opposition of that most important resource, some local notables for leadership.

Of course, the absence of a counter campaign does not mean that there is no opposition. School elections, except perhaps some renewal levies, have the built-in opposition of a substantial number of persons with a preference for not paying property taxes. Also it surely is a rare community that does not have several persons with specific dissatisfactions about the schools, and several who object to some aspect of the project, such as the design or location of a proposed building.

The unrespectability of appearing to oppose the welfare of children and schools may explain the dearth of organized opposition campaigns. Roberta Sigel has furnished a precis of one instance. Downtown property interests, under the banner of The Citizens Committee on Public Issues, defeated a Detroit levy in 1957 by "a clever theme and smart timing." The opposition remained quiet until the final week, and then launched a barrage of publicity. The pitch did not contest the need for school funds, but instead suggested that there was a better and cheaper way, namely by floating bonds. That ploy offered the voter-taxpayer an opportunity to eat his cake and have it, and absolved him of any guilt in voting No.[68]

The counter-campaign activists are not exclusively affluential businessmen. "The Committee for Education Under Freedom" at Sherwood, Ohio was some farmers, whose literature was called "vicious" by another farmer—the president of the school board.[69] In Bowling Green, the frenetic opposition leader was not a local notable, although the support of a banker-property-owner provided the opposition with sufficient funds for a media campaign. Even if some large taxpayers are the nucleus of the opposition, the bulk of their followers are likely to be low-income, blue-collar people.

What is the appropriate strategy for schoolmen in dealing with the opposition? The usual advice of the pros is to ignore it; "concentrate on organizing the home camp."[70] When a canvasser encounters opposition, he should not argue. "He should state his own position positively, and support it by focusing on the objectives to be achieved for children," but he should not waste time in fruitless argument.[71] School speakers should avoid extemporaneous public argument with opponents; "they can easily twist any facts and figures."[72] The logic of this strategy is for school campaigners to keep attention focused on their data and their arguments, and not permit the opposition to befog matters or deflect the discussion to the terrain of its choice and advanatage. Play your game, not your opponents. A reported example occurred in a San Diego campaign where the opposition tried to link the bond issue to the school district's de facto segregation problems. The schoolmen avoided the booby trap by insisting that the two matters were separate issues.[73] This does not mean that opposition arguments are to be ignored. Far from it; the handbooks for canvassers and speakers provide pat responses for the anticipated opposition arguments. Also, of course, school campaigners try to avoid disparagement of opponents and their arguments.

Two Detroit Campaigns

Surprisingly few comprehensive descriptions of campaigns are available.

Most accounts are unpublished memoranda filed away for reference in future elections. The following descriptions of two levy campaigns in Detroit are from an unpublished monograph by Professor Roberta Sigel.[74]

Detroit voters in 1957 deviated from their traditional support of schools by rejecting overwhelmingly a 3 mills levy. That alarmed the school board, since a 4½ mills levy would expire in 1959 and more than that was needed. The disturbed school people carefully analyzed the 1957 defeat to ascertain their mistakes, and promptly launched a series of activities looking to 1959. That twenty-four months effort was perhaps the most gigantic campaign ever waged in the nation. In April 1959, the board submitted a 7½ mills levy, deliberately employing a combination strategy, and simultaneously submitted a $60 million bond issue.

The stunning 1957 defeat was largely because of the weak and late prolevy campaigning, the scant promotion by the press, and the adroitness of the aforementioned counter campaign. The Citizens Committee for Proposition D was formed only five weeks in advance of election day, and it expended only $30 thousand. It comprised representatives of numerous organizations, who were expected to reach their respective constituencies, but evidently that expectation was unfulfilled. Inadequate attention was given to the mass media. The newspapers endorsed the levy very late and did little promotion of it. The entire campaign was too little, too late. The low-visibility campaign may have been because of overconfidence and, perhaps, a strategy to avoid arousing opposition. If so, the strategy failed.

The initial stage of the 1959 campaign was the formation of a Citizens Advisory Committee on School Needs, whose membership was a veritable galaxy of Detroit notables with George Romney as chairman. The committee proved to be more than another letterhead. It raised a large budget with which to employ consultants for a series of studies, and its reports numbered six volumes. Its work over eighteen months was widely publicized, and its reports documented the need for a higher levy. Although another committee was organized to conduct the subsequent campaign, the CAC actually participated extensively by supplying content for the campaign advertising and literature.

Buttressed by the CAC recommendations, the school board chose to ask for 7½ mills as one proposition. The strategy was to compel voters to grant the addition because of the necessity of some extramillage. The dire consequences of a defeat of the proposition were a prominent theme of the campaign. The superintendent told Detroit parents that defeat would mean *inter alia* one month less school, half-day sessions at several schools, and discontinuance of summer school. If the renewal and the addition had been separated the results might have been quite different.

This time the campaign committee was organized four months in advance. The Citizens for Schools Committee was another galaxy, "the Committee of 100." Its plans and campaign calendar reflected lessons from

1957. It executed not only a massive publicity campaign, but also door-to-door canvassing, and an election-day push to get out the vote. The canvassing enlisted ten thousand volunteers, the largest effort in Detroit's history. The canvasser did more than distribute literature; he talked to the voter and ascertained his attitude, which was posted on a file card. If the voters seemed undecided or deficient in information, literature was left and a return call was made. The file cards were used by poll watchers on election day in a concerted effort to get all the favorably inclined voters to the polls.

Citizens for Schools

9 February 1959

Calendar for the Campaign

February 2-16   Completion of organization, city-wide and in each school area. Preliminary briefing of committee members. Distribution of reports of the Citizens Advisory Committee on School Needs. Investigating organizations in each area. Analysis of voting statistics by precincts and schools. Start block organization. Secure endorsements of power groups.

February 16-27   Continuation of the above. Start the speakers program, distribution of materials, solicitation of funds, registration of voters. Begin press and radio-TV announcements. Do preliminary poll of voters. Secure full support of school groups.

March 1-20   Accelerated campaign with weekly distribution of material. Step up press, radio, and TV coverage. Intensive speaking program. Meeting of all principals in district groups. Meetings of community groups. Stickers and button distribution. Heavy instruction on voting procedures.

March 20-April 5   Block-by-block canvassing of the city by 10,000 volunteers. Advertising giving endorsements in city and community papers. "All out" radio and television campaign. Preparation for anticipated opposition and be prepared to meet with intensive counterattack. Final distribution of materials. Active participation by church, synagogue, and similar groups. Speakers at every conceivable meeting. Postal card mailing. Major meeting using popular TV personalities. Completion of election-day organization.

April 6   Get out the vote. Poll watchers' challengers, and literature distribution at the polls. Provide baby sitters and taxi service.[75]

In addition to plentiful advertising, the media were induced to promote both propositions vigorously. A tremendous variety of pamphlets, flyers, and posters were produced. Some were brief and simple, aimed at the man with little time or little education; others were detailed, aiming to explain how schools are financed and what would be accomplished with Propositions A and B. The recommendations of the Romney committee were given the widest distribution. The literature was sufficiently diversified to address all segments of the population, and it was not lacking in the use of emotional appeal. The following items were distributed in volume:

"Why Should We Suffer?" (distributed by high school students)

"Your Child's Future Is in Your Hands" (16 pages, color, illustrated)

"Questions and Answers About the School Propositions" (8 pages)

"Facts You Should Know" (4 pages, by League of Women Voters)

"Some Facts and Figures" (4 pages, by League of Women Voters)

There was an avalanche of communications to parents through PTA meetings and literature carried home by the children.

The timing of the campaign was worked out carefully. A Calendar of events was worked out so that the campaign would reach a summit of interest a day or two before the election. Qualified speakers addressed hundreds of meetings, and thousands of school employees worked energetically. The committee had adequate funds; $65 thousand was expended for printing literature and $27 thousand for advertising. The campaign "pitch" was designed to foster school-community relations, and speakers were instructed to do three things: (1) Tell the people the facts as they relate to the schools. (2) Inform them how the money will be spent in clear, concise terms. (3) Make sure the people understand the consequences in case the millage and bond proposals fail.

The success of this Herculean campaign was spectacular. It attracted sixty-eight thousand more voters than the 1957 election, and evidently about thirty thousand switched! The volume of No votes shrank by 30 percent and the volume of Yes votes doubled. Twenty-two percent of the respondents in a postelection survey said they had switched.

Capitalizing on its successful experience, the Citizens for Schools issued a long report containing suggestions for the future—a veritable campaign handbook. The general suggestions were:

Preparation—Begin planning the committee well in advance.

Organization—Decide early whether to organize on a school basis, a precinct basis, or a combination. Carefully select subarea workers who can be depended on to work.

Finance—Urge the citizenry to underwrite their share of the campaign.

Communication—Develop materials which are brief and to the point. Vary the materials between school areas. Keep committee workers and the community informed.

A Continuing Program—Between campaigns, maintain a skeleton organization.

There were more than a hundred specific suggestions, such as: Organize a workshop to assess the campaign. Motivate the small fraction of teachers who didn't work this time. Maintain the block organization. Continue to use children in the program, the most effective workers of all, but with due caution. Have better instruction to poll workers. Prepare a campaign manual.

There is no magic formula, however, as Detroit's 1972 debacle attests.

Notes

1. James S. Ginocchio, "Local Tax and Bond Referenda in Ohio," (thesis, Bowling Green State University, 1970), p. 58.

2. For example, Toledo superintendent Fred Dick, who as of 1968 had a perfect record of fourteen successful campaigns in four different school districts. *The Blade*, Toledo, Ohio, March 24, 1968, p. 2.

3. Michael Y. Nunnery and Ralph B. Kimbrough, *Politics, Power, Polls, and School Elections* (Berkeley: McCutchan Publishing Corporation, 1971), p. iii.

4. Ibid., pp. 1-36.

5. Ibid., p. 19. Copyright 1971. Reprinted by permission of the Publisher.

6. Ibid., p. 21. Copyright 1971. Reprinted by permission of the Publisher.

7. Ibid., p. 19.

8. Ibid., pp. 14-24, 33-36.

9. Ibid., p. 5.

10. Roe L. Johns and Ralph B. Kimbrough, *The Relationship of Socioeconomic Factors, Educational Leadership Patterns and Elements of Community Power Structure to Local Fiscal Policy* (Washington: Office of Education, 1968).

11. R.V. Smith et al., *Community Organization and Support of the Schools* (Ypsilanti, Michigan: Institute for Community and Educational Research, 1964), p. 2.

12. Ibid., pp. 45-62, 125.

13. Ibid., p. 123.

14. Richard F. Carter and John Sutthoff, *Communities and Their Schools* (School of Education, Stanford University, 1960, mimeographed), pp. 1-30, 69-70, 238.

15. Ibid., p. 26.

16. Ibid., p. 15.

17. Ibid., pp. 16, 29-30.

18. Ibid., pp. 69-70.

19. Nunnery and Kimbrough, op. cit., pp. 104-108.

20. Schoolmen should be aware that surveys of referenda voting are hazardous, because of the problem of what in the trade is euphemistically called "respondent error," deriving from a strong disposition to honor majority values. Numerous respondents are not eager to say that they voted, or intend to vote against the school levy, the retarded-children levy, or a fair-housing ordinance—particularly to an interviewer for the school campaign organization. The self-serving maxim of survey research that "respondent error" is random and washes out can be woefully wrong. For example, 73 percent of the sample in one case study said they voted Yes, but the official election vote was 54 percent Yes. In another instance, 75 percent of a huge sample said they voted affirmatively, but the official tally was 64 percent. The Austintown survey was successful in coping with "respondent error." The sample results were within 1 percent of the official tallies in both elections, and also had the appropriate size drop-off between the November and December elections. That accuracy was achieved by drawing the sample from the registrants who had voted in November, by incorporating in the interview schedule internal checks of veracity, by being alert to the danger, and by using only three veteran interviewers with knowledge of the community and skill at achieving rapport.

21. Ginocchio, op. cit., p. 59.

22. Frederick M. Wirt and Michael W. Kirst, *The Political Web of American Schools* (Boston: Little, Brown and Company, 1972), p. 97.

23. Smith et al., op. cit., pp. 46-47, 57.

24. Roberta S. Sigel, "Election with an Issue: Voting Behavior of a Metropolitan Community in a School Fiscal Election" (unpublished study, 1960).

25. The ratio of combinations and new levies was 10 to 17 in Ohio in 1962 but only 1 to 25 in 1972. If a combination is a calculated gamble, evidently Ohio officials have become more cautious than Michigan officials.

26. Smith et al., op. cit., p. 58.

27. Nunnery and Kimbrough, op. cit., p. 107.

28. A repeat election in "Midwest County" lost because it was held only fifteen days after the first defeat, too little time for influencing the electorate. Lawrence Iannaccone and Frank W. Lutz, *Politics, Power, and Policy: The Governing of School Districts* (Columbus, Ohio: Charles E. Merrill Co., 1970).

29. Smith et al., op. cit., pp. 49-50.

30. Ibid., pp. 15-16, 45-58.

31. Ginocchio, op. cit., p. 60.

32. Sigel, op. cit.

33. Opinion leaders were found in all social strata in the Elmira voting study. Bernard R. Berelson, Paul F. Lazarsfeld, and William N. McPhee, *Voting* (Chicago: University of Chicago Press, 1954), pp. 109-115.

34. Co-option of the establishment was so successful in Birmingham that no organized opposition developed, in contrast to the two previous elections. Smith et al., op. cit., p. 59.

35. Wirt and Kirst, op. cit., pp. 108-109.

36. For example: "In Eugene numerous people and groups made demands on the school board for various programs of special education. An association to help retarded children urged a class in high school for them and for admission of children with IQs less than 60. Groups periodically urged expansion of the program for the individually talented. There were repeated demands for ninth grade football, and the PTA pushed for kindergartens." Robert E. Agger, "The Politics of Local Education" in *Governing Education*, ed. by Alan Rosenthal (Garden City, N.Y.: Doubleday, 1969), pp. 67-68.

37. William W. Allen, "Steps to Successful Campaigns for School Bond Issues and Tax Referenda," *Illinois Education* 56, no. 6 (February 1968): 257-59.

38. Nunnery and Kimbrough, op. cit., p. 111.

39. Nicholaus Englehardt as reported in the Bowling Green, Ohio *Sentinel-Tribune*, June 9, 1970.

40. Ibid., p. 110.

41. *The Blade*, Toledo, Ohio, March 24, 1968, p. 2.

42. Ibid.

43. Agger, op. cit., pp. 76-77.

44. Smith et al., op. cit., p. 60.

45. *The Blade*, Toledo, Ohio, January 26, 1969, p. 4.

46. Akron *Beacon Journal*, November 18, 1970, p. 2 of editorial section.

47. For a generous supply of Detroit literature and other things, the authors are indebted to Reginald Ciokajlo, assistant to the superintendent.

48. From Tallmadge and Twinsburg, Ohio, as reported in the Akron *Beacon Journal*, October 28, 1970.

49. From the Bowling Green *Sentinel-Tribune*, September 6, 1967.

50. From Mantua, Ohio, as reported in the Akron *Beacon Journal*, October 27, 1970.

51. From Fremont, Ohio, as reported in *The Blade*, Toledo, Ohio, May 29, 1970.

52. Allen, op. cit., p. 258.

53. Otis A. Crosby, "How to Make Bonds a Winning Issue," *Nation's Schools* 72, no. 1 (July 1963): 27-28.

54. A major finding of the Erie County study; see Paul Lazarsfeld et al., *The People's Choice* (New York: Columbia University Press, 1944).

55. Nunnery and Kimbrough, op. cit., p. 116.

56. Anon., "How One District Reversed a Bond Defeat," *School Management* 6, no. 3 (March 1962): 93-95.

57. Crosby, op. cit., p. 28.

58. Anon., "How to Win a Lost Bond Vote," *School Management* 8, no. 11 (November 1964): 73.

59. Nunnery and Kimbrough, op. cit., p. 118.

60. *The Blade*, Toledo, Ohio, February 12, 1969.

61. *The Blade*, Toledo, Ohio, June 1, 1969.

62. Wirt and Kirst, op. cit., p. 97.

63. Bowling Green *Sentinel-Tribune*, September 26, 1967.

64. From conversation with officials of the MEA, July 20, 1973.

65. Iannaccone and Lutz, op. cit., p. 172.

66. The superintendent of Ravenna, Ohio as quoted in the Akron *Beacon Journal*, October 30, 1970.

67. Bowling Green *Sentinel-Tribune*, October 27, 1969.

68. Sigel, op. cit.

69. *The Blade*, Toledo, Ohio, February 13, 1969, p. 25.

70. Boyd Carter and Ted DeVries, "Ten Commandments of Successful School Tax Campaigns," *The Clearing House* 42 (December 1967): 210-212. Their ten rules are: Know where you stand, before attempting to convince the public. Enlist the aid to citizens to champion your cause. Stay in the background and function as a research source. Ignore your opposition. Build your campaign around an emotional appeal. Use inexpensive brochures. Don't threaten the public. Don't count on newspaper support, i.e., editorial support. Concentrate on the "yes" voters. After the issues pass, don't forget the public; continue an aggressive public information program.

71. Nunnery and Kimbrough, op. cit., pp. 119-120.

72. Carter and DeVries, op. cit.

73. Dorothy Thompson, "An Informed Public 'Buys' Bonds," *American School Board Journal* 155, no. 1 (July 1967): 18-22.

74. "Election with an Issue." This is largely in Professor Sigel's words, with some paraphrasing and condensation.

75. From *Report* of the Citizens for Schools Committee, Detroit, 1959.

5

Bond Elections: Issues and Strategies

School bond elections have important elements which are absent or less prominent in operating levy and budget elections. They are more episodic and may be more spectacular because of the size of the proposed expenditures. They may be rather frequent in some school districts with mushrooming populations; but, in most communities, school bond elections are extraordinary events occurring only once in fifteen or twenty years. The national ratio of bond elections annually to the number of school districts is 1:15, although it is distinctly greater in some states—being 1:10 in Arkansas, Illinois, Oklahoma, and Texas; and 1:6 in Michigan, Minnesota, New Jersey, and Ohio. It is surprising that, except in small districts, the voting rate is no greater than in tax levy elections (see Table 3-2).

Bond elections in metropolises are distinctive in two respects. The amounts necessarily are large in absolute terms and they are for extensive capital programs rather than single projects. The 1959 Detroit bond issue was $60 million; issues of $25, $40, and $90 million were voted during 1972 in Cincinnati, Toledo, and Columbus. Outside metropolises, bond proposals normally are for specific projects—a new high school or two new elementary buildings, an addition or a renovation. The mean value of the proposals during 1971 was $3.1 million; most of the issues approved were less than $3.1 million.

It follows that voting is qualitatively different in metropolitan and nonmetropolitan school districts. In metropolises, the question is whether to authorize a construction *program,* the components of which are known only slightly by the voters; and most voting decisions necessarily become primarily a function of the voter's standing attitudes, notably his general attitude toward public expenditures and taxes, his valuation of public schools, and his confidence in school authorities—an affirmative vote is an expression of faith in school officials and their judgment.

In nonmetropolitan areas, however, voting decisions on bond proposals are also related to the attributes of a specific construction project. There voting has the closest correspondence to consumer decisions in the marketplace and the circumstances are well nigh optimal for rationality in voting. The voter is not obliged to make a decision on the basis of faith in the wisdom of school officials. The object of the expenditure as well as the price tag is explicit and visible: "Shall $6,805,000 and a tax levy of 4.8 mills be authorized for remodeling Jackson elementary school and constructing a new high school with a vocational wing and a swimming pool and a capacity of 1,550 students?"[1]

Propositions usually are presented with considerable precision and are accompanied by architect's drawings and other exhibits. Thus the campaign workers at Napoleon, Ohio, gave the electorate ample opportunity to learn that the $3 million facility would occupy sixty-five acres; would accommodate a 50 percent expansion of enrollment; and would contain a space science laboratory, an instructional materials center, air conditioning, and an olympic size swimming pool.[2] The proposal for a second high school by the New Trier, Illinois school board included artists' sketches and detailed facts and figures to demonstrate that New Trier West would be an "educational twin" of the prestigious New Trier East.[3]

The specificity of these proposals furnishes advantages to both sides in the election. The proponents have an explicit commodity for "sale," one with appealing benefits to a large portion of the populace. Numerous persons in addition to parents may perceive benefits from, for example, athletic and vocational education facilities, and the psychic income from a handsome monument may be very substantial. Thus, the expensive price tag of New Trier West generated little criticism, in fact it won votes, since a high quality school was regarded as beneficial to property values, and the school board's description of the expensive facility "converted voter apprehension into general approval."

The sword cuts both ways. Opponents have a broad target which affords abundant opportunity to find objectionable aspects: "mistakes" in design, wasteful "frills," and "poor planning." The location of a new building almost certainly will be wrong in the eyes of some voters, and while some critics charge that the project is extravagant the very same proposal may be criticized for being inadequate. Indeed a project often presents so many targets for criticism that subterfuge may be the strategy used to oppose bond proposals. "There is ample opportunity for detractors to fix on objectionable minor aspects in an attempt to confound the entire proposal."[4]

Strategies and Campaigns

The design of a bond proposition is crucial to its success, and more important than the subsequent campaign propaganda. "The trick," says Alan Clem, "is to put together the proper combination of variables"—location, purpose, design, facilities, price—that will attract the requisite affirmative vote. Obviously, the proposition must include everything that will maximize the favorable vote and minimize the unfavorable vote—not an easy matter since features that appeal to some voters may alienate others, while the wishes of many voters may be unknown and unpredictable.

A defeated proposal is not usually abandoned. Instead, the situation is reassessed and the variables are adjusted, perhaps by changing location, building additional units, lowering (or raising) the cost, or by adding or subtracting certain facilities such as auditoriums, swimming pools, parking lots, and special-purpose rooms. The revised proposal does not necessarily carry a smaller price tag; frequently the cost is increased. Columbus, Ohio voters rejected an $80 million proposal in 1971 and approved a $90 million one in 1972.[5] The art of coalition building with a drafting board involves considerably more than the price tag.

Other strategy decisions relate to timing and the style and methods of campaigns. Timing is a more significant decision for bond than levy elections because of their episodic nature and the longer incubation period of proposals. The issue must not be scheduled prematurely before community elites have been convinced of the merits of the proposition. A proposal may be postponed to avoid coincidence with bond proposals of other jurisdictions or until some consensus has been achieved on a critical question such as the location. One reason for the initial defeat of the New Trier school board proposal was that it preceded any consensus about location and the question of whether to expand the existing high school or build another. The board did not repeat those mistakes. Before the second effort, it had convinced the public that alternative locations were unsuitable or unavailable and it had engaged a consulting firm to do a population study, whose results demonstrated conclusively that enrollment increases would require an additional school.[6] Conversely, protracted planning and talking is not without hazards.

We talked about the need for ten years and lost the interest of our people in the process. Too many moved in or out. Children grew up and finished school. Many persons indicated that perhaps we did not urgently need the building because the Board of Education moved so slowly.[7]

A major tactical decision for bond campaigns is the active-passive option, i.e., a vigorous, large-scale campaign or a modest, low-key one. The latter choice may occur when the school officials are confident of success or it may be a calculated tactic to avoid arousing opposition. Low-key campaigns probably are more frequent than we are aware, since they make fewer newspaper headlines than the all-out campaigns. Occasionally one is tried and then the other. In one of the cases recounted below, after two arduous campaigns failed by narrow margins, the school board successfully resorted to the other extreme of no campaign and a minimum of publicity prior to the third election. "I doubt," said an observer, "if this method would have worked if the need had not been shown in the earlier effort."[8] The more common pattern is an unsuccessful low-key campaign followed by an intensive campaign in the repeat election (or elections). In New Trier, where only one school proposal had been defeated in the sixty years of the school district, the confident board chose a minimal campaign—no volunteer campaign organization, no public relations firm, not even a citizens advisory committee—but the repeat effort was a maximum, saturation-level campaign.[9]

Bond campaign activities are the same as those of levy campaigns with one addition, pictures and blueprints of the project. Unless the proposal is minor, prior consultation with the local power structure probably is even more important for bond than for tax and budget elections. A concerned-citizens committee of local notables seems to be an indispensable fixture of bond campaigns.[10] The distinctive, last-ditch theme of levy and budget campaigns is the prophecy of cutbacks if the proposal loses; bond campaigns have an equivalent pitch; split sessions or temporary makeshift classrooms. "We'll be on half-day sessions in two or three years if the new school vote fails."[11] The New Trier school board added emphasis to that theme by purchasing some mobile classrooms, to the embarrassment of the burghers of that affluent community.[12]

Although every school bond election may be unique in some aspects, there are some recurrent topics of controversy, patterns of support and opposition, and characteristic coping behaviors by school officials. The task for schoolmen is to fashion a winning coalition by the design (and redesign) of the proposition and the sales pitch of the campaign. Another way of describing the activities of a controverted school bond issue is that they are the processes for resolving the controversies endemic in such community decisions and achieving a consensus. The issues and the consensus-building processes may be illuminated by the following resumés of eight controversies, each of which entailed two or more elections. The cases, located in four states, are a middling sample: a large Southern city, a gold coast suburban community renowned for the quality of its schools, a small rural community whose bucolic placidity was disturbed suddenly by a residential subdivision wave and an influx of outlanders, and five prairie cities.

Cape City

Cape City, the core of one of the largest metropolitan areas in the South, is said to have a history of hostility toward school bonds.[13] The initial referendum of the bond issue discussed here resulted in a two-to-one defeat. A fifth of the pupils were on half-day sessions and another fourth were in substandard classrooms by the time of the second election, which, after two years of planning and a Herculean campaign, achieved an abnormal turnout and an affirmative vote of 54 percent.

A postmortem of the initial defeat indicated several important campaign errors: The factual documentation of school needs had been insufficient. Public opinion polls had not been used to secure information for planning. The releases to the mass media were unattractive. The campaign had been poorly organized and had not utilized some effective grassroots techniques. The members of the local establishment had not been mobilized on behalf of the proposition. Organization for the second election began.

To assemble impressive data of the system's capital needs, even though it was documenting the obvious, the superintendent engaged a consultant team of university professors and representatives of the state department of education. After examination of the physical plant, demographic data, and the financial resources of the school district, the consultants recommended a dozen new buildings and additions to thirty others at an estimated cost of $30 million.

Three opinion polls and a postelection mail survey were conducted, using systematic samples drawn from the registration rolls and interviewers not identified with the school system. The initial poll for planning purposes preceded the election by nine months and its announcement by four months. The data indicated slight voter knowledge of the crowded and obsolete facilities and considerable opposition to the idea of a bond issue in Spanish-speaking areas and neighborhoods where the new construction proposed in the preceding election would have promoted racial desegregation. There were, however, some encouraging signs: the large proportion of "undecided" responses and numerous favorable respondents who had not voted in the previous bond election.

The gigantic campaign left few stones unturned in the effort to educate the public, to influence the undecided, and to get out the favorable voters. A poll three weeks before the election indicated the campaign's effectiveness. Nearly all respondents knew that a referendum was impending, three-fourths planned to vote, and a bare majority said they would vote Yes; only a seventh remained undecided. There was considerable apprehension about the cost of the proposal, and it was viewed in some quarters as a racial integration device. Three-fourths of the respondents had received the school message either by direct mail or through the mass media. Nevertheless, the campaign leaders decided to intensify the volume of propaganda in the balance of the campaign. The final pre-election poll disclosed a slight increase in Yes responses, the same fears and pockets of opposition, and some evidence of overkill.

The racial integration issue became a serious hazard. The opposition proclaimed that a vote for the bond issue was "a vote for integration." School spokesmen, insisting that this was an unrelated issue, received valuable assistance from a local newspaper, which, in addition to editorial support, ran a feature series on the problems of the school district, emphasizing that the bond proposal and the integration issue were separate matters.

The mistake of ignoring the influentials of Cape City, whose power structure apparently is a monpolistic archetype, was not repeated. As a starting point for the second election, superintendent and board members cultivated the influentials assiduously. After conversations with several individuals, a conclave of twenty notables occurred in the General Steel Corporation offices to consider the data presented by the schoolmen. The influentials were receptive, but they agreed only to meet a week later, obviously a stall to enable them to "check around." At the second meeting, they agreed to support a bond issue of $25 million, rather than the $30 million desired by the schoolmen, with the understanding that they would support another issue in a few years if conditions justified it. The schoolmen accepted the deal.

The Citizens Advisory Committee of fifty notables, chaired by the president of General Steel, took responsibility for financing the campaign—quite adequately. Other influentials comprised the Publicity Advisory Board and the one-hundred-fifty member Speakers Bureau. Thus, the resources of the political system of Cape City were at the disposal of the schoolmen. The organized resistance of the first campaign was largely scotched. Over seventy organizations endorsed the proposition; the mass media gave strong editorial support as well as generous coverage. The support of the influentials, said the superintendent, "was a tremendous factor in the bond passage."

New Trier

New Trier Township consists of six villages, with an aggregate population of sixty thousand, located on Chicago's North Shore adjacent to Evanston. That community of commuting businessmen is one of the most affluent residential areas of the nation and famous for the quality of its schools. Each of the villages has an identity and an elementary school system. The only significant institution of New Trier is the prestigious high school; and when, in the 1960s, the school board tried to cope with its burgeoning enrollment, the village loyalties and conflicting interests created complications and controversies that have been the subject of a fascinating case study of school politics.[14]

New Trier school district is an extraordinary polity, one with an incredible consensus on values and goals, seemingly conflictless—the schoolman's dream of a school government without "politics," guided exclusively by the professional norms and judgments of the educators. The election system is designed to that end. The office seeks the man; candidates are tapped at village caucuses and run unopposed. The populace eagerly delegates all policy making to the board, which in turn defers to the judgments of the professionals whose decisions (and ample budgets) have made New Trier a renowned institution for forty years. The consensus, confidence in the board, and deference to professional expertise are so extraordinary that no levy or bond proposal had ever been defeated prior to the expansion controversy.

Community pride in its school and belief in its quality led the school board to respond to the rising enrollment of the 1950s by proposing an expansion which, it said, would be adequate for twenty-five years. The villages ratified the proposal overwhelmingly, but the enrollment projection proved faulty, and by 1960 the enrollment again exceeded the rated capacity. Further expansion was dubious, because the site had only twenty-four acres. The board's effort to secure a small amount of land by condemnation of a residential strip boomeranged, the first defeated referendum in the history of the district. In retrospect, the decision to expand rather than build at another location was a $6 million mistake, and the public's confidence in the infallibility of its officials was shaken.

Confronted with the necessity of more classrooms, the school board considered the alternatives: more buildings at the existing site, contracting with elementary districts to retain ninth graders, a new school for ninth graders, one for ninth and tenth grades, or another four-year high school with the district partitioned. After consultation with the professionals, but not the public, the board concluded that another four-year school was technically, although perhaps not politically, the most feasible solution. They selected a site, issued a map demarcating two attendance areas, and scheduled a bond election for purchase of the designated site.

The campaign consisted of public meetings in each of the elementary districts, where the board explained the wisdom of its two-schools decision and the site selection. The meetings did not manufacture consensus; the board encountered vociferous opposition and a host of criticisms. The newspapers were bombarded by critical letters. Northfield officials objected to locating the new school in their little village; numerous people favored other sites; others intensely opposed the two-schools concept, arguing that the new school necessarily would be inferior and/or that it was a social segregation scheme by which residents of the west would get "separate but equal" schools. The districting map was a fatal faux pas. The proposition carried east of the partition line and was rejected overwhelmingly by the precincts of the proposed New Trier West. The board's unilateral decision was defeated, the second instance in sixty years that benevolent despotism failed in New Trier.

The reasons for the defeat were clear to no one, but the board realized that a different *modus operandi* was required. It established a large Citizens Advisory Committee representative of all the villages, to evaluate the alternatives and propose a solution. On the committee's recommendation, a firm was engaged to do a population projection study, which predicted increasing enrollment until 1980 and in amounts much larger than prior assumptions. Thereupon the CAC recommended a second high school at another site, which ended the one-school-versus-two controversy as the community accepted the fact that another four-year school was necessary.

The site question continued to be vexatious, with ardent advocates of six locations and confounded by conflicting village interests. Thwarted by the village trustees in an effort to acquire the Winnetka site recommended by the CAC, the board reevaluated the other sites, and finally concluded that the Northfield site was the best one available. So one year after the previous election, the electorate voted again on purchase of the Northfield site, this time with the price tag doubled.

The board's campaign strategy was based on its mistakes in the previous election. The new campaign had three propaganda arms: the New Trier Information Committee, an ad hoc group of resident public relations executives; the Committee for Two New Triers of one thousand block workers; and the Student Action Committee, which did canvassing and sponsored advertisements. The board held no neighborhood public meetings, because those had stimulated village chauvinism and furnished platforms for the opposition. This time the opponents were obliged to fight a battle of newspaper ads, which were expensive and obliged them to identify themselves as adversaries.

Other strategies included the embarrassing purchase of six mobile classrooms. The most astute one was the announcement that it would be "premature" to determine attendance areas before the new building was completed, and that the board favored the "major villages concept," i.e., that students from the larger villages should be in both schools—a nice solution of the volatile social segregation issue.

The Northfield site purchase was approved by a two-to-one margin by an electorate that had achieved a consensus on two schools, if not on the site, and that expansion could be deferred no longer. Nine months later the electorate voted four-to-one for a $9 million building whose appearance, specifications, and cost seemed to convince nearly everyone that it would be truly an "educational twin" of New Trier.

Okemos

The conflict over schools in Okemos, Michigan, a rural school district of seven thousand on the perimeter of East Lansing, was distinctly more typical than that at New Trier. Indeed, it must have been duplicated in scores of once-rural communities as city populations have spilled into the countryside and subdivisions have mushroomed with two, three, or six children in each of the new ranch houses or split levels.[15]

Cities are polyglot; suburbs are homogenous and frictionless. Suburban areas in the throes of heavy immigration and rapid transition are neither. The Okemos school district has distinct residential categories: the sleepy, unincorporated village; several large, established subdivisions; some highway strip settlements; and the open country dotted with the homes of blue-collar workers and some part-time farmers. The occupants of the subdivisions—Lansing businessmen, university faculty, and other professionals—are all new residents; most are college graduates and below middle age; and none are penniless. The composition of the nonsubdivision area is more variegated; but it is principally blue collar with a substantial proportion of long-time residents and retirees.

The immigration created an acute problem of school expansion and also contributed the diversity of values, and views about educational policy, that made the problem conflictual. With the high school bulging and two elementary schools on split shifts, the imperative need for construction was incontrovertible; there was, however, strong disagreement about what kind of school to build. The school board proposed a bond issue to provide a new high school, two elementary schools, and remodeling of existing structures. The proposition lost by a narrow margin in the highest turnout election in the history of the school district. Thereupon the board scaled down the proposal by deleting new elementary buildings and called another election.

The voting in the two elections was virtually identical. The community was about evenly split and no one budged. The supporters of the bond issue were principally parents of school children and the newcomers in the bourgeois subdivisions (the same people); the opponents were principally the old timers, nonparents, retirees, blue-collar workers, and other residents outside the subdivisions. The initiators of the first bond package were the "Parents and Taxpayers for the Bond Issue," all of whose members were professors or business or government executives.

Some community residents who opposed the issue felt that school decisions were being made by a nonrepresentative minority of the community. They felt that these self-appointed leaders were acting without regard for the opinions of others in the district. Indeed, at meetings held by the sponsoring group, the impression was made (erroneously or not) that anyone opposed to any portion of the proposal did not care about the education of the young people of the community. No discussion was allowed as this was an 'informational' meeting. This apparent overbearing attitude irritated many persons who attended the meeting.[16]

The reasons for the identical voting even after the proposal had been

Table 5-1
Three School Bond Elections in Okemos, Michigan

Election	Amount (million)	Projects	Votes Yes	No
First	$3.5	High school & two elementary	814	888
Second	2.6	High school only	797	890
Third	2.1	High school less "frills"	1247	253

Data source: Gary King, *Conflict Over Schools.*

Table 5-2
Correlates of Voting at First Election (percent Yes)

Residence		Ocupation	
Subdivision	52	White collar	57
Nonsubdivision	35	Blue collar	25
Parental status		Education	
Parents	59	More than H.S.	63
Nonparents	25	H.S. or less	32

Data source: Gary King, *Conflict Over Schools.*

trimmed were the sharp community cleavages; the fact that the bond issue had become an emotional one between "we" and "they"; and because the organized opposition, led by a retired army officer, directed its fire at the "frills" in the proposed high school—the swimming pool, auditorium, technical center, and campus-type building plan. For the opposition, those became symbols of extravagance and "progressive" education. In fighting those "frills," they were fighting the newcomers and their wrong fiscal and educational philosophies.

The tallies of the second election demonstrated the obduracy of the opposition. The "Parents and Taxpayers" were obliged to capitulate to secure any action at all. The "frills" were deleted from the blueprints for the third election, and the frilless high school was endorsed overwhelmingly by the electorate. Some weariness with conflict and a feeling that circumstances did not allow longer delay may have contributed to the lop-sided vote.

For an observer, some intriguing questions linger. Could the bourgeois cosmopolitans have avoided acute community conflict by including some of the more conservative "localites" in their planning group or by making their initial proposal more modest? Would they have achieved more by that strategy or would it have been less because of less incentive to the proponents of change? How much change should be sacrificed for peace?

Cities of the Prairie

City is a misnomer for any address in South Dakota, but the elections of five school districts in that prairie state, which were studied by Alan L. Clem, augment our sample as representative of small independent communities. They appear to be typical with two qualifications. South Dakota requires a 60 percent majority vote, which was one reason that those communities had election marathons, an aggregate of twenty plebiscites. These perceptive descriptions are essentially as written by Professor Clem with some condensation.[17]

Belle Fourche was the scene of four elementary school bond elections during two years. During the first campaign, strong opposition developed in the fourth ward to the proposed $225 thousand elementary school. That low-income, northern section of the city wanted two schools, one to be located in that section. The proposal lost overwhelmingly, getting only seven votes in the fourth ward.

Thereupon the school board proposed $395 thousand of bonds for twelve classrooms and simultaneously asked the voters to state their preference for one or two buildings. A majority voted for two buildings, but only 56 percent endorsed the bonds.

For the next election, a different tactic was employed to assuage the feelings of the north ward. The proposition was one building at the edge of town, with the provision that buses be provided in lieu of a second building. Some elements argued that one school would perform the function of "integrating" Belle Fourche. The fourth ward emphatically rejected that proposition and it was defeated. The *Daily Post* commented that:

There will always be oppostion to any plan proposed, but until we clear up, once and for all, by a clear-cut election, the matter of two schools, our community will continue to be split and the split will feed the fires of every unsavory movement that man has conceived.

We need schools and we call upon the school board members to join in immediate action, before this controversy wrecks our schools and drives away our teachers.

The school board responded by proposing $400 thousand for two buildings. The fourth ward turned in a thumping majority and the proposition carried. The residents of the northside got their own school.

During five years, Canton residents voted five times on proposals for grade schools. Four times the proposition was to construct a central school on the edge of the business district. At each successive election the price tag was marked up appreciably. The third and fourth efforts secured a majority of the votes, but fell short of the requisite 60 percent. The fifth proposition was for two buildings, one on each side of the city, and it garnered two-thirds of the votes cast. Wards I and II of Canton are higher status areas than wards III and IV. In each of the elections the affirmative vote was distinctly higher in wards I and II.

Mitchell residents voted on four variations of a new high school building. Three proposals received a majority, but not the requisite 60 percent. The slight variations in the amount of each proposal seemingly had scant influence on the outcomes. Evidently in Mitchell, as in Okemos, there were critics of frills. For the fourth election the school board dissected the project into three propositions: a classroom section, a gymnasium, and an auditorium and music section. Curiously, all three propositions passed handily. It would appear that more consensus had evolved over the eighteen months and the consensus was for a school with a full complement of amenities, but one can not be certain about that since the turnout of the last election was substantially less than the preceding ones. The volume of Yes votes dropped only slightly, but the number of negative votes dropped by half.

The Vermillion school board devised a cost-sharing arrangement with the city council and presented the electorate a joint proposal: a school district bond issue of $950 thousand for a new high school and a city bond issue of $330 thousand to cover part of the cost of a gymnasium-auditorium unit to serve both the high school and the community generally. The school bond issue secured the requisite three-fifths majority, but the city bond issue fell short by a bare fifteen votes. At a repeat election, the city bond issue again fell short of a three-fifths majority. "Rejection of the city bond issue," commented the newspaper, "put an end to the present building plans as presented by the school board." It did; at the third election the proposition was $1.02 million for the school building only, which carried.

There were profound contrasts in the voting of the wards, reflecting status differences and the location of the proposed building. The affirmative vote was consistently above 70 percent in the eastern wards and consistently below 40 percent in the western wards. The result, Clem observes, "seems to reflect the usual reluctance of low-income areas to support school bond issues, but also the fact that Vermillion's new school was to be built at the eastern edge of the city."

After a $1.85 million bond proposal for a high school had failed thrice, Watertown school officials devised two strategies which proved to be sagacious. In deference to criticism of the project's amenities, at the fourth election the original proposition was split into separate issues: a high school building and a civic arena. Even though the cost, $2.5 million, was much greater, both passed when standing alone, as occurred at Mitchell. That result demonstrated that the principal root of the opposition was not "frills," but the thorny problem of location, and the board achieved success by its adroit handling of that central issue.

At the preceding elections the proposal was for building on a tract acquired by the school board at the eastern edge of the city. The acquisition had seemed high-handed to some, and there was muttering that the project would enrich some property owners in that vicinity. The officials agreed to hold a plebiscite on the location issue. Simultaneously with the fourth bond election, voters marked a ballot indicating preferences among three locations. Possibly the school strategists preferred listing three options rather than two, in the expectation that opposition to the eastern plot would be split. To guard against the possibility that lack of a majority on the location preferential vote would thwart the fruit of a victory on the bond issue, it was stipulated that if none of the sites received 50 percent of the vote, there would be a run-off between the two top locations.

The location question attracted the interest of a great many persons who had not previously felt deeply involved, with volunteer partisans for each of the locations working mightily to get the school building in their part of town. The question became, in the words of one observer, "not *whether* a new high school should be built, but *where* it would be built." With attention diverted away from *should,* the price, and frills, and to *where,* and with all partisans optimistic that their preference might win in the plebiscite, the school board's preference won and the bond issues carried in every ward! Not surprisingly, the heaviest majority was in the eastern and higher status wards.

Observations

Few inconsistencies are visible in these eight examples of strongly controverted bond elections, and the small sample seems adequate to support a few generalizations. One of the clearest implications is that schoolmen and their eager partisans are not inclined to read the election returns as a categorical NO. Instead they look for clues about how the proposal and the campaign can be modified to build a majority. Hence, most school construction proposals usually reappear in modified form and eventually pass. This attests to the place of education in the American creed. Schools do get built, if not today then tomorrow, despite the hazards of referenda and even supramajority rules. This generalization, however, may not be as valid in an era of stable school population. All of these cases were in the era of the bulging schoolhouse.

Fashioning a winning proposal is more difficult in a supramajority state. Had the standard been a simple majority, the Dakota cities would have had nine rather than twenty elections. The supramajority may delay projects, but in Dakota in that era it was not an effective lid on expenditures.

The amount of the bonds was something of an issue in most of the cases, except New Trier, but never the exclusive one, and usually was less significant than some nonpecuniary ones. Apparently that was so even for the tax-conscious opposition in Okemos, for whom the "frills" were such important symbols, and who were battling the newcomers. Also, frills are not necessarily fatal. In both of the Dakota cities where they were segregated on the ballot, the electorates—a whole 60 percent—voted for them. In two of the Dakota cases and in New Trier, winning propositions were more expensive than some defeated ones. Evidently, among nonpecuniary issues there is nothing more important than the location of buildings, or whether "we get a building," although in New Trier the location issue was bound up with the other nonpecuniary issues.

Turnout distinctly affected outcomes in five of these cases. Apparently the high turnout was essential for the Cape City building program. Support correlated positively with turnout in two of the South Dakota communities and negatively in two. There were, however, no inconsistencies in the association of social status and voting direction. Voting patterns will be examined in later chapters, after consideration of some other dimensions of levy and bond elections.

Notes

1. The ballot proposition in Jackson school district, Massillon, Ohio, November 6, 1973. Akron *Beacon Journal,* July 18, 1973.

2. *The Blade,* Toledo, Ohio, April 8, 1968.

3. Louis S. Masotti, *Education and Politics in Suburbia* (Cleveland: Western Reserve University Press, 1967), p. 102.

4. Alan L. Clem, "Money and Schools: Campaign Strategy in School Bond Elections," *Public Affairs* (Governmental Research Bureau, University of South Dakota, February 15, 1964), No. 16, p. 5.

5. Another instance of a positive association of turnout and approval—the unsuccessful vote was at the low-turnout May 1971 primary; the successful one was at the 1972 presidential election.

6. Masotti, op. cit., p. 73.

7. Clem, op. cit., p. 6.

8. Ibid.

9. Masotti, op. cit., pp. 84-89.

10. An interesting variation in co-opting the community elite occurred at Fostoria, Ohio. LIFT was a civic action group, nominally at least not the creature of the school board, with additional interests. Its support helped push the affirmative vote to 49 percent in the third election and victory at the fourth one. *The Blade,* Toledo, Ohio, September 26, 1967.

11. The superintendent of Napoleon, Ohio schools quoted in *The Blade,* Toledo, Ohio, April 16, 1968.

12. Masotti, op. cit., p. 88.

13. This resumé is drawn from ch. 7 of Michael Y. Nunnery and Ralph Kimbrough, *Politics, Power, Polls, and School Elections* (Berkeley, California: McCutchan Publishing Corporation, 1971).

14. Masotti, op. cit.

15. Gary W. King et al., *Conflict Over Schools* (East Lansing: Institute for Community Development, Michigan State University, 1963).

16. Ibid., p. 32.

17. Clem, op. cit. Professor Clem does not bear responsibility for our condensation nor for some of the additional inferences we have drawn from the incidents.

6

Communication, Knowledge, and Influence

Referenda campaigns are viewed by school forces as a gigantic communication offensive. Torrents of messages are dispatched, but how much communication occurs? And with what effects? To what extent do campaigns achieve their manifest purpose of augmenting the electorate's knowledge? How much influence is exerted and who are the influential?

Referenda campaigns are communication processes about which little is known except what goes on at the transmitting end. Although the activities and strategies of the campaigners are easily observed, considerably less is known about the less visible activities and tactics of the opposition, and there is a dearth of anything beyond speculation and casual observations about the effects of referenda campaigns: How much of the campaign messages actually gets through? What proportion of the voters receive information and via which channels? What is the extent and accuracy of the voters' knowledge? How much are voters influenced and what influences them? These aspects of school elections have been almost totally neglected by the research to date. One reason for this neglect was mentioned in one voting study: "Formulating a questionnaire to measure these nebulous matters is exceedingly difficult, and we were not very successful."[1]

Four surveys of school referenda have taken some soundings about communication processes in referenda: Roberta Sigel's study of the 1959 Detroit election (described in Chapter 4), a 1970 study of levy defeats by the Washington Temporary Special Levy Study Commission, and our surveys of referenda in Bowling Green (1966) and Austintown (1970), Ohio. (Table 8-1 furnishes additional information about those surveys.) Some communication measurements are reported by a survey of public works referenda in DeKalb County, Georgia, 1961. And a study of school-community relations by the Stanford University Institute of Community Relations included a survey in one city during a school bond campaign.

Communications Channels

"Two channels stand out as means by which voters learn about the schools. Newspapers lead the other mass media as useful channels; personal communications follow in usefulness."[2] In the Stanford study, a sample of voters interviewed in "City D" at the time of a school bond election were asked which channels were "useful" sources of information about schools. Nearly all nominated newspaper articles and half mentioned school bulletins. Conversations with friends were regarded as useful by two-thirds of the sample; however that was less important for the bond issue, as only a fourth had discussed it in conversation.

The same information sources pattern pertained for the Bowling Green electorate. Newspapers were the foremost source, personal communication was second in frequency, and public communication (pamphlets) was a close third. The preeminence of newspapers as an information source is the inevitable product of three givens of school elections: most voters are not parents of school children, most people do not attend the public meetings where the school proposal is discussed, and the press is inclined to be generous in reporting school news and publishing campaign press releases. The importance of the press relative to other communication channels is a function of the scale of the school district. Sigel's measurements of influence indicate that the press was the exclusive source of information about the school proposals for the bulk of Detroit voters. Alternative channels may be far more important in smaller communities: e.g., a doorbell campaign may reach nearly all of the electorate in a small city, as in Birmingham; and 60 percent of the Bowling Green sample reported having seen pamphlets or leaflets. Leaflets could be the principal information channel if they were read. Two were delivered to every door in Austintown, but two-thirds of the naysayers in the sample said they had not seen a leaflet.[3]

School levy campaigns cannot rely simply on giving the pitch to the PTA, the luncheon clubs, and a few ad hoc public meetings. Two-thirds of the Bowling Green electorate did not hear the school orators at any public meeting; and less than a fifth of the electorates in Austintown and Bowling Green attended PTA meetings. It does not follow that PTAs are ineffectual and unimportant for communication; they may communicate via the mass media to a large portion of the populace, as occurred in the Detroit campaign.

Selective Exposure and Perception

The pioneer voting studies discovered the importance of conversation as a source of information about politics; the presence of a multitude of informal opinion leaders sprinkled through all social strata; the selectivity of conversation; and the two-step characteristic of the communication process, from the mass media to the mass of voters via the opinion leaders.[4] Our limited evidence indicates that these observations are equally valid for school referenda. Some school elections, particularly in a metropolis, may elicit little discussion; some elections, particularly in smaller communities,

Table 6-1

Communication Channels Useful to Voters of City D for Acquiring Information About Schools

(Percent nominating each as "useful")

Mass Media		Public Communications		Personal Communication	
Newspapers	88	School bulletins	49	Friends	68
Television	34	Speeches by school		School personnel	16
Radio	25	representatives	31	Others	10

Data source: Carter, *Voters and Their Schools,* p. 205. $N = 400$.

Table 6-2

Sources of Information About the Bowling Green School Levy

	Yes	No	Not Sure
Did you read anything about the school levy in newspapers?	320	44	6
Did the *Sentinel-Tribune* endorse or oppose the levy?	191	4	176
Did you see a television program about it?	38	317	12
Did you read a pamphlet or leaflet about it?	216	147	8
Did you hear the levy discussed at a PTA meeting?	69	298	2
Did you hear it discussed at a neighborhood meeting?	39	322	1
Did you discuss the school levy with friends and neighbors?	223	139	4

Data source: Hamilton and Marlow, "Survey of Voting on Tax Levies," p. 12.

Table 6-3

Conversation in Austintown: Own Levy Position Related to Position of Persons Mostly Talked With

Talked with persons	Levy Position	
	Pros	Cons
For	27%	2%
Against	33	68
Both	18	11
No discussion	22	19

Source: Cohen, *Voting Behavior,* p. 155.

generate a lot of talk. A "school crisis" can generate a lot of discussion even in a metropolis. Sixty percent of the Bowling Green sample had discussed the school levy with friends and neighbors, and four-fifths of the Austintowners had discussed it with either members of the family, neighbors, or work associates.

Who talks to whom and with what effects? The Elmira voting study reported that conversation was overwhelmingly between persons with similar characteristics, backgrounds, and opinions.[5] That definitely also is true of referenda conversations. Three-fourths of the conversations in Austintown were between persons who agreed about the bitterly controverted school levy. There was, however, a sharp contrast between the communication patterns of the pro and con voters. The pro voters talked to slightly more con than pro people, but the conversation of the con voters was amazingly one-sided. Ninety percent of their conversations were with like-minded people! By that selective exposure the con voters secured a lot of reinforcement, encountered no strain from cross pressures, and probably acquired little new information. The principal product of the talk about the school levy evidently was reinforcement rather than acquisition of information or the testing of ideas by debate.

Selective exposure to information was noted by the Stanford study. Yes voting is associated with the voter's choice of information sources. When his choice is school personnel and publications, the likelihood of Yes voting is high. "The favorable voter turns to the schools for information, while the apathetic or unfavorable voter merely turns away to talk to his like-minded friends."[6] Although newspapers and friends are the most frequently used sources for learning about schools, usage of those channels is unrelated to Yes voting.

Concomitant with selective exposure are selective perception and incongruence of the perceptions and attitudes of pro and con voters. Those phenomena were measured with respect to three of the "facts" most pertinent to the Austintown levy elections. Three-fourths of the voters knew that most of the prospective levy revenue was earmarked for teacher salaries, which were lower than in neighboring Youngstown, a matter that was well publicized in the two levy campaigns. In advance of the repeat election, school authorities warned that cutbacks might be necessary and also stated that "If the levy fails, there is no assurance the schools will continue to operate. We are facing a financial crisis." Another salient "fact," of course, was "high taxes."

Although pros and cons equally heard that most of the levy revenue was designated for teacher salaries, they got different messages about the salary level in Austintown. Half of the pro voters perceived the Austintown salaries to be lower than in Youngstown, but only a fifth of the cons shared that perception. The naysayers did not want to know that the Austintown

Table 6-4
Contrasting Perceptions of Pro and Con Voters in Austintown (percent)

Austintown teacher salaries are:[a]	Pros	Cons	School Authorities said schools would close:[b]	Pros	Cons	Taxes are:	Pros	Cons
Lower	48	12	Yes	33	43	Too low	15	1
Same	30	39	No	54	46	About right	62	34
Higher	17	27	Don't know	13	11	Too high	22	65
Don't know	7	12						

[a] "Are the salaries of Austintown teachers mostly higher, lower, or about the same as in Youngstown schools?"

[b] "Did the school authorities say that if the levy failed again that the schools might have to be closed for an indefinite period?"

salaries were lower. A voter does not exert himself to secure information incompatible with his attitudes, and if it is thrust on him, he may disbelieve it. A common response in the interviewing went like this: "They tell you they're lower, but I don't believe it."

Conversely, more con than pro voters got the message about cutbacks and the possibility of school closing. That message, particularly the hint of closing, was an illegitimate "tactic" in the eyes of the cons, an effort to coerce the voters—blackmail. Fewer pro voters perceived a threat of closing, perhaps because of their greater trust of school authorities.

Another sharp contrast appeared in the perceptions of the identities of levy supporters and opponents. Most pro voters perceived the levy supporters to be parents and the opponents to be retirees and others on fixed incomes. The con voters perceived teachers and other school employees after more money as the levy supporters and perceived the levy opponents to be homeowner-taxpayers. (See Table 9-4.)

The greatest difference of all was in the perceptions of Austintown taxes, which were viewed by the pros as about right or even too low, but were too high in the eyes of two-thirds of the cons. Patently that item was also a measure of their attitudes toward taxes, the very attitude so greatly responsible for all the incongruent perceptions. In referenda, as in other elections, voting decisions are largely a function of the voter's values, which cause selective exposure to information and operate as a perceptual screen; the information that filters through is interpreted within the framework of those values.

Also, the voter's values and predispositions determine how much confidence he has in the judgments of others, as well as his susceptibility to influence and by whom—a major dimension of selective exposure. Another prominent contrast between the yeasayers and naysayers in Austintown was their *professed* openness to influence. Most of the pros professed that they would place some confidence in the judgments of the principal sources of information about the school levy, but two-thirds of the cons said they would not be influenced by these sources, not even by the comments of friends. An obvious explanation for their rejection of the newspaper, chamber of commerce, and PTA is that all of those were pro-levy, but most cons did not even acknowledge any influence by friends, even though their conversations were almost exclusively with other cons. This appears to be related to their lower scores on a political efficacy scale and higher scores on a political alienation scale. Alienates are not trusting people. Persons with a strong sense of political efficacy can be open to the counsel of others, since they have no sense of inferiority or fear of being dominated.

The yeasayers' exposure to information was considerably greater than the naysayers', who did not attend meetings and two-thirds of whom said they had not seen the leaflets that were distributed to every house. That

Table 6-5
Willingness of Austintown Voters to Be Influenced (percent)

By	Greatly		Slightly		Not at all	
	Pros	Cons	Pros	Cons	Pros	Cons
Austintown Leader	13	2	39	22	48	76
Chamber of Commerce	18	9	37	26	44	65
PTA	21	7	45	23	34	70
Comments of Friends	5	3	42	35	52	62

"On a school election, would you be slightly influenced, greatly influenced, or not influenced at all?"

contrast was the natural result of the situation and the difference in the composition of the pros and cons. A majority of the pros, but less than 40 percent of the cons were parents. The pros were somewhat higher in social status, and hence involved in more communication networks. Furthermore, the public sources of information—newspaper, meetings, and printed literature—were hospitable to the values and predispositions of the pros but not the cons, who therefore restricted their exposure almost entirely to conversation with like-minded friends. Evidently the Austintown information exposure patterns were not atypical. A study of a nonschool bond election found two patterns of exposure. "Those who voted in favor of the issue were high exposure types, and those who were opposed were low exposure types."[7]

Voters' Knowledge

Professor Sigel attributes the strong influence of newspapers on school referenda voting in Detroit to the voters' sense of a knowledge deficit. How adequate is the electorate's knowledge of the important issues upon which it must pass judgment in referenda? Although this has been a subject of debate since the origin of state initiative and referenda systems in the first decade of this century, actual data about it are virtually nil. This is partially because measuring it is difficult; only one of the school election surveys has attempted it.

During the week after election, voters at Bowling Green were asked the purposes of the four fiscal propositions on which they had voted—the ballots had carried explanations of each proposition. The responses were 95 percent correct for two propositions, 80 percent for one, and 60 percent for another (ironically the one that passed). The school board had announced a list of cutbacks if the levy failed. Eighty percent of the voters got that message, and 70 percent were aware that teacher salaries were below the regional average. On the other hand, about half were unaware of the local newspaper's endorsement of the school levy. Two-thirds did not know how much the school levy would have cost them, but perhaps that was not essential information in that situation since anyone could surmise that four simultaneous expenditures would have more than a slight effect on his tax bill. Although this survey certainly did not measure the adequacy of the electorate's information for making sound judgments, it does demonstrate that the people at Bowling Green were not apathetic and that they were paying attention to the election propositions.[8]

Surely, Bowling Green was an atypical case. The conditions were optimal for voter interest and information: a small community, ninety square miles and twenty thousand population; four fiscal propositions at once, one of which was a repeat, strongly contested by an organized opposition; and simultaneously a bitter school redistricting controversy. Indeed interest was so keen as to produce an 80 percent turnout, and for numerous voters the propositions were more important than the concurrent election! Probably more typical was the information level in Austintown, where only 40 percent of the electorate heard the school-closing warning by school authorities and only a third knew—or at least acknowledged—that teacher salaries were less than in adjacent Youngstown.

Voter knowledge was low in the only other case study that reports even fragmentary data, a survey of a bond election in DeKalb County, Georgia. For that extraordinary election, a cafeteria of ten public works projects, few voters exerted themselves to acquire information and few were aware of the positions and activities of civic and professional organizations. The "basic thread" was the "extensive immunity to argument, information, or persuasion. Both sets of voters followed their own preconceived notions of their own and the county's needs."[9]

Voter knowledge may be distinctly greater in school elections than most other referenda, since a large fraction of the electorate has abundant opportunity to acquire information from their school children and direct observation. Thirty percent of the voters in the Detroit election described in Chapter 4 said they were influenced most by first-hand knowledge of school needs acquired as parents, participation in PTA, or school employment.[10] That figure appears to be close to the upper limit of information from direct contacts except for small communities and new housing developments. Parents of children enrolled in the school system were 42 percent of the registered voters in Bowling Green and 32 percent of the adults in Birmingham. PTA members were a third of the adults in Birmingham and 38 percent of those voting in Austintown. Adding school employees, the proportion of adults with current, direct contacts with the schools is likely to range between 30 and 40 percent.

It follows that knowledge about specifics of school elections should be distinctly greater among yeasayers than naysayers. School levy voters in eighteen Washington school districts were queried about teacher and administrator salaries and asked to evaluate their school board, teachers, and administrators. The "don't know" responses were two or three times more frequent among naysayers than yeasayers.[11]

Voter knowledge may possibly be more adequate for bond than operating levy referenda. Many people are likely to know something about the condition of their school buildings, whether facilities are obsolete, rooms are overcrowded, or the roof leaks. Except in metropolises, most bond issues are for construction of specific buildings, whose location, scale, facilities, and price tags have been well publicized. "Most of the schoolmen feel that this decision is within the competence of voters, who can—they think—see when structures need replacement or classrooms are overcrowded."[12]

Reliance on the Advice of Authorities

The basic premise of Nunnery and Kimbrough's campaign handbook for schoolmen is that voters are disposed to heed the counsel of school officials, the press, and community elites. The stated "reasons" of pro voters in Bowling Green reflect deference to the pronouncements of the school board. To quote one farmer, "I know three members of the school board, and if they say. . . ." When asked "Who supported the levy?" a third of the yeasayers in Austintown did not say parents or teachers; they said civic leaders, churches, and business.

In most political controversies, expert advice is abundant on both sides and anyone can choose his "experts." In this regard, school referenda present a polar contrast, since distribution of the supportive "authorities" is usually asymmetrical. All the authentic "experts" with the appropriate technical information inevitably are arrayed on one side, since the experts are the very promoters and direct beneficiaries of the proposition—their advice may be technically superb, but it certainly is not detached or balanced. Authoritative guidance is also distinctly unbalanced when school levies or bonds are promoted by prestigious civic leaders, the pillars of the community and the possessors of generalized authoritativeness by virtue of their status in the community.[13]

Such imbalance limits the use of authoritative guidance. Naturally people with an initial predisposition against a school proposal for whatever reasons—Catholics objecting to "double taxation," opponents of "high taxes," or critics of the new math—make scant use of the information and advice proferred by the "authorities" on the matter. The sources of influence cited by the Detroit sample were exclusively pro-levy, and no con voters in Austintown or Bowling Green cited the advice of any authorities as "reasons" for their decisions. Evidently the amount of reliance on the guidance of authorities in school referenda is inverse to the competitiveness of the election.

Opponents talk principally to other opponents of high taxes, tend to disbelieve the school campaign propaganda, and are intensely resistant to influence by community elites. There are patent reasons why naysayers make slight use of the usually abundant information and advice of authorities. It is the wrong advice, and one does not need experts to tell you that taxes are bad and high. Many of them distrust the local establishment generally and school officials specifically.

Here is another spring of alienation sentiment and hostility in strongly contested school referenda. Opponents of "waste" and more school taxes or the "frills" in that new building, or those peeved at a teacher, can readily perceive themselves as the beleaguered underdogs in an unfair contest with the entire local establishment, which is trying to "foist this on us taxpayers." Given the roots of their opposition, few such opponents are likely to feel much need of advice from technicians, newspapers, or the local notables, and they may resent the dearth of expressions by elites of the rightness of their position.

This picture should not be overdrawn. Community elites are not always monolithically behind school proposals, the citizens committee may be only a veneer of elite support. Occasionally opponents can secure endorsement of the rightness of their position and active assistance from some high-status individuals. Others may be conspicuous by their neutrality. The opposition in Okemos was led by a high-status individual. Some local notables were active in the organized opposition at Bowling Green, including a distinguished banker (and very large landowner). Sigel credits the defeat of the Detroit levy in 1957 to the propaganda of downtown property owners masked as the Citizens Committee for Public Issues. Elite disunity is likely to make a referendum competitive, and in some communities it may be a *sine qua non* for a defeat.

The Influencers

Hard data about influence is pitifully meager in the case studies of school elections, although it is evident enough that the volume of influence was slight in some of them. The most extensive measurements are of the 1959 Detroit election, one where a phenomenal amount of influence was exerted by the campaign—22 percent of the voters switched from their positions in the 1957 election. The Detroit sample was asked, "What influenced you

Table 6-6

Influences Cited by Detroit Voters (percent citing each source)

Press	43	PTA meetings	10
Television	15	PTA literature sent home	15
Radio	11	Doorbell canvassing	9
People	11	Citizens Action Committee & other organizations	14
Personal knowledge of school needs			31
Cited no outside influence			34

Source: Roberta Sigel, *Election with an Issue*, p. 79.

most in making your decision?'' Roberta Sigel writes of the responses:[14]

Nothing stands out as much as the important role of the mass media. Over half of the population was influenced by the press, radio, or TV. Next in importance were all the civic organizations combined—over one-third felt their pull. Almost as many respondents, however, were influenced by the school directly and their acquaintance with it. Only 10 percent were influenced by other people.

Organizations played a crucial role, but not those that are customarily thought of as influential. All the organizations that exerted influence were school-connected—the PTAs and the citizens committees. Only the PTAs were mentioned frequently by respondents, but the prestigious Citizens Advisory Committee on School Needs and the campaign Citizens Action Committee exerted influence invisibly by supplying material to the PTA and the media. It was not directly, but through the media that the committees reached the populace.

Propaganda, however, was not the exclusive vehicle of influence, since almost a third of the sample said they had been influenced by personal knowledge of school needs. Table 6-6 is an illustration of the asymmetry of information and advice. Thirty-four percent of the respondents had not been influenced by any external scource—almost precisely the proportion of No votes in the election.

The Detroit case is conspicuously inconsistent with the conventional wisdom about voting since the Erie County study: that campaigns have slight net effect on election tallies, that the principal influencers are opinion leaders and reference groups, and that the media are not molders, only purveyors of information to reinforce previously established preferences. Sigel offers a two-part explanation for the extraordinary influence of the Detroit campaign and the potency of the mass media. Referenda are not elections. Absent are the usual guides for voting decisions, party labels and prominent candidate names. The voter is called upon to pass judgment on a question that is complex, remote, and about which he has a paucity of knowledge.

The problem being complex and essentially of a professional non-political nature (or so he thinks), he'll look for guidance from sources which have this greater professional knowledge. Where he would blithely ignore the press in a gubernatorial election, he'll accept it on a school issue on the assumption that the newspaper writers are better able to judge school needs than he is.[15]

The fragmentary data of other referenda case studies do not contradict that logic or its factual postulates, but neither do they indicate any great influence on voting decisions or that the mass media are Pied Pipers. In the DeKalb County public works referenda, newspapers ranked first, but did not monopolize influence; many voters said they had been influenced by county officials or personal contacts. Only 4 percent said they had switched positions during the campaign and all of those ascribed that influence to personal contacts. The investigators concluded that in that low-turnout election there was very little influence achieved as "both sets of voters followed their own predispositions."[16]

In three communities where the authors have observed strongly contested, and unusually large-turnout school levy elections, no one was able to exert much influence. The Bowling Green school levy was fulsomely reported by the newspaper and endorsed in a front page editorial with no visible effect. The levy lost twice in Austintown notwithstanding support by the newspapers, church leaders, and the chamber of commerce. Levies were defeated six times successively in Youngstown despite press support.

Apparently the 1959 Detroit election was rather a deviant case. Perhaps the extent of influence exerted by elites and the media is a function of three variables; the unity of community elites, the amount and skill of the campaign, and the competitiveness of the election. Naturally elites and the press can exert considerable influence if there is no serious opposition and the measure will be carried by a landslide. Evidently the 1959 Detroit campaign of two years preparation was so massive and effective that it overwhelmed the resistance and became an unbalanced if not quite an uncontested election.

The Power of the Press?

Sigel's *leitmotif* is the power of the press in school referenda. "No element approached the press influence, which influenced far more people than TV and radio combined. Its nearest rival was not any other mass medium nor any organization, but people's acquaintance with their schools."[17] That is consistent with the (poorly documented) conventional wisdom of textbooks, e.g., "newspapers probably have a greater impact on local issues and elections . . . the local newspaper may be almost the only source for weighing school board candidacies or the desirability of a community bond issue.''[18] That is only speculation based on a bagatelle of impressionistic evidence and logic: Press power is slight in national elections because of the structured situation; voters' choices are determined primarily by party attachments reinforced by milieu and reference groups, and secondarily by candidate images and issues, which allows slight opportunity for the press to influence voting. Referenda are antipodal unstructured situations, posing questions of a complex, technical, and remote nature about which many voters have a dearth of information. Ergo, there is a strong propensity of voters to rely on newspapers for information and to be guided by editorials and the tenor of news columns by local reporters.

The logic is sound enough, but the weight of empirical evidence is *contra*. The Detroit case is the only school referendum study that reports great press influence. The press did not exert much influence in the DeKalb County referenda even though the newspapers unanimously plumped for the measures. School levies lost in Austintown, and Bowling Green, and, repeatedly, in Youngstown despite press support. Logically, newspaper influence should be maximal in elections where the voter is overwhelmed by a multitude of referenda questions. Mueller, however, found by examination of ballots in an election with nineteen propositions that the editorial advice of the Los Angeles newspapers had scant effect. ''It seems likely that there is no major impact of newspaper recommendations on proposition voting.''[19] We have observed numerous other instances of propositions losing despite enthusiastic press support. Metropolitan government schemes have lost repeatedly in Cleveland and Detroit. At Akron a county charter lost despite strong support by the single newspaper, as did an ambitious annexation scheme at Lansing, Michigan, which was a pet project of the newspaper publisher. Open housing lost in Toledo despite endorsement by *The Blade*, renowned for its political influence.[20]

The power of the press in referenda is considerably myth. The press is relied upon heavily by the public as a source of information, the foremost one for most voters, and the newspapers' characteristic willingness to publish school promotional releases as news or feature stores is a big asset for schoolmen. The effect of editorial endorsements, however, ranges widely from the pole of the Detroit case to instances like Austintown and Bowling Green where its impact is almost nil, except as reinforcement for the pros and perhaps of the cons as well. Possibly more influential is the subtle editorializing of feature stories by a sympathetic school news reporter, who may be the eager unofficial press agent for the school campaign. Press impact on school election tallies is attenuated by behavior patterns of the populace. More pros than cons expose themselves to the school election information in the press, and there is greater resistance among the cons to guidance from the press. Intense opposition to a proposition may produce a condition of strong resistance to influence from any source. Hence the power of the press varies inversely with the competitiveness of referenda, and—ironically—inversely with the need of schoolmen for press support.

The textbook speculations in their hedged phrasing are not incorrect; the Detroit case attests that occasionally press influence is profound. Hence the task is to specify the conditions that govern its strength, which can be done by reference to the elements of the logic for the inference that press power is greater in referenda than authentic elections: (a) referenda are unstructured situations, (b) the voters' dependence on the press for information and advice, and (c) their proclivity to accept the guidance of the press. Postulate b requires clarification. It is not the objective need for advice and information; it is the subjective need. The objective need of most voters may be great in most referenda, but frequently the subjective need is not.

Press power varies with the extent that those postulated conditions actually obtain in a referendum. Why was press power negligible in Austintown and Bowling Green? Those situations were not unstructured. For 80 percent of the electorates they were structured as much or more than a presidential election, and the subjective need for advice was nil for all but a few voters.

The empirical evidence indicates that press power is affected by several factors which may be enumerated as a paradigm. The influence of the press on referenda outcomes is a function of: (1) the scale (population) of the jurisdiction; (2) the technicalness of the issue and its remoteness from voter experience; (3) the extent that the issue is perceived as technical; (4) the extent that voters perceive a direct personal stake, benefits or costs, in the issue; (5) the extent that voter decisions are based on deeply rooted values and preferences; (6) the extent that community elites are united and aligned with the press; and, occasionally (7) trust of the local press, e.g., the Toledo *Blade* v. "those lying Atlanta papers," or generalized distrust of elites stemming from an unusual amount of political alienation as in Corning and Youngstown.

Conditions of the 1959 Detroit school levy were optimal for press influence: a metropolis, and one with a large black population predisposed to vote Yes if the campaign could activate them; community elites united and so energetic that there was not a significant opposition campaign; and a press that labored mightily to promote the levy. By 1972 conditions had changed. The school levies encountered resistance from far more people whose predispositions derived from deeply rooted values—opposition to taxation and racial antagonism—invulnerable to press influence. Similarly, in Youngstown the press had little influence in the face of intense antitax sentiment and political alienation.

Some nonschool referenda fill out the paradigm. Although press power appears to have been substantial in numerous state and large-city bond referenda, it has been ineffectual in promoting metropolitan government charters—situations in which numerous people perceive some stake in the status quo; elites are divided; and the opposition has been successful in exploiting ignorance, fear, and prejudice. Press power is maximal, *ceteris paribus,* for minor, technical amendments of state constitutions. It was about nil in the antipodal situation of open housing referenda.[21]

It follows that press power is likely to be less in school referenda, when controverted strongly, than for most other subjects. Schools are less remote from personal experience, a very large portion of the populace perceives an important personal stake—benefits or costs, it may not be perceived as a technical matter, and it relates to deeply rooted values. As competitiveness of school referenda increases, press power is likely to drop sharply.

Notes

1. Howard D. Hamilton and Byron Marlowe, "Survey of Voting on Tax Levies in Bowling Green," p. 11 (unpublished).

2. Robert F. Carter, *Voters and Their Schools* (Institute for Communications Research, Stanford University, 1960), p. 205.

3. Sylvan H. Cohen, *Voting Behavior in School Referenda: An Investigation of Attitudes and Other Determinants by Q Technique and Survey Research* (dissertation, Kent State University, 1971), p. 156.

4. Cf. Bernard R. Berelson et al., *Voting* (Chicago: University of Chicago Press, 1954), ch. 6.

5. Ibid.

6. Carter, op. cit., p. 207.

7. Alvin Boskoff and Harmon Zeigler, *Voting Patterns in a Local Election* (Philadelphia: Lippincott, 1964), p. 80.

8. Hamilton and Marlowe, op. cit., pp. 10-14.

9. Boskoff and Zeigler, op. cit., p. 87.

10. Roberta S. Sigel, *Election with an Issue: Voting Behavior of a Metropolitan Community in a School Fiscal Election* (unpublished), p. 79.

11. Temporary Special Levy Commission, *Summary Report and Research Reports* (Olympia: Washington Legislature, 1971), vol. 1, pp. 344-355.

12. James S. Ginocchio, *Local Tax and Bond Referenda in Ohio* (thesis, Bowling Green State University, 1970), p. 83.

13. Cf. Victor A. Thompson, *Modern Organization* (New York: Knopf, 1961), pp. 66-73.

14. Sigel, op. cit., p. 77.

15. Ibid., p. 21.

16. Boskoff and Zeigler, op. cit., pp. 87-91.

17. Sigel, op. cit., p. 77.

18. James Macgregor Burns and Jack Walter Peltason, *Government by the People* (Englewood Cliffs, New Jersey: Prentice-Hall, 1969, 7th edn.), p. 630.

19. John E. Mueller, ''Voting on the Propositions: Ballot Patterns and Historical Trends in California,'' *American Political Science Review* 63 (December 1969), pp. 1204-1206.

20. Cf. Reo M. Christenson, ''The Power of the Press—The Case of the Toledo *Blade,*'' *Midwest Journal of Political Science* 3 (August 1959), pp. 227-240.

21. Cf. Howard D. Hamilton, ''Direct Legislation: Some Implications of Open Housing Referenda,'' *American Political Science Review* 64 (March 1970), pp. 132, 136.

7 School Referenda and Community Conflict

Newspaper accounts of school crises indicate that acute community conflict is a significant element of some school referenda. Conflict was intense in the Okemos and New Trier bond elections and it surely was substantial in the South Dakota cases, since each involved three, four, or five elections before the issues were settled. The Cape City election was an example of adroit conflict management by schoolmen. By cooptation of the community elite beforehand, they minimized the amount of opposition by preempting its potential leadership and thereby delimited the scope of community conflict. With the assistance of the influentials and the press, they also succeeded in containing the menacing racial segregation issue. Patently, however, the election did involve considerable community conflict and the closeness of the election shows that the campaign and precampaign activities achieved a victory for the schoolmen but not a solid community consensus.

The cases in Chapter 5 are illustrative of the conflicts characteristic of bond elections, i.e., school construction issues. The patterns are somewhat different in tax levy elections; hence this chapter contains brief accounts of the severe conflicts that attended levy elections in five communities observed by the authors at close range. These vignettes may be more meaningful if preceded by some discussion of the nature of community conflict, drawing on analyses in social science literature.

Schools and Conflict

One way of viewing and explaining the structures of American public education is that they are elaborate arrangements for minimizing the frequency, scope, and intensity of conflict. Thus, schools are isolated from ''politics'' by the devices of the independent school district, nonpartisan election of board members, and the appointment of professional superintendents; the bulk of policy making is defined as technical decisions, to be made by professionals applying technical criteria rather than by public discussion and elections; and board members are expected to be passive, delegate authority generously to the educationists, and habitually defer to their judgments. It follows that bond, levy, and budget elections are aberrant graftings on the structure of the school polity, which, instead of insulating it from conflict, do the very opposite by assigning fiscal decisions to the electorate, thereby maximizing the arena of discussion, decision making, and politics.

Indeed, it is ironical that school districts are the only governments whose fiscal decisions are extensively subject to referenda, as the president of the Youngstown board of education complained following the sixth consecutive levy defeat:

We don't vote on whether or not to build a highway, where to place it, and how to finance it. At least not in a general election. Why should the community be voting on similar educational concerns?[1]

No structural magic can immunize schools from conflict and there never is a shortage of conflict for school officials. Witness the spectacular controversies over sex education, prayer, racial segregation, and even so-called technical concerns such as "tracking." Those volatile issues aside, schools cannot be conflict free, since they are political systems which, in Easton's definition, make authoritative allocations of values. They are political entities, and they are engaged heavily in political activity.[2] School finance is one of the most fecund breeders of conflict; controversy over who shall pay how much for local education is omnipresent in varying degrees of intensity, with or without referenda. It does appear, however, and schoolmen strongly believe, that the referenda system augments the amount of conflict rather substantially. Furthermore, when highly controverted referenda approach the scale of serious community conflict, other unresolved educational issues are likely to compound the disagreements over school financing.

Conflict management necessarily is one of the foremost, most continuous, and most delicate tasks of school officials. Conflict potential must be considered in the strategy decisions preceding referenda and during campaigns. The essence of the problem for schoolmen is how to secure voter approval of school "needs" with the minimum of opposition and conflict—an ideal that sometimes is unobtainable.

One can distinguish two different conflict situations in controverted school referenda, two alignments of the electorate. One characteristic pattern is that of school forces on one side and tax resisters and school critics on the other. Accommodation between those two factions is a difficult feat, sometimes impossible given the "win" or "lose" structure of referenda. The other common alignment is one in which school officials are caught in the middle of contending factions and are obliged to try to resolve the conflict. Most of the bond election cases in Chapter 5 were in that pattern.

Conflict over schools is moderated to some extent by the general consensus on the importance of public education, just as it usually is fanned by disagreements over means to that end. That ambivalence occasioned Masotti's caution to "be careful not to accept the school district as just another political system."[3] He offers this explanation of the potential of this system for both cooperation and conflict:

Traditionally, education has occupied a favored position in the hierarchy of public services; a general consensus has developed, based ultimately on Jeffersonian ideology, concerning the value of a good educational system. An individual is against education at the risk of community opprobrium, although conflict is common over sub-issues—personnel, curriculum, school finance, district organization, and facilities—wherever communities are unable to agree on explicit criteria of a "good" educational system.[4]

School officials trade on the "favored position in the hierarchy of public services" that education enjoys in managing the inevitable conflicts that arise in their bailiwicks. That "favored position" is something of a two-edged sword, however, as illustrated by the comments of an assistant superintendent of a suburban system: Following a successful levy campaign, he described the joy of "communicating" with local citizens, telling the "school's story," and rediscovering the favored position that education enjoys among his electorate. But this official's parting remark put these observations in perspective: "Still, with inflation and all, I certainly would not want to have to go to the people right now to ask for more money."

Conditions Requisite for Community Conflict

A prominent monograph on community conflict postulates that community conflicts are triggered by events having three specific characteristics: The event must touch upon an important aspect of community life; it must affect the lives of community members differentially; and it must be an event about which citizens feel that something can be done.[5] Certainly, within the tradition of locally operated and controlled schools, school referenda will touch upon an important aspect of community life. Despite centralizing trends, the local character of schools remains vital, and they continue to be heavily financed from local revenue. In scale, physically and financially, and in the concern and attention of the citizenry, schools are the foremost community institution. So much community life is centered about its schools that school districts are the most significant boundaries of many communities, especially those with a single high school.

Patently, the effects of school financial proposals on community members are differential; that is what the hubbub is all about. Some people stand to derive substantial benefits, as well as some costs; others, usually more numerous, will incur costs but no direct, material benefits. School referenda are the clearest instances of what Lowi has termed redistributive policies. School forces naturally try to play down the redistributive character of their proposals. If the intended purpose of a tax levy is to provide a new salary schedule for teachers, it will be portrayed as a measure essential for "maintaining the quality of our schools." Another standard campaign theme is that "everyone" benefits from good schools.

The reallocation of resources via referenda is so palpable and substantial that it cannot be disguised, and it is the principal basis for the "choosing up of sides," as the voting data in Chapter 8 will verify. The characteristic alignment in levy elections of school forces versus tax resisters and school critics approximates the cleavage between those who either earn their daily bread at schools or educate their children there and those without children in the public school system. Numerically, school forces are the vocal minority; but referenda are events in which the great silent majority can and does signal where it believes its interests lie. Cries of "double taxation" from Catholics[6] or "overtaxation" from farmers or businessmen and retirees,[7] complaints of "free loading" directed against renters[8] or "nest feathering" against school authorities and teachers,[9] these and similar charges of "unequal sacrifices" and "unequal gains" are often part of the vigorous and emotional dialogue of these redistributive events.

Numerous issues, problems, and grievances do not generate community conflict, because the populace perceives that little or nothing can be done; but in school referenda every adult can do something. There are various definitions of "the problem," but both supporters and opponents of ballot proposals perceive that something can be done. For persons dismayed by "high taxes," either local or federal, "this is the one opportunity to say no." Those who complain about unequal sacrifices and unequal gains can vote against the school levy or budget with impunity and anonymity. Their capacity to act negatively is likely to be reinforced by perceptions that the revenue or proposed facilities are unnecessary and their confidence that education is "too important" to permit schools to close, if at all, for any great length of time, regardless of the election outcome.

Opponents of school proposals envision three possible results from electoral defeats: (1) schools will therefore economize, and/or manage their finances "more honestly"; or (2) another referendum will be held with a lower "price tag," or even the same one but the day of reckoning will have been postponed with some "saving"; or (3) repeated defeats will compel "tax reform." The most vocal critics of the property tax and "high taxes" fervently hope to shift the incidence of taxation to some other source, any other source. That hope was responsible for the successive defeats of the Detroit school levies in 1972; it has become an important factor in numerous communities and some states.

School loyalists, also, may "do something" about the problem as they define it. Their cause is virtuous, given the exalted place of public schools in the American creed; they have a ready-made organization and no lack of other resources. There are few, if any, limitations on the rights of yeasayers to mobilize the community to "save our schools." When a proposal is defeated, they may resubmit it as often as state law permits—and they do.

Referenda and Conflict Dynamics

The referendum process increases the probability of acute community conflict. A plebiscite expands participation; campaign rhetoric and mobilization activity fan the flames of controversy; the situation becomes a struggle between "we" and "they"; and the controversy becomes compounded by the surfacing of other community frictions, as disagreement turns into antagonism.

A protracted levy controversy may set in motion an unfortunate chain reaction, as, for example, when a school board, desperate after one or two defeats, announces specific drastic retrenchment measures that will be necessitated if the levy is rejected again. Passions and civic participation escalate; the opposition cries "wolf" and "blackmail"; and the measure is defeated. When the beleaguered board moves to fulfill its campaign promises, it incurs about equally the wrath of its supporters and opponents and faces the prospect of wholesale resignations, teacher strikes, and even a parents' strike, as in Bedford Township.

The probability of conflict is increased by any expansion of participation in policy making, but there are peculiar reasons for school referenda to do so. Referenda spotlight and exacerbate tensions between government by a representative minority and policy making by an Athenian populist type of citizen involvement, as well as the tensions between professional management and political accountability.[10] Referenda violate the policy-making model preferred by schoolmen and their supporters—a model in which decisions are made by Burkean "virtual" representatives, influenced by their professional training, colleagues, and norms on one hand and their seasoned judgment of community folkways and mores on the other. That model is predicated on the assumptions that school officials are primarily responsible for delivering a vital service and that their performance should be judged on how well they achieve sound educational goals (effectiveness) and manage resources (efficiency). Politics is a last resort on their part when effectiveness or efficiency are threatened. The role of the electorate is to ratify decisions that promote sound educational goals, to provide school board members who are committed to high educational standards, and to warn officials when the community finds their behavior unacceptable. In the educators' model, school officials are, in William Gamson's conceptualization, the *authorities*, those who make the binding decisions, "the recipients or targets of influence and agents or initiators of social control." The members of the electorate are the *partisans,* those who seek favorable decisions.[11] The essence and peculiarity of referenda is that the roles are reversed, the authorities are the many, the electorate, and the partisans are the few, the schoolmen. The role reversal is more apparent than real in uncontested referenda, but in contested cases school officials must redouble their efforts and build a coalition in order to change their minority status; they are obliged, as Nunnery and Kimbrough advise, to exert political leadership.

Both sides in contested referenda have incentives to expand participation, since the outcome is determined by a count of ballots. The rhetoric is *about* the ballot proposition, but the contest is *over* the audience, since victory is likely to hinge on which side is more successful in inducing the most members of the audience to participate. At first glance this seems to be a peculiarity of plebiscites, but it is characteristic of all political conflicts in an open society as Elmer Schattschneider has pointed out.[12] Political conflict, he suggests, is analagous to a street fight and consists of two parts: a few individuals actively engaged at the center and an audience attracted to the altercation. The scope of the fight is expanded as spectators are moved to become involved. The strategic decisions for the protagonists revolve about inducing members of the audience to become allies or excluding parts of the audience from the fight. Occasionally, schoolmen employ an exclusionary strategy by conducting a low-key campaign or none at all. Schattschneider's comment that "Competitiveness is the mechanism for the expansion of the scope of the conflict. It is the *loser* who calls in the outside help,"[13] explains some of the phenomena of expanding participation in a school referendum conflict.

A referendum, it would seem, inexorably contributes to the solidifying of partisanship by limiting the ranges of choice, by barring compromise, and by compelling everyone interested to align with one of two camps. Most issues are prisms of many sides and a corresponding variety of possible compromises; but once an issue is cast into a ballot proposition, only two choices remain, with no further possibility for compromise. At that point it fits Michael Nicholson's dyadic representation of conflict: "A conflict exists when two people wish to carry out acts which are mutually inconsistent."[14] A referendum dichotomizes a community into "two people." It is presumed to be an expeditious way of settling matters, although the frequency of repeat school elections casts some doubt on that, but it is hardly a decision-making mechanism that minimizes conflict.

There is a set of self-fulfilling responses that originates in part from the expectations the "two persons" hold relative to each other's behavior.

Protagonists tend to act toward each other in such a way that those expectations are most likely to be realized. We refer to the stereotypic images of school referenda "others": private-regarding, overly tax-conscious electorates (as seen by school loyalists) and politically motivated, empire-building school officials (as seen by opponents). Each side has some proof of the existence of those images; previous referenda are the sources of those stereotypes. The contest between yeasayers and naysayers appears to be to some extent a product of anticipatory behavior relative to those stereotypes and to some extent a confirmation of their "truth."

School supporters who campaign vigorously for a favorable electoral outcome, no matter how clever, cannot escape the dilemma of telling the taxpayers what they do not want to hear, that the proposition (except levy renewals) will raise taxes (but for a worthy cause). Opponents are expected to, and do, communicate their displeasure with this news as "irate taxpayers" who question the school system's needs, its management of available resources, the fairness of the tax, the timing of such taxation. Since schoolmen know that dialogue only too well, they are prepared to respond to it even before it materializes.

Archetypical of such anticipatory behavior is a cartoon brochure of the second Detroit levy campaign during 1972. On the cover is a cartoon of an individual with dollar signs for eyes, perspiring profusely, obviously agitated, and labeled: "This is an Irate Taxpayer. . . ." The brochure's portrayal of the behavior of the Irate Taxpayer looking for a leprechaun is an amusing example of behavior expectations as seen from the perspective of school supporters. This is political conflict at an advanced stage; in Schattschneider's schema the *loser* is pulling all the stops in order to broaden the scope of conflict to include those among the audience still on the sidelines. The brochure certainly is not aimed to convert any tax resisters and its stridency reveals the desperation of the school forces.[15]

Campaigns by "those in favor of schools," may have the flavor of a crusade, which can be exasperating to naysayers, who thereby are placed on the defensive. Frequently their countering tactic is to shift the ground of the conflict from the issue on the ballot to a general issue that discredits the proponents of the measure. This often entails overt or covert accusations of the schools, e.g., "mismanagement of funds" or "too many frills."

Such diversification of the issues, as Coleman points out, serves two functions: It gains new adherents and increases the solidarity of those already committed.[16] It also escalates the level of controversy. Coleman has generalized this pattern of community controversy: (1) specific issues give way to general ones; (2) new and different issues emerge; and (3) disagreement turns into antagonism.[17] The danger at that point is the surfacing of other community cleavages that are only peripherally related to the original issue of the referendum; and school officials may be in the unenviable position of being caught in the middle, as in the Campbell and Bowling Green cases described below.

Political alienation is a sentiment that contributes substantially to the conflict in numerous school referenda and occasionally is the most potent force of all. A referendum may attract discontented alienates into the arena, since it offers such a convenient and rare opportunity for those with intense feelings of powerlessness and distrust of the holders and symbols of power in the community to give vent to their frustrations by resisting "them" who are trying to foist this proposal on "us."[18] When a school measure becomes the occasion for a substantial amount of such protest politics, the controversy inexorably will escalate in the pattern of Coleman's developmental paradigm. The alienates will inject additional and perhaps quite extraneous issues, the issue on the ballot will be generalized and beclouded, and disagreement will be transformed into antagonism. The impact of alienation in the Austintown, Corning, and Ithaca elections will be discussed in Chapter 9.

Another cause of antagonism is the disinclination of school forces to accept an electoral defeat as final. The naysayers view this as a violation of the rules of the game, a flagrant disregard of the will of "the people," and harassment. "When the school people lose, they just keep holding elections until they get what they want." Naysayers also are aware that as the electoral situation worsens for the schools, they step up the intensity of "asking" the electorate for support. For the second or third election the school board is likely to announce a list of cuts of school services if the levy or budget is defeated again. If that does not work, school officials may play their last card by announcing, with the blessing of their supporters, plans for a temporary suspension of operation at the date that the treasury will be exhausted. The repeat election is the ace in the hole for school forces. Naysayers view announcements of cutbacks, shutdowns, and repeat elections as threats and blackmail—and they are. Harried school forces view them as vital information and realistic tactics—and they are. This disparity in perceptions between the protagonists is both cause and effect of the community polarization that may occur in school referenda.

The school elections described below illustrate the content and dynamics of acute community conflict. They are not representative of school elections in general, because each of the five communities was confronted with an authentic school crisis.

Bedford Township, Michigan (1967)

The Bedford Township school crisis was described by a reporter as "the hottest emotion-ridden issue the township has faced in recent years."[19]

Community polarization corresponded to the pattern described by Carter and Sutthof:

> . . . school and community leaders arrayed against voters—organized or unorganized. These leaders are usually selected representatives of the voters; yet they face their most critical evaluation after they are elected when their policies are subject to review.[20]

Indeed, the working-class bedroom community of Bedford Township was the site of an extremely "critical evaluation" of its financially liberal (by community standards) school board—a process that included mass meetings, parents picketing and blocking school buses, a student boycott, and a threat to recall the school board. Conflict was triggered by the school board's proposal of two levies aggregating 20 mills in order to relieve an impending large deficit.

The most obvious aspect of the controversy was intense polarization over economics. On one side, the school board and its supporters were willing to incur a deficit in order to maintain what they considered a minimal level of educational services for a system with a rapidly climbing enrollment. As that faction saw the problem, there was no choice but to place the schools at the mercy of an electorate that had rejected twelve of sixteen propositions during the previous six years. On the other side, opponents insisted that the school system should live within its means and were adamant in their unwillingness to bail the school board out of a deficit which the board estimated could reach a million dollars. The projected deficit came as a shock to the financially conservative community, and the search for a scapegoat was the order of the day. As usual, school supporters nominated the stingy electorate for that role; the antitax faction nominated the profligate school board.

Another element of the controversy was the question of power and authority. There was little cross-cutting of cleavages in Bedford Township; the alignment of the financial issue corresponded with the split over the question of the legitimacy of the school decision makers. Prior to a recent election, the school board was dominated by financial conservatives who never engaged in deficit financing. Indubitably the conservative board was in tune with the ethos of Bedford and its authority was rooted in that genre of legitimacy as much as its election. The legitimacy of the liberal board, which had ignored the signals of an electorate that had voted so frequently against property taxes, surely was weaker. The policy of the new board was to resubmit issues until they were successful. After five elections, the electorate had finally acceded to the wishes of the board and the Good Schools Committee by approving a 5 mills levy in February. Now, only ten months later, the board was asking for 20 mills. The severity of the crisis over power and authority was demonstrated by a move among dissidents to recall the school board.

A third breeding ground for conflict was the political culture of Bedford, whose population boom was related to its low tax rate and the lower cost of new homes than in neighboring Toledo. The obverse side of the coin is the dearth of amenities, e.g., no sidewalks, water, or sewerage systems. Bedford is distinctly a caretaker community that eschews "extras." A concomitant of the caretaker policy, unfortunately for the tax-conscious Bedford citizens, is that there is no industry to share the tax burden for schools. Probably, the financial condition of Bedford schools had always been stringent and precarious, and they had operated in the black only because of the tight-fisted control of a conservative school board.

The township's ethos was not disguised; it accepted the imperative to live within its means, those of a caretaker regime. The existence of the Good Schools Committee and the election of a liberal school board shows that a substantial faction in the township rejected the caretaker image and service level. In the face of the deficit, the liberal school board added teachers for expanding the elementary art and music curriculum. Bedford's financial controversy was also a controversy over educational policy, values, and beliefs.

The sequence of disorderly events during the financial crisis fit our generalizations about the dynamics of bitterly contested referenda. Perhaps the Bedford case illustrates that conflicts are likely to have a lengthy history, sometimes beneath the surface of community events. The deep cleavage in Bedford antedated the crisis; the referendum of 1967 was a catalyst for the conflict. Since the incidents of the crisis were hardly therapeutic, surely the cleavage remained after the excitement was over.

Bowling Green, Ohio (1966-1967)

The defeat of a school levy in May 1966 was a shock for Bowling Green, a college town with some pride in the quality of its schools and an unbroken record of passing school measures. The defeat was narrow, and the school board rescheduled the levy—at a higher rate—for November. A formidable, organized opposition emerged to campaign against it, and the school forces mounted a strong campaign of which the most prominent feature was the school board's announcement of a list of cutbacks that would be adopted to balance the budget if the levy should fail. Unfortunately for the schools, the November ballot also contained three other expenditure proposals, and the school levy lost by a 1 percent margin. The fall of 1966 produced an extraordinary commotion for that sedate community.

A post-election survey revealed a sprinkling of criticisms of the schools, but not a substantial amount. Everyone knew that two factors accounted for nearly all of the naysaying, objection to "high" property taxes and the dissatisfactions of the residents of the two rural townships that had just joined the school district. It was obvious that the levy would not have lost in May or November if the Westwood district had not joined the city district. That was particularly disconcerting for some parents and school loyalists, since Bowling Green had accepted Westwood as a generous response to the plight of a district whose high school had been "decommissioned" by the state board of education.

The overwhelming No vote in the Westwood area was rooted in taxation, geography, and history. When compelled to relinquish their own identity, there was strong disagreement about what to do within Westwood, with strong opposition within the township most distant from Bowling Green to the decision to join the city. That legacy of bitterness was quite visible in the post-election survey. A large levy was understandably unappealing to the farmers and the less affluential nonfarm residents of the Westwood area, coming immediately after their taxes had been hiked by merger with the high-rate city district. Parents in the western part of the expansive district, fifteen miles away, were legitimately distressed by the long bus route; and some Bowling Green residents objected to busing in the Westwood children "to crowd our schools." The merger entailed some distinct difficulties and strains. The dilemmas of the Bowling Green school district were the product of events and conditions which no one planned, caused, or could control.

Defeat of the levy presented the school board with an agonizing choice: whether to cancel the new salary schedules promised the employees and the teachers, with the distinct risk of injury to a good faculty, or adopting the austerity measures it had announced before the election—curtailment of supplies, higher lunch prices, consolidation of bus routes, no transportation for high school children within the city limits, discontinuance of band and of music, art, and physical education in the elementary schools.

When the school board members arrived for their meeting, they confronted a packed hall of agitated parents assembled to resist the cutbacks. The meeting lasted until one o'clock with tension so thick it could be cut with a knife. Parents from Westwood were hostile to both the board and Bowling Green residents, and the Bowling Green parents were bitter since they had supported the levy that Westwood votes had defeated. The board acceded to some modifications, but it resolutely adopted the austerity program. During the balance of the school year, there were a lot of dissatisfied people.

The officials, however, took energetic steps to ameliorate conditions. The Bowling Green students and faculty welcomed the Westwood students fulsomely, and Westwood residents were invited to participate in decision making. The board instituted a Citizens Advisory Committee to Study School Operations and Finance, chaired by a Westwood farmer. After extensive surveys and a stream of well-publicized reports, the Committee recommended a levy of the same size as before, which unencumbered by other expenditure measures on the ballot, passed in November 1967, with slight resistance. The crisis was resolved by judicious measures and a year of marriage.

Youngstown (1966-1969)

December 13, 1966 was Responsibility Day in Youngstown according to the school campaign literature. "A day for ALL citizens to vote for THE SCHOOL TAX LEVY." Election tallies, however, exhibited a different notion of responsibility on the part of 70 percent of the electorate. Thus began a protracted school crisis with six consecutive levy defeats, culminating in the first shutdown of a large school system, as the 1968 Thanksgiving vacation extended to New Year's day, and Youngstown achieved the most national publicity since the bloody steel strikes. The conflict came to subsume other community controversies, which compounded the vicissitudes of the schoolmen; this account therefore is even less complete than the preceding descriptions.

One of the intertwined controversies that handicapped the school forces and contributed signally to the Responsibility Day fiasco was the rivalry between the Education Association (the YEA), a long-established unit of the National Education Association, and the new, militant Federation of Teachers (the YFT). Shortly before Responsibility Day, the YFT, supported by the city labor council, conducted an abortive strike for recognition, which failed when members of the YEA crossed the picket lines—a cardinal sin in a labor-oriented steel town. Recognition by the school board of the YEA as the bargaining agent elicited cries of favoritism and augmented the hostility of unionists.

Another problem plaguing the schools was a residuum of the past: social distance between school officialdom and a large segment of the electorate. Actually the distance was narrowing during the crisis period, but the change was not highly visible. Numerous voters perceived the school board and the superintendent as a continuation of, in a reporter's words, "the intrenched establishment" of old-stock Youngstowners—Protestant, business-professionals antipathetic to the labor movement. Municipal politics reflected the ethnic, religious, and prolabor composition of the community; but the schools had been the preserve of the upper-middle class. Many voters were unaware that new leadership was emerging, and therefore did not support the new superintendent or the school board despite its changing complexion.[21]

Table 7-1
School Levy Elections in Youngstown

Election	Mills	Yes	No	% Y
Dec. 13, 1966	5	7,646	18,551	29
May 2, 1967	7½	13,504	24,722	35
Nov. 7, 1967	6	19,281	24,856	44
May 7, 1968	12	16,612	22,555	42
June 5, 1968	12	11,326	19,171	37
Nov. 5, 1968	12	25,836	27,192	49
May 6, 1969	12	27,320	20,515	57

The lack of public confidence in school officials was discussed by a newspaper feature story before the seventh election:

. . . this lack of confidence was a major factor in the defeat of the previous levy proposals.

A restoration of confidence, perhaps, is the first need for gaining a more favorable response on public school issues. It also appears that the levy failure partly resulted from being caught in a cross fire.[22]

The school board lost support at both ends, receiving only lukewarm support from the establishment it had replaced and getting short shrift from the discontented sector of the populace, which failed or refused to notice the changing composition of school officialdom.

The "old" board and the "old" superintendent had incurred the wrath of influential labor leaders. During the crisis period, the new board had two major collisions with labor leadership. One was recrimination over the defeat in a referendum of a proposal to establish a community college. Labor leaders charged that the school people were responsible by way of their passivity, and there was talk that labor might retaliate against the schools.[23] The other dispute—recrimination over the bargaining election between the rival teacher organizations—was coincident with the sixth levy election, and involved heated exchanges in the mass media. Local union chieftains backed the YFT, but the YEA won the election decisively. The labor council president accused the school board of being antilabor and tilting the election. The school board president retorted at a press conference, and charged that a labor leader was responsible for the levy defeat in November 1968. Then the YFT demanded the board president's resignation.[24]

The school board made a unilateral contribution to the reservoir of distrust by the foolish strategy of the June 1968 special election. After four defeats, the desperate board resorted to the sleeper strategy, truly a "quiet election"—no media publicity, no billboards, and no literature. That strategy was foredoomed, since there is a strong positive turnout-outcome relationship in Youngstown (see Table 7-1); it was a bad *faux pas* which smacked of the oligarchical ways of the old school establishment and left a bitter taste.

The following January, the changing board acquired a new president, an indefatigable leader who was popular with unionists and the voters. His open style helped to dispel the public distrust and went some way toward washing out the accumulated bitterness. The board reduced the distance between itself and the public by a series of open meetings.

Three other ingredients of the Youngstown travail are important components of school referenda in any metropolis today: the "taxpayers' rebellion," the changing racial and social composition of the schools, and the religious-ethnic resistance to the levies. The taxpayers' rebellion was significant, but needs no elaboration as it was no different from the tax-related referenda conflicts previously described.

The Youngstown school district was in a period of transition, in many ways disintegrative and disruptive. The transition was unmentioned in official school communications and only obliquely in the newspaper, but its side effects showed up in the election tallies. During the period, the enrollment of black children rose to 40 percent of the total. There were problems of discipline, and rumors of racially related incidents pervaded the atmosphere. The flight to the suburbs was headlong, and there was a minor flight within the city to parochial schools, especially from those high schools that had "changed" radically. The official word was that there was no racial aspect to the levy defeats, but blacks sensed that there was, and so did school officials, who worried about it—off the record. Euphemisms crept into the dialogue of the levy elections, e.g., "children of renters," "expensive vandalism in the schools," and "children of parents on welfare." In some less-refined circles euphemisms were not used.

The Catholic vote was also a touchy subject in Youngstown. Although Catholic leaders called for support of the levies, it was not always forthcoming, especially in the ethnic enclaves that complained of "double taxation." According to a school official, many of the ethnics were industrious, thrifty people who had earned their money by labor in the steel mills, and did not "want to share their affluence with other minorities."[25] The ethnic-Catholic voting indubitably was important, but not susceptible to accurate measurement except in one solidly ethnic ward which had the highest turnout and the most naysaying in every election.

Since most of the elements that contributed to the levy defeats tended to go together, one has to be cautious lest the end product, the Youngstown levy resister, becomes stereotypic. That became a concern of the school forces. In the seventh election, they carefully avoided stereotyping the opposition or offending any segment of the electorate. The conciliatory effort included a survey commissioned by the chamber of commerce to "ascertain the reasons for the failures" and to provide "guidelines for future action by the Board of Education."[26] The tone, terminology, omissions, and diplomatic conclusions of this report reflect, rather than scientific analysis, an attempt to create an atmosphere conducive to passage of the levy and to resolve the crisis in a community racked with recriminations directed against ethnic, religious, racial, and labor groups. Obviously the report writers were well aware of the volatility of their subject and the need for therapy. The report is a model of diplomacy, written to offend no one, to remedy rather than exacerbate the situation.

A climate favorable for the school levy was achieved on the seventh try. An unexpected contribution was a successful arm-band campaign by the school children. The deliberately low profile of the school board aided both the contagion of "Join the Arm Band" and the canvassing done by parents. The campaign visibly generated support from a cross-section of the community, although victory could be interpreted as another instance of the electorate finally "giving in" when it was weary of conflict.

Austintown, Ohio (1970)

Twice within the space of five weeks, voters in Austintown rejected a new operating levy, and in 1971 they twice rejected a capital improvements levy. It was not until May 1972 that the community passed by a slender margin a combination operating and maintenance levy. This account is restricted to the conflict surrounding the 1970 elections.

The series of defeats and the rancor is surprising in view of the relative affluence of the community. Austintown is quite unlike Bedford Township. It is largely middle class, and has middle-income tract housing, modern apartments, new commercial development, and light industry. It is the epitomization of the family-centered suburb of shopping centers, new schools, and wide expanses of grass.

In 1970 this "suburbia USA" was in the throes of a conflict over attempts to raise the school millage to the level of neighboring and less affluential communities. Teacher salaries were lower than in surrounding communities, and the teachers were restive. The school board also was caught in the middle over deficit financing. As in Bedford, some vocal members of the community were critical of deficits.

Pervading the dialogue of the conflict was the persistent rumor that school money had been mismanaged. The new stadium came under fire —costs exceeded the estimates. After clamoring for that symbol of virility and success, the community was having second thoughts about the upkeep expense. The schools tried to soften the situation by publicizing that its equipment and buses were stored under the grandstand, but that made no impression on the dissident voters who talked about "some graft in that stadium deal." On the local talk show, in letters to the editor, and even at school meetings, the school administration was accused of everything from aloofness to mismanagement of funds.[27]

On the other side of the issue, support for the schools was visibly evident from the churches, professional groups, businessmen, and all the organizations of note. On the surface it appeared that the coalition of local elites would carry the issue, with only scattered resistance from some vocal dissenters. There were, however some clues that all was not well. During the question periods of the public meetings conducted by the school officials, there always was some hostility toward the school establishment. The complaint was repeated often that the schools did not like to answer questions and resented any sign of opposition.

Why should school measures generate so much hostility and lose repeatedly despite the backing of local elites in a suburb that looks like a natural for support of schools? The explanation is its location and the composition of its population. Austintown is contiguous to Youngstown, whence came many of its residents. In a sense, it has imported the problems of Youngstown, especially the ethnic, religious, and unionist opposition to property taxes.

Austintown is a union town; unionists and their spouses outnumbered other voters in 1970; and nearly two-thirds of the unionists rejected the school levy, which was endorsed by a majority of the nonunionists. Controlling for parental status reveals not only was the levy opposed by unionists who had children in the school system, but that their support rate was even slightly less than that of nonunionist voters without school children.

Of course, union membership per se is not the full explanation of Table 7-2; it is a surrogate for status variables and attitudinal configurations. Political alienation, the important attitude in the Corning and Ithaca bond elections, was significant in Austintown. One of the strongest correlates of the voting was political alienation, the incidence of which was greater among the unionists. Thirty percent of the unionists scored high on a political alienation scale, compared to 17 percent of the nonunionist voters. The levy support rate of parents high on the alienation scale was only 30 percent, compared to 80 percent for the parents that scored low on alienation. The support rate of nonparents high on alienation was 10 percent.[28]

School elections in Austintown are affected very considerably by two overlapping demographic variables, ethnicity and religion. The association of those variables and the levy voting is shown in Chapters 8 and 9 (Tables 8-7 and 9-7). Only a fourth of Austintowners are of British stock; there are equal numbers of Catholics and Protestants; a significant number of children attend parochial schools.

Table 7-2

Voting in Austintown by Union Affiliation (percent favorable)

	Parents*	(N)	Nonparents	(N)
Unionists	43	(100)	29	(97)
Nonunion	67	(78)	45	(83)

*Of children in Austintown school system.
Source: Cohen, *Voting Behavior in School Referenda.*

The composition of the population and some political alienation appear to be the roots of the difficulties of Austintown schools and the conflict. The large proportions of unionized manual workers, European ethnicity, and Catholics contribute to the widespread opposition to property taxes. The large proportion of Catholics augments the redistributive character of school taxes. Political alienation contributed to confounding the levy question and shifting of the issue, as diffuse discontent was projected on the school establishment. After two years of conflict and four levy defeats, a new superintendent was able to expand the base of school support and secure passage of a levy (barely); but a repetition of the events of 1970-1971 is not an impossibility.

Campbell, Ohio (1973)

School opened in September 1973 at Campbell with a strike by both teachers and employees, the second strike resulting from three levy defeats during the preceding sixteen months. School officials broke the strike by invoking the penalty provisions of the state law forbidding strikes by public employees and threatening to hire replacements of the strikers.[29] This is an extraordinarily complex and multifaceted community conflict in which the financial issues are intertwined with a struggle for control of the schools and controversies over curriculum, purchasing practices, and personnel policies.

School politics in Campbell traditionally have resembled courthouse politics—personal, private-regarding, and parochial. Supply and equipment contracts usually were not put up for bids, but let to friends, and always local firms. Promotions, especially to the rank of principal, also were treated as patronage and reserved for local boys. A new superintendent in 1973 did not adhere to the traditional political style. He appointed a principal from outside the system, and he made purchases by bids. His deviant behavior sparked a struggle for control of patronage by those who had influenced those decisions and saw their influence diminishing. Control of mundane school decisions was an important factor in the defeat of a levy in July 1973.

One of the most conspicuous elements of the imbroglio has been the discontent of the teachers, displeased with salaries and various economy measures by the superintendent. Prior to a levy election in May 1972, the superintendent reduced the teaching staff. If that was intended, inter alia, to influence the voters, it did not succeed, for the levy lost. The teachers struck and schools were closed for two weeks. Prior to the next levy effort in April, the new superintendent announced another reduction in force; some nontenured teachers would be liberated. And the levy failed again, although by a small margin. Not surprisingly, the subsequent salary negotiations between the board and the teachers association stymied and remained stalemated until after the next levy election in July. By that time, teacher apprehensiveness and dissatisfaction were compounded by the report of an ad hoc "fact finding" panel, and some teachers even joined the opposition to the levy. In September they struck again.

The "fact finding" panel, chaired by a prestigious local judge, was created to study the salary negotiation impasse and furnish third-party counsel. The panel's report in July surely did not facilitate the negotiations, since its observations and uninhibited advice were largely extraneous to the salary negotiations matter. However, the report, which appears to be an astounding instance of a body exceeding its mandate, was not without consequences, especially for the next levy election.

The report asserted that the superintendent's salary ($25,000) was "much too high"; the per pupil costs in Campbell were "relatively large"; and an austerity program was in order; kindergarten should be discontinued and perhaps art and music teachers should be eliminated. The most spectacular observations and advice challenged the legitimacy of the school authorities:

The Board of Education has significant (sic) money to operate a good, efficient school system with well-paid teachers; but it must operate that system according to law, and not for the purpose of paying political obligations or employing relatives and friends.

Until the board does this, it is not entitled to, nor will it receive the support of the citizens of Campbell.

It may be that the board, as now constituted, cannot accomplish this goal. If this is so, then the only cure for the present financial condition of the schools of Campbell is the resignation of the present board and the election of a new board.[30]

Declining the invitation to resign, the flabbergasted and outraged officials replied to the report point by point. They even found themselves defending a type of politics that they did not espouse, one they had inherited and were in the process of changing. They also tried to enlist the ethnic attachments of the community by charging that the panel's report was an attack on "the Slavics, Greeks, Italians, Negroes, and Puerto Ricans of

Campbell."[31] Evidently the rebuttal was ineffective. The school levy a few days later was slaughtered by a vote of three to one.

The sovereign people had spoken three times and the third time with a stentorian voice that should settle everything. Actually nothing was settled by the July election or the audacious panel's report which added so much fuel to the conflict. Nor were things settled when the schools reopened two weeks late, after the teachers and employees were "persuaded" by invocation of the Ferguson Act. Another levy election was scheduled for November, accompanied by the announcement that if the levy should fail the treasury would be bare by December.[32] Another vacation was in sight for Campbell children.

Incidence of Conflict in School Referenda

Intense conflict and polarization of a community are only occasional features of school referenda, but how occasional is unknown. In six of the nine case studies of school referenda voting that have come to our attention community conflict had reached crisis levels and polarization had dominated the community stage for more than election day or a few weeks before or after.[33] Most of those crises were measured in months or years rather than weeks, with peaks of tension around election time. The important point is that as episodic as these conflicts were, they were not insignificant affairs. As Schattschneider contends, there is an infinite number of potential conflicts at any one time in any modern society, *"but, only a few become significant . . . A democratic society is able to survive because it manages conflict by establishing priorities among a multitude of potential conflicts."*[34]

Newspaper reporting indicates that in the competition among local conflicts, a high priority is generally assigned to controverted school elections. They are front page news for the community, for surrounding communities and sometimes for the state. The most dramatic ones acquire national attention, sometimes from unlikely media. Youngstown voters received the "Laugh-In" television program's "Flying Fickle Finger of Fate Award."

Recently, the incidence of crisis-level conflicts seems to have been greatest in Ohio, Michigan, California, Missouri, and West Virginia, probably in that order of descending frequency. All these states have *both* school levy and school bond referenda. Logic suggests that this compounds the problem of going to the people for financial support of public education. The incidence of crisis appears to be roughly proportional to the volume of referenda, occuring more often in those states where the schools might be

Table 7-3

Distribution of California School Levy Elections as an Indicator of Stress

Percent YES Votes	Percent of Elections			
	1966-67	1967-68	1969-70	1971-72
Below 35	17	7	11	10
35-44	20	18	24	23
45-54*	28	24	33	29
55-64	16	24	16	14
65 & over	19	28	16	25
N	(209)	(120)	(261)	(177)

*Marginal contests, indicator of stress.

Data source: California Department of Education.

said to be in "double jeopardy," with tax as well as bond elections, and where operating levy or budget elections are most frequent.

How can the incidence of conflict be measured? Newspaper accounts are a rough but unreliable indicator since newspaper practices vary. Some play down local conflict, or may not report it, perhaps merely for lack of a feature writer; some seem to play it up in order to assist the "good guys." The volume of school "closings" is an utterly unsatisfactory measure. Although closings are indubitably indicative of community conflict at an advanced stage, few conflicts are climaxed by a suspension of operation, e.g., this occurred in only one of the preceding five illustrations of community conflict, and have occurred in only a few states.

A better measure is the frequency of repeat elections, one of the conflict-spiralling mechanisms and an almost invariable feature of crisis-level conflict. The scheduling of a repeat election indicates the existence of conflict, which the repeat is likely to increase by a more intensive campaign and by antagonizing the naysayers. Thus, the frequency of conflict is substantial in some states, as witness the number of repeat elections.

Another measure has been offered by Wirt and Kirst—the proportion of close elections. They suggest that elections where the results are in the 45-54 percent range reflect sharp cleavage and a "stressful environment."[35] By that yardstick, most school elections are not intensely conflictive. The proportion of "stressful" levy elections in California, for example, ranges from a fourth to a third annually. This may be the best available measure of the incidence of community conflict in school elections but it is not a precise one. It is a direct measure of the amount of consensus, but it is only an indicator of community conflict. Some close elections may be low-intensity affairs, and conversely elections that are not close can occur in a distinctly "stressful environment," e.g., Campbell and Youngstown. It appears to be a good indicator of the relative amount of community conflict, from year to year or for interjurisdictional comparison.

The data of Table 7-3 furnish additional support of the hypothesis that the incidence of community conflict is roughly proportional to the frequency of referenda. Observe the correspondence between the proportion of elections in the "stressful" zone and the annual volume of elections. Evidently this relationship holds both within a state and between states.

Conclusion

The motif of conflict ought not be overdrawn lest the impression be conveyed that all conflict is an unmitigated evil for schools or that the public school system is on the verge of collapse. Emphasis of the new-fashionable systems theory on "system maintenance" and its processes seems to have led to an epidemiological view of conflict. One of the endlessly repeated cliches is that "conflict threatens system stability and system maintenance"; with respect to school referenda conflict this is hardly more than a half truth. Certainly referenda conflicts affect the stability of some school systems, but they do not seriously threaten system maintenance—even in Youngstown or Detroit. Sooner or later a referendum conflict subsides and is replaced by other issues in the school district. Racial conflict, not infrequently an ingredient of referenda conflict, may be an authentic threat to system maintenance in some communities.

Social science also has its counterpoint, in this instance the theory that conflict in general and community conflict specifically is not entirely dysfunctional.[36] Thus, a moderate amount of controversy in school elections could be said to be beneficial as a stimulant of the citizenry's interest and participation, by requiring schoolmen to reply to objections to the proposition and to miscellaneous criticisms, by quickening officialdom's sense of responsibility, and by making the election a vehicle for the acquisition by more citizens of more information about their schools than would likely occur in a conflictless referendum. It has been noted that conflict may even be a unifier—eventually. Possibly the Birmingham and New Trier controversies were instances, as the final outcome of each was a considerable consensus. How frequently that felicitous outcome occurs is unknown. One suspects that acute community conflicts rarely have a net gain. Nor is conflict beneficial if it persists, becomes chronic, and develops deep cleavages and durable animosities.

Conflictual referenda have additional significance for schoolmen. Strenuous campaigns and the attendant conflict are hard on the myth that schoolmen are not politicians. With referenda, few schoolmen can escape conflict and politics; unless they are willing to accept austerity indefinitely, they have to accept both, as did the school principal who remarked, "at least we can say that we are one defeat nearer to victory."[37]

In conclusion it may be well to remind ourselves that school referenda and community conflict are not synonyms, and that there appears to be no shortage of conflict about schools in those states with few or no referenda. In most elections there is a distinct majority pro or con, something of a community consensus about the matter; some referenda, in fact, are not at all conflictual; e.g., some Oregon budget elections are unanimous.[38]

Nevertheless, the volume of conflict attendant to school referenda is substantial, even though adequate measurement is lacking; and this seems to be a significant liability of the system. It would be difficult to argue that plebiscitary democracy in school districts inhibits the incidence of conflict or that it is a very efficacious instrument of conflict resolution. Further, we are inclined to regard conflict as an important criterion for appraising policy-making institutions. In subsequent chapters we will consider other criteria pertinent to appraising school referenda, but at this point we turn to an investigation of voting behavior in school elections.

Notes

1. Paraphrase of personal discussion with the president of the Youngstown Board of Education during the seventh levy campaign. He voiced similar sentiments as a panelist at a forum sponsored by the League of Women Voters of Greater Youngstown held at Chaney High School, February 27, 1969.

2. Thomas H. Eliot, "Toward an Understanding of Public School Politics," *American Political Science Review* 53 (December 1959), p. 1035.

3. Lewis H. Masotti, *Education and Politics in Suburbia: The New Trier Experience* (Cleveland: The Press of Western Reserve University, 1967), p. 7.

4. Ibid., pp. 7-8.

5. James S. Coleman, *Community Conflict* (New York: The Free Press, 1957), p. 4.

6. This was a factor of unknown proportions in the six school levy defeats in Youngstown, Ohio from December 1966 to November 1968. That this theory received national recognition is evident from the reference of Robert E. Agger and Marshall N. Goldstein, *Who Will Rule the Schools: A Cultural Class Crisis* (Belmont, California: Wadsworth Publishing Company, Inc., 1971), p. 2, to "opposition to public school taxes by a parochial school constituency as in Youngstown, Ohio. . . ."

7. Howard D. Hamilton and Byron Marlowe, "Survey of Voting on Tax Levies in Bowling Green" (unpublished).

8. This was evident in Austintown. One of the authors of this book personally completed over half of the surveys in that study and he was impressed with the generally shared image of renters as "nontaxpayers" vis-a-vis public education and the anger that this image called forth from levy supporters as well as nonsupporters.

9. Sylvan H. Cohen, "Voting Behavior in School Referenda: An Investigation of Attitudes and Other Determinants by Q Technique and Survey Research" (unpublished dissertation, Kent State University, 1971), p. 159.

10. Agger and Goldstein, op. cit., p. 1, on the juxtaposing of representative and direct democracy; Robert L. Lineberry and Ira Sharkansky, *Urban Politics and Public Policy* (New York: Harper & Row, Publishers, 1971), pp. 110-112 on the tension between professional management and political accountability.

11. William A. Gamson, *Power and Discontent* (Homewood, Illinois: The Dorsey Press, 1968), p. 18.

12. E. E. Schattschneider, *The Semi-Sovereign People: A Realist's View of Democracy in America* (New York: Holt, Rinehart and Winston, 1960), pp. 1-19 and 62-77.

13. Ibid., p. 16.

14. Michael Nicholson, *Conflict Analysis* (New York: Barnes & Noble, Inc., 1970), p. 2

15. The Leprechaun Search Committee, Detroit, Michigan (pamphlet).

16. Coleman, op. cit., p. 10.

17. Ibid., pp. 9-11.

18. Wayne E. Thompson and John E. Horton, "Political Alienation as a Force in Political Action," *Social Forces* 38 (March 1960), p. 191.

19. Patricia Schreiner, "Turbulence in Education: Bedford Township," *The Blade*, Toledo, Ohio, December 10, 1967, Section B, pp. 1 and 2.

20. Richard F. Carter and John Sutthof, *Communities and Their Schools* (Stanford, California: Stanford Institute for Communication Research, 1960), p. 14.

21. Clingan Jackson, "Confidence Is Key to School Levy," *Youngstown Vindicator*, January 26, 1969, pp. 1 and 4.

22. Ibid.

23. Richard J. Baker, "Youngstown Schools Face an Uncertain Future," *Ohio Schools*, January 3, 1969, p. 20.

24. *Youngstown Vindicator*, November 26, 1968, p. 1.

25. John Morton, "The Voters Won't Pay More, So Ohio City's Schools Will Close," *The National Observer*, November 26, 1968, p. 2.

26. "YSU to Probe Voters' Motives on Schools," *Youngstown Vindicator*, January 31, 1969, p. 4. The "probe" was J. Kiriazis and S. Hotchkiss, "Community Attitudinal Survey of Youngstown Voters on School Tax Levies" (manuscript, Youngstown State University library).

27. Cohen, op. cit., p. 164. Of the voters who did not support the levy, 25 percent listed "mismanagement of funds" as their reason; another 8 percent listed the superintendent of schools, whose style was irritating to some local citizens.

28. Ibid., p. 214.

29. "Campbell Takes Action in Strike—Plans to Hire New Teachers," *Youngstown Vindicator*, September 16, 1973, pp. 1 and 8.

30. Tim Yovich, "Judge Finds Funds Ample—Suggests Campbell School Board Quit,"*Youngstown Vindicator*, July 19, 1973, pp. 1 and 10.

31. Tim Yovich, "Angered Over Panel's Report—Campbell School Leaders Rap Judge," *Youngstown Vindicator*, July 22, 1973, p. 1.

32. *Akron Beacon Journal*, September 4, 1973, p. 5.

33. The case studies are listed in Table 8-1.

34. Op. cit., p. 66, with italics added.

35. Frederick M. Wirt and Michael W. Kirst, *The Political Web of American Schools* (Boston: Little, Brown, 1972), p. 108. Reprinted by permission.

36. Cf. Lewis A. Coser, *The Functions of Social Conflict* (New York: The Free Press, 1956).

37. Morton, *loc. cit.*

38. During 1972, school budgets were approved unanimously in seven small Oregon districts, and nearly so in fifteen others.

8 Voting Patterns—the Correlates

Although referenda voting is not random, the voting patterns are hazy because of the paucity of measurements. The reasons for this deficit are not obscure: Data are inaccessible; only a few states collect aggregate vote tallies; and there are no statistics that relate votes to the attributes or attitudes of the voters. The ecological analysis method, explained below, is not feasible since census data are not compiled for school districts, and unfortunately surveys are difficult and expensive.

School Election Surveys

The initial method of voting research was ecological analysis, computing correlation coefficients of census data with election tallies by wards, precincts, or counties. There has been hardly any application of ecological analysis to school elections. It was applied to fiscal referenda in Cuyahoga County and Chicago in a famous study of public regardingness by Wilson and Banfield, but only one of those bond and tax elections was a school measure.[1] Their findings, however, match those of subsequent survey studies and will be noted below. Alan Clem observed, without computations, that in the South Dakota bond elections treated in Chapter 5 voting was associated with the social status of wards.

The survey, direct measurement, has become the principal method of voting research because of the severe limitations of the ecological method, which restricts investigation to only the census variables and also is vulnerable to the "ecological fallacy." That is, one may find a strong correlation between, for example, ethnicity and voting on fiscal propositions, but since it is not known how "ethnics" actually voted, the association could be spurious. For school referenda there is the additional limitation that census data do not fit school districts.

Survey studies of school elections are fugitive literature, obscure pamphlets, mimeographed or not published in any form. We have located nine with data that are sufficiently extensive and comparable to be useful. Only two are comprehensive; hence the number of cases varies in the subsequent tables. The data have distinct limitations. Independent studies undertaken for different purposes pose the familiar problem that the data are classified in various ways, but that is not an insurmountable obstacle.

177

Moreover, any liabilities are more than offset by the novel elements in several of the studies. Most of the samples are small, which bars refined categories and handicaps the application of controls in analysis. The set is a good assortment; the cases are from four states and include two metropolises, three suburbs, two medium-size cities, and a rural-urban school district. Three were school levy elections, three were bond issues, and two were both. Two were incidental to an investigation of alienation (Corning and Ithaca), one was a case study of community conflict (Okemos), one was a diagnosis of school-community relations (Birmingham), and the others were explicit investigations of voting behavior.[2] One was not a survey of a single community; its sample was from eighteen Washington school districts where levies had lost. The investigation of levy failure for the Washington Temporary Special Levy Study Commission was a combination mail and telephone survey, and one of the three studies with large samples.

The nine surveys provide ample data for investigating the association of voting with the voter attributes treated in presidential voting research—e.g., education, income, and occupation—plus those attributes of peculiar significance for school elections—parental status, age, and religion. Economic variables should be more influential in fiscal referenda than in office elections; hence the association of voting with home ownership, property tax payments, and tax/income ratio are examined. We also have gleaned some data for appraising the validity of the community integration theory, which has been advanced as an explanation of school election voting. Finally we turn to causal analysis, which hitherto has not been explored for school elections. Attitudes will be the frame of analysis in Chapter 9.

Social Status Variables

The principal determinants of social status in America are education, occupation, and income, in that relative order.[3] Each of these attributes is important in presidential elections; they are considerably more important in school referenda. The promoters of school proposals are highly educated; they usually are supported by the community elite, and formal education is most highly valued by the people who have the most of it. Furthermore those people usually have the means for paying taxes. The only surprise in Table 8-2 is the strength and regularity of the association. The refined categories of the Bowling Green study (Table 8-14) show the full strength of the correlation. The Corning case, however, shows that occasionally this association may be dampened almost to the vanishing

Table 8-1
School Referenda Surveys

Location	Year	Sample Size	Voted	Sampling Method
Austintown, Ohio	1970	362	362	Every twentieth registered voter that actually voted in November
Birmingham, Mich.	1961	490	209	Probability sample of dwellings
Bowling Green, Ohio	1966	385	322	Every fifteenth registered voter
Corning, New York	1957	197	164	Proportion of voters per precinct
Detroit, Michigan	1959	900	400	Sampling of 118 key precincts
Ithaca, New York	1958	205	160	Proportion of voters per precinct
Okemos, Michigan	1958	113	83	Every tenth residence
Youngstown, Ohio	1968	999	847	Every fortieth registered voter
Wasington State	1970	715	715	Voters in eighteen school districts

Sources: See note 2.

point by other influences, in that instance acute community conflict and alienation.[4]

Surprisingly, only four of the case studies measured income; as one said, it was thought to be "too sensitive." The findings of the three that did inquire about the income of the respondents are remarkably uniform. Endorsement of the school levies by voters in the top income bracket was more than twice the rate of those in the bottom bracket. Wilson and Banfield obtained the same result by ecological analysis; the survey data prove that the correlation was not spurious. They reasoned that this pattern demonstrates "public-regardingness" on the part of numerous upper income voters, since their property taxes are larger and they benefit no more and sometimes distinctly less from the public services involved. We will examine this hypothesis later.

Occupation, the status element that Wilson and Banfield could not examine by ecological analysis turns out be one of the most distinct correlates of referenda voting. The association was strong and strikingly consistent in all of the case studies that examined it except the Detroit study, which found no difference at all![5] The Okemos case conformed to the pattern of Table 8-4; the school construction proposal was endorsed by 25 percent of the blue-collar voters and by 57 percent of the white-collar voters.

Professionals are the most enthusiastic supporters of school expenditures, distinctly more so than businessmen and far more so than manual workers. One would expect professionals to be pro-education; but they are also the strongest supporters of other referenda proposals, such as metropolitan charters, health and welfare programs, and open housing laws,[6]

Table 8-2
Vote Distribution by Educational Level (percent favorable)

Years of School	Bowling Green	Youngstown	Birmingham	Corning	Ithaca	Okemos	Austintown	Washington
1-8	30	38	} 35	} 23	} 43	} 32	} 24	41
9-11	40	48						46
12	49	56					45	50
13-15	57	} 71	} 53	} 31	} 69	} 63		53
16+	88						73	79

Table 8-3
Vote Distribution by Income (percent favorable)

Family Income	Austin- town	Bowling Green	Youngs- town	Wash- ington
0-3000	9	38	} 42	} 38
3-5000	25	39		
5-7000	36	40	} 57	} 60
7-10000	40	42		
10-15000	52	70	70	63
15000	60	72	89	67

Table 8-4
Vote Distribution by Occupation (percent favorable)

	Austin- town	Bowling Green	Corning	Ithaca	Wash- ington
Farmer	—	26	} 27	} 37	42
Manual worker	33	37			56
White collar	33	71	43	59	61
Managerial	50	61	} 49	} 72	59
Professional	85	84			82

which indicates that they are the most public-regarding segment of the electorate.

Variables of Peculiar Significance for School Elections

The age, parental status, and religious preference of voters are of extraordinary significance for school referenda. Curiously, age was investigated by only four of the surveys, but those are sufficient; the association is unambiguous. The significance of the strong association of voting with age was noted by the investigators in Washington, where a levy must secure a 60 percent majority. "People over 50 opposed the levy. Considering the fact that those over 50 constitute a sizeable proportion of the levy electorate (47 percent of our sample), it is no wonder the levies lost."[7] The smooth regressions of Table 8-5 correspond to the frequency of parents of school and pre-school age children, and also to the frequency of retired persons, who—having neither school children nor income—are one of the least supportive groups. Sixty percent of the retirees voted against the Bowling Green levy and three-fourths of them voted against the new school in Okemos.[8] We have observed during interviewing that parents of pre-school

Table 8-5
Vote Distribution by Age (percent favorable)

Years of Age	Bowling Green	Okemos	Youngs-town	Wash-ington
21-29	74	} 57	} 60	66
30-39	69			73
40-49	60		} 56	62
50-59	49	} 44		} 45
60	45		47	

Table 8-6
Vote Distribution by Parental Status (percent favorable)

	Austin-town	Bir-mingham	Bowling Green	Detroit	Okemos	Wash-ington
Parents*	52	80	60	76	59	69
(N)	(176)	(143)	(135)	(?)	(63)	(319)
Others	35	40	41	56	26	47
(N)	(182)	(131)	(187)	(?)	(41)	(358)

*Of children in the school system.

age children are ardent supporters of school propositions; they were the most supportive group in the Birmingham sample.[9]

One study of voter attitudes and knowledge concluded that "understanding" of school issues is unsatisfactory, because "the voter understands the situation largely in terms of his own child's need. This is hardly understanding at all; it is a personalized perception. The voter reacts as a consumer to the product."[10] The survey data are partially consistent with that generalization; a large portion of the voting decisions are consistent with judgments as consumers of a product. Parents of children enrolled in the school system and those with toddlers consistently vote "yes" more frequently than the balance of the electorate. School referenda, however, are not purely a parents versus taxpayers contest. Indeed, if they were, few school measures would prevail, because the parents are a minority in most districts.

The pertinence of religious affiliation or preference to school referenda is common knowledge, but its significance is widely mooted, partially because its significance is so situational, being a negligible factor in numerous communities with no parochial schools. It was of slight effect in Bowling Green, where there was only a small elementary parochial school and transportation and science instruction were furnished by the school

Table 8-7

Vote Distribution by Religious Preference and Parental Status, Austintown School Levy

	Catholic		Protestant	
	Pct. Yes	(N)	Pct. Yes	(N)
Parents of children in Austintown schools	34	(82)	61	(91)
Parents of children in parochial schools*	32	(50)	—	—
Voters with no children in Austintown schools	35	(88)	37	(84)
Total	35	(170)	51	(175)

*Overlaps with other categories.

district.[11] But it was quite influential in Austintown and in Detroit, where the "core of resistance is to be found among citizens with children in parochial schools."[12] This is a delicate subject, which people prefer to ignore or minimize, and which is rarely measured. Only four of the case studies report any data, and only one is comprehensive. Fifty-eight percent of the parents of parochial school children said they voted for the Detroit levy, compared to 89 percent of the public school parents, and 68 percent of the nonparents. The Birmingham levy was supported by 40 percent of the parochial and private school parents, by 42 percent of the nonparents, and 80 percent of the public school parents.[13]

Possibly the trend of increasing subsidy of parochial education under the child benefit rationale may erode this variable, but it still is consequential in Austintown, an ethnic community. There most of the Catholic children are enrolled in the public schools, which also provide the transportation for parochial school children. Catholic leaders supported the school levy, with no visible effect—the pocketbook, and perhaps habit, was much the stronger influence. Being a "consumer" did not influence the Catholic voters; Catholic parents with children in the public schools were no more supportive of the levy than were the parents of parochial school children or nonparents. "Religion," however, was by no means the exclusive cause of the levy defeat, since the support rate of Protestant nonparents was low. We will examine the relative strength of the principal variables in the Austintown case presently.

Occasionally there may be some association of sex and voting. Women were more favorable to school proposals in five of the six cases that report that variable, but the difference was statistically significant in only three instances. The female support rate was six percentage points higher in the Detroit sample, eight points higher in the Washington sample, and much higher in the Youngstown sample.[14] In Birmingham, men were slightly

Table 8-8
Voting Patterns of Owners and Renters (percent favorable)

	*Bir-mingham	Bowling Green	Corning	Ithaca	Wash-ington
Owners	44	47	44	65	55
(N)	(370)	(275)	(88)	(137)	(633)
Renters	52	65	34	74	78
(N)	(70)	(46)	(76)	(23)	(46)

*More than half of the Birmingham sample did not vote; other data are of those respondents that reported they voted.

more supportive, verbally, but women supplied more "active support" by a substantially higher voting rate.[15]

Property, Taxes, and Income: the Voter as Economic Man

The existence of the anachronistic "taxpayer" requirement for voting in the referenda of fourteen states, until eliminated by the Supreme Court in 1970, is evidence of the durability of the illusion that renters are not taxpayers and the currency of the presumption that property ownership is a potent or even the paramount determinant of voting on fiscal propositions, with renters presumably voting for free services in opposition to "taxpayers." If that supposition were correct, the Supreme Court's decision might boost the passage rates substantially in those fourteen states. However, four surveys, (Table 8-8), which furnish data on the association of property ownership and voting, demonstrate that admission of renters to the polls is unlikely to have revolutionary effects for three reasons. Renters are a small fraction of the populace in many communities, they vote less often than owners, and frequently their voting pattern is not profoundly different from the "taxpayers."

The proportion of renters varies tremendously between communities. They are less than a fifth of the adult population of many communities, e.g., Ithaca and Bowling Green; only a third in suburban Birmingham; but about half in Corning; and they may be a majority in metropolises. Almost invariably, however, renters are a minority of the de facto electorate of school elections, because of their low participation. They were only 7 percent of the Washington sample. Occasionally the participation differential is tremendous. In Birmingham, 46 percent of the propertyowners had voted but only 10 percent of the renters.[16] The extent to which the participation differential has been the result of long residence requirements for registration remains to be seen now that they have been reduced by Supreme Court decisions.

The property requirement presumes an "economic man" theory of voting, which is, in the words of Wilson and Banfield, that the informed, rational voter "tries to maximize his family income or self-interest narrowly conceived by estimating both the benefits that will accrue to him and his family if the proposed expenditure is made and the amount of the tax that will fall on him" and votes for the larger amount.[17] The economic man theory has maximal plausibility for renters; their cost-benefit computations are so simple unless they are sophisticated about tax incidence. Wilson and Banfield investigated the economic man hypothesis by correlating affirmative votes with income and home ownership, and concluded that it does not hold for wealthy people, who often vote against their economic self-interest, but it does hold for renters. They found that in non-homeowning areas, the voters "almost invariably support all expenditure proposals," often at rates of 80 percent. Renters at least vote "as if" they were economic men.[18] The surveys, however, indicate that in school referenda renters are not much more likely than property owners to vote as economic men. Although renters are usually somewhat more supportive, the differences are not profound.

The data of Table 8-8 supplement the Wilson and Banfield findings and qualify their generalizations. They are not necessarily contradictory, since they relate to different categories of expenditure and different types of communities. Evidently expenditure proposals are more appealing to renters within than outside metropolises, which suggests differences in sophistication about tax incidence. Also in a small community other forces, such as the volume of political alienation in Corning, may extinguish the owner-renter differential or even reverse it. (See Table 9-5.) Middle-income homeowners are unenthusiastic about expenditures, as the Wilson and Banfield data show, but they also are more discriminating, and schools are more appealing to them than most referenda items,[19] since a large fraction of them are consumers of education, whereas they are not consumers of urban renewal projects or county hospitals.

If voters are economic men, true maximizers, voting in school referenda should correlate negatively with the amount of property tax of the voters, since public schools are of approximately equal benefit to people in all tax brackets. The Wilson and Banfield data, however, indicate that, exclusive of renters, the reverse is true. They report positive correlations of yeasaying with both income and amount of property owned.[20] The limited evidence of the school election surveys is *contra*. The association of yeasaying and property tax amount in the Washington sample, as reported by the respondents, was distinctly negative. At Bowling Green, where the tax liability of respondents was ascertained from county records, the correlation pattern was a bell curve. In both samples levy support was least among the large taxpayers. The pattern of the Washington sample may be the modal one, not only because the sample was a composite from eighteen school districts, but also because a third of the Bowling Green voters were rural residents. In rural areas, the amount of property tax does not match such surrogates as income or value of residence. We repeat, the association of referenda voting with some variables is related to the type of community.

The impact of property tax on voting, of course, is not the objective amount; it is "how you look at things," the voter's feelings. "Do you think taxes in Austintown are too low, too high, or about right?" That perception was potent; it was consistent with 70 percent of the vote decisions. If the 33 Yes voters who thought taxes were too high were parents, then four-fifths of the Austintowners voted in a manner appropriate for an economic man. "No doubt, relatively few voters make a conscious calculation of costs and benefits," say Wilson and Banfield.[21] That speculation is not supported by the Washington data, and even less so by the Austintown and Bowling Green data. There may be more economic men in the voting booth than they suspected.

What determines a voter's judgment that taxes are "too high" or "about right"? It might be the taxes in Washington rather than in Austintown, but it also might be related to his income. Grouping the Austintown and Bowling Green samples into five property tax and five income intervals made possible the five-interval scale of tax/income relationship in Table 8-11.[22] Renters were excluded. Parents were segregated to neutralize that factor and to observe the comparative strength of parentage and economics. Economics prevailed over parentage when parents had an unfavorable tax/income situation; and among nonparents altruism prevailed only among voters with a very favorable tax/income relationship in Bowling Green and not at all in Austintown. Economics was distinctly the stronger force in Bowling Green. At first glance, the two appear to be equal in Austintown, but notice how many parents voted No. The school levy evidently was an economic question for most of the voters in both communities.

The data confirm logic. The important variable is the tax/income ratio rather than the absolute amount of either, and for numerous voters the calculus is less a matter of weighing benefits against costs than of weighing tax and income. A voter need not struggle long to weigh his nebulous personal benefit or look up his property tax records if he is retired, or poor, or a large property owner, or merely feels that taxes are too high. Nor is the voting decision difficult for those with a very favorable tax/income ratio, who can easily take an "enlightened," altruistic view of public expenditures.

There was a substantial amount of economic rationality in the voting in Austintown and Bowling Green, and examination of the populations of the tax/income ratio intervals is illuminating.[23] The unfavorable intervals con-

Table 8-9
Vote Distribution by Tax Amount

Voter's annual tax amount	Bowling Green		Washington Districts	
	Pct. Yes	(N)	Pct. Yes	(N)
$0 (renters)	65	46	78	46
$1-199	40	91	60	186
$200-399	55	112	57	159
$400-699	60	46	55	60
$700-999	33	15	36	33
$1000 or more	9	11	43	28

Table 8-10
Perceptions of Taxes and Voting in Austintown

"Taxes are?"	Pct. Yes	(N)
Too low	92	24
About right	58	156
Too high	21	160

Table 8-11
Vote by Tax/Income Ratio (percent favorable)

	Bowling Green		Austintown	
	*Parents	Others	*Parents	Others
I level below T:				
Two intervals	26	17	{ 44	{ 17
One interval	47	23		
Same I and T level	51	24	55	21
I level above T:				
One interval	51	45	41	30
Two intervals	73	69	64	43

*Of public school children. Renters are excluded.

tain farmers, retirees, and a few manual workers.[24] White and blue collar workers are distributed across the three intermediate intervals. Businessmen are in the favorable intervals. The most favorable interval embraces, predominantly, professionals—Wilson and Banfield's "public-regarding" voters.

The Community Integration Theory

The degree of community integration, a variable found to be relevant in fluoridation referenda,[25] was hypothesized by the Birmingham study as a major determinant of the level of community support for schools and of voting in school referenda. The foundation of this voting hypothesis is essentially the same as the alienated voter theory: "analysis of formal memberships reveals two distinct populations; the active, participating segment, and a more isolated, non-participating segment." The hypothesis is that the "anomic segment" will be less supportive of schools, because it is "alienated from community affairs" and outside the communications network that generates community consensus. Therefore, disinterest and opposition are primarily in the "anomic segment," which usually is apathetic but occasionally organizes as an ephemeral protest group to oppose a levy or bond issue. Thus, the (one) levy defeat in Birmingham despite no organized opposition was attributed by the investigators to the apathy and inconspicuous opposition generated by "community anomia"—a type of opposition that is not produced by organization, but derives from the fact that many people are not organized, are not integrated into the community.[26]

That is a plausible hypothesis of community support level, one which seemed particularly apropos to Birmingham, a community with a high migration rate and massive nonvoting by newcomers in school elections. It is a good theory of nonvoting, but the evidence of its influence on the direction of voting is unimpressive. Certainly it is useful as a guide to locations of support and for campaigning, but the weight on voting decisions attributed to it by the Birmingham study appears to be an instance of sociologists overburdening a favorite horse.

Sociologists regard formal organization membership as an index of community integration. Not surprisingly, the Birmingham data and the Austintown replication confirm that participation in school elections and yeasaying correlate with organizational activity, but the data are unimpressive for several reasons. There was no showing in the Birmingham study of actual alienation among the nonjoiners, and such crucial variables as parentage and social status were not controlled. In fact, in both Birmingham and Austintown, yeasaying was not associated with organizational membership per se, only with membership in the PTA and church-related groups.[27] Furthermore, the association of yeasaying and rate of organizational activity is largely epiphenomenal, a reflection of social status. The

Table 8-12
Organizational Activity and School Levy Voting

	Average Meetings per Month			All Joiners	Non-Joiners
	None	1 or 2	3 plus		
Pct. YES votes					
Austintown	37	49	58	52	40
Birmingham	46	66	69	63	47
Pct. NOT voting					
Birmingham	43	38	32	37	60

Table 8-13
Memberships and Voting on the Austintown School Levy (percent favorable)

	Members	Nonmembers
Clubs	42	44
Lodges	44	43
Church related	51	39
PTA	60	33

association of social class and organizational activity has been thoroughly documented.[28]

Causal Variables

Association is not necessarily causation; some strong associations are "spurious correlation." The preceding data have identified the attributes of Yes and No voters and the extent to which various variables are associated with the direction of voting. The strength of these associations may or may not be proportional to their actual influence on voting decisions. Discovering causation, a slippery business at best, requires an analysis undertaken by only two of the survey studies. Spurious correlation is detected by controlling some variables, i.e., neutralizing them by either partial or multiple correlation, or by cross-tabulation with some variables controlled. An example of the latter is Table 8-11, where the influence of parental status was segregated from the summary economic variable, tax/income ratio.

Partial correlation coefficients, the coefficient for each variable with all the others controlled, were computed for the Bowling Green election.

Table 8-14
Strength of Variables in Bowling Green School Election

	Coefficients of Simple	Correlation Partial
Urban residence	.35	.26
Occupational rank	.43	.23
Education	.26	.05
Age	−.23	−.03
Parental status	.18	.13
Income	.24	.03
Property tax pay't.	−.18	−.18
Tax/Income ratio	.33	.24

Comparison of the simple and partial coefficients conveys two important messages. The association of age, income, and even education turned out to be largely epiphenomenal—they faded under controls. Occupation, parental status, property tax, and tax/income ratio emerged as the strong causal variables, with occupation strongest of all.

Other variables occasionally may be extraordinarily influential. Thus at Bowling Green, for an election in a geographically atypical district at a unique historical juncture, the foremost determinant of voting was place of residence, rural or urban; and amount of property tax was stronger than parental status. Two variables absent in Bowling Green were major determinants in Austintown, where the strongest influences were ethnicity, occupation, parental status, and religious preference in that order. Alienation was the strongest force in the Corning and Ithaca elections. Communities are not uniform.

Notes

1. James Q. Wilson and Edward C. Banfield, "Public Regardingness as a Value Premise in Voting Behavior," *American Political Science Review* 58 (December 1964), pp. 876-887.

2. The studies in the order listed in Table 8-1 are: Sylvan H. Cohen, *Voting Behavior in School Referenda: An Investigation of Attitudes and Other Determinants by Q Technique and Survey Research* (dissertation, Kent State University, 1971); R.V. Smith et al., *Community Organization and Support of Schools* (Institute for Community Research, Eastern Michigan University, 1964); Howard D. Hamilton and Byron Marlowe, *Survey of Voting on Tax Levies in Bowling Green* (unpublished); John E. Horton and Wayne E. Thompson, "Powerlessness and Political Negativism: A Study of Defeated Referendums," *American Journal of*

Sociology 67 (1962), pp. 485-493; Roberta Sigel, *Election with an Issue: Voting Behavior of a Metropolitan Community in a School Fund Election* (unpublished); Wayne E. Thompson and John E. Horton, "Political Alienation as a Force in Political Action," *Social Forces* 38 (1960), pp. 190-195; Gary E. King et al., *Conflict Over Schools* (Institute for Community Research, Michigan State University, 1963); J. Kiriazis and S. Hotchkiss, *Community Attitudinal Survey of Youngstown Voters on School Tax Levies* (unpublished); Temporary Special Levy Study Commission, *Summary Report and Research Reports* (Olympia: Washington Legislature, 1971), vol. 1, pp. 333-348. Another survey is reported in Robert E. Agger and Marshall N. Goldstein, *Who Will Rule the Schools: A Cultural Class Conflict* (Belmont, California: Wadsworth, 1971). We have not used those data, because the questions relate principally to a kindergarten proposal rather than the simultaneous budget election, but they are consistent with the content of this chapter.

3. Social status is far more complex in Europe. Cf. Johan Galtung's eight-factor status scale in James N. Rosenau, ed., *Domestic Sources of Foreign Policy* (New York: Free Press, 1967), p. 174.

4. The 1959 Detroit election provided another example of a weak association of educational level and voting decision; 75 percent of the respondents with an elementary or secondary education and 83 percent of those who attended college said they voted "yes." Two factors contributed to the small difference: the large number of Blacks in the elementary education category and the fact that the levy carried by a large margin, two to one. All variables fade in a consensual election. Also there evidently was considerable fibbing to the interviewers.

5. The finding of no appreciable differences between occupations in the Detroit case strains credibility, but the factors mentioned in the preceding footnote would diminish the difference.

6. Cf. Howard D. Hamilton, "Voting Behavior in Open Housing Referenda," *Social Science Quarterly* 51 (December 1970), pp. 715-729; John H. Bowden and Howard D. Hamilton, "Some Notes on Metropolitics," in Jack Gargan and James Coke, eds., *Political Behavior and Public Issues in Ohio* (Kent: Kent University Press, 1973), pp. 274-293.

7. Washington Levy Study Commission, op. cit., p. 335.

8. King et al., op. cit., p. 20; and Hamilton and Marlowe, op. cit., p. 18.

9. Sixty-one percent of the respondents with children under 6 supported the Birmingham levy, compared with 49 percent of those with children age 6-18, and 35 percent of those with no children under 18. Smith et al., op. cit., p. 30.

10. Richard F. Carter and John Sutthoff, *Communities and Their Schools* (School of Education, Stanford University, 1960), pp. 3, 14.

11. Hamilton and Marlowe, op. cit.

12. Sigel, op. cit.

13. Smith et al., op. cit., p. 117.

14. Sigel, op. cit.; Kiriazis and Hotchkiss, op. cit., p. 39.

15. Smith et al., op. cit., p. 33.

16. Smith et al., op. cit., p. 52.

17. Wilson and Banfield, op. cit., p. 876.

18. Ibid., p. 879. Wilson and Banfield's generalizations could be fallacious if they were based on correlations, since a high coefficient could occur with only slight differences between the voting of renters and homeowners if the pattern was geographically uniform, but their data on this topic were not coefficients.

19. Ibid., p. 883.

20. Ibid., p. 881.

21. Ibid., p. 876.

22. Credit for this idea belongs to Byron Marlowe, research director of the Ohio Educational Association, who assisted with the Bowling Green survey.

23. Interviewing revealed that, all the propaganda notwithstanding, there continues to be a rough correspondence between ability to pay and the maligned general property tax. In numerous instances, respondents said that they belonged at the same interval on both scales.

24. The tax/income ratio exerts a potent influence on the beliefs of retirees, although it is less valid as an index of ability to pay for them than for other people; indeed numerous retirees have abundant resources, even though perhaps less liquidity. This has become of some moment for school referenda. From the absence of any federal income tax liability, the retirees have come to feel that they should be entirely tax exempt. The feeling is strong, but the logic is not. They are not exempt from income taxes; they simply have paid all the taxes on their income. Occasionally schoolmen endorse the efforts of retirees to secure exemption from the property tax, on the assumption that this will facilitate school elections; but this is a vicious circle and a losing game, since exemption of retirees boosts the rates of the rest of the electorate.

25. Cf. Maurice Pinard, "Structural Attachments and Political Support in Urban Politics: The Case of Fluoridation Referendums," *American Journal of Sociology* 61 (1963), pp. 513-516.

26. Smith et al., op. cit., pp. 12-15, 85.

27. Ibid., pp. 112-113.

28. Cf. Charles R. Wright and Herbert Hyman, "Voluntary Memberships of American Adults: Evidence from National Sample Surveys," *American Sociological-Review* 23 (June 1958), pp. 284-292.

9 The Voter's Decision-Making Process

The preceding data on the correlates of school referenda voting illuminate the identities of who decides Yes or No, but they furnish only clues about the process by which voting decisions are made. Actually, there are two decisions, *whether* and *how* to vote. They may be related; the stimulus to vote may also determine how. This is a difficult area of investigation and there has been scant effort to expose the voter's decisional process in referenda voting.

The extent to which voters are obliged to make a conscious decision whether to vote is largely a function of the date. The decision is automatic for most voters when a referendum coincides with a presidential election, except in metropolises, where an amazing number of voters make the decision not to participate by failing to mark the proposition ballot—a third of them in Detroit (Table 3-17)! Since those "nonvoters" are disproportionately Blacks—the ethnic group which Chicago, Cleveland, and Detroit data show to be the most favorable toward all fiscal measures—those instant nonvoting decisions are a serious loss of potential support for school proposals.

When a school issue is scheduled as a special election or even concurrently with a school board election, an authentic decision and some time and effort are required of voters; and for most special elections three-fourths or more of the "whether" decisions are negative. In that circumstance, *which* persons decide to vote may well determine the outcome of an election, depending on the direction and extent that the low-turnout electorate is a skewed one. School officials can affect the whether decisions marginally by campaigns, but much more by their choices in scheduling school proposals either concurrently with major elections or as specials.

Theories of Referenda Voting

Scarcely any effort has been made to ascertain a voter's decisional process in referenda, primarily because they lack the glamour of presidential elections and the easily available mountains of data accumulated by the periodic national election surveys. We suspect it also is partly because local government attracts the attention of relatively few political scientists, school districts least of all. Apparently a tacit assumption of political scientists is that study of local voting is bootless—because it is hopelessly idiosyncratic. That assumption is even more plausible for referenda since "election" is a misnomer. Referenda are acts of legislation and hence, one might presume, there could be no patterns in the voters' decisional process which is necessarily specific to each item of legislation, and related to the way the voter "sees" its merits. We disagree. The data of the preceding chapter show that school voting is not unstructured. Furthermore, Wilson and Banfield have found impressive evidence that some voting patterns are common to all fiscal referenda.

Two partial theories of referenda voting have emerged accidentally, the alienated voter theory and the political ethos theory, two of the most celebrated concepts in social science currently. A comprehensive theory of how a voter decides school issues is offered by Roberta Sigel.

We theorize that he is guided by self-interest (as he perceives it) and is much more swayed by outside influences, such as the press, than in partisan elections. Schools being close to his experiential level, he will make his decision on the basis of self-interest (wanting no more property taxes, wanting good schools for his children, etc.), but when he cannot perceive his self-interest easily (could the schools get along on the money they have, or do they really need more?), he will look for guidance.[1]

Note that this statement contains a hedge, "as he perceives it," which rather begs the question and makes the hypothesis irrefutable. Sigel's self-interest hypothesis is partially at variance with the other theories. One asserts that in some referenda considerable voting decisions are products of political alienation; the other asserts that some categorical groups tend not to rely on self-interest as their voting guide because they are imbued with public-regardingness. The survey data also furnish impressive verification of those theories. If one accepts Sigel's hedge, the alienation and self-interest theories are compatible; the alienate definitely perceives his negative voting as in his self-interest. But when four-fifths of the alienates vote No, as in Corning (Table 9-5) and Austintown (Table 9-6), some are parents whose votes may not be consistent with any dispassionate assessment of self-interest. Indeed, "as he perceives it" makes anything self-interest.

No legerdemain can fully reconcile the self-interest and public-regardingness theories. Of course, some votes inconsistent with self-interest can be explained by voter ignorance, but when middle-age farmers and other large taxpayers vote for school issues there is no misperception of self-interest. These two theories could be reconciled by sophistry. As Wilson and Banfield say, the essence of public-regardingness is "to take the welfare of others, especially that of 'the community,' into account as an aspect of their own welfare,"[2] but to call that a species of self-interest is to obliterate the distinction between private and public interest. An alternative sophistry would be that they are merely alternative notions of the public interest. Truly, but they are profoundly different definitions of the public interest, one equating private with public interest. The data of Wilson and Banfield did not permit them to specify the parameters of private- and public-regardingness voting in referenda. Survey data are more useful for that task.

It is plausible to view the alienation and public-regardingness (or ethos) theories as important qualifications of the largely valid proposition that school referenda voting is guided by self-interest. Although there is much coincidence of alienation and private-regardingness, they are distinctly different phenomena and occasionally, alienation may be the more important. Our own research has disclosed other attitudes that are significant in school election voting. Our task is to analyze the data for evidence of the extent to which voting decisions are predicated on self-interest, public-regardingness, alienation, and the other attitudes that we have observed. We are aware of four methods of investigating the voting-decision process: self-report, attitude measurement, inference from demographic correlates of voting, and Q analysis. The latter is reserved for the next chapter.

Self-Report: Stated "Reasons"

It may seem that the best way to illuminate voter decision processes would be simply to "ask the people." Our experience has demonstrated, however, that it is not a very satisfactory method. Many respondents are nonplussed by "What were your reasons?" and the answers are likely to be cliches. If the voter had a conscious reason, it may be deliberately concealed or not conveyed by his words. The responses may be so varied as to defy standardization, "coding"; although this difficulty can be alleviated some by limiting the voter's response, as in the Austintown survey, "What was the most important reason that influenced your vote?" The fundamental weakness of self-report is that voting causation is so complex that the response will be only a partial and perhaps a quite superficial explanation. Only three of the surveys considered here inquired about reasons.

In the Washington survey, the (395) affirmative voters gave four principal reasons for supporting the school levy (frequency of mention in parentheses):

1. Voter has always supported education, it's a matter of principle. (122)
2. Referred to specific needs of the district—teacher salaries, new buildings, books, etc. (112)
3. A member of the family is attending school.(101)
4. Children (in general) need a good education—an explanation often offered by people whose children are no longer in school. (81)[3]

Table 9-1
Stated Reasons for Affirmative Voting

Austintown	Pct.	Bowling Green	Mentions
The children need it	45	Schools need money	115
Schools need money	26	To raise teacher salaries	53
Want better schools	15	The value of education	46
Fear of closing	6	Have children in school	19
Other reasons	8	Other reasons	15
(156 Yes voters)	100	(158 Yes voters)	133

Table 9-2
Stated Reasons for Negative Voting

Austintown	Pct.	Bowling Green	Mentions
Taxes are too high	28	Taxes are too high	48
Mismanagement of funds	25	Revise tax system	32
Not needed; economize	17	Not needed; economize	32
Unfair tax	10	Dissatisfaction with district merger	13
Dissatisfaction with superintendent	8	Other dissatisfactions	18
Other reasons	12	Other reasons	16
(201 No voters)	100	(164 No voters)	159

Reasons 1 and 4, half of the responses, are essentially expressions of commitment to support of education—the voter's attachment to the American creed; a fourth are explicit acceptance of the claims by school authorities regarding "needs"—the official rationale of the levy; and a fourth are candid expressions of the voters' concern for the welfare of their own children—what Carter and Sutthoff dub the consumer orientation.

Those same reasons were reported in the Ohio communities—in more or less the same proportions in Austintown, but distributed differently in Bowling Green, where most of the yeasayers mentioned agreement with school authorities that more revenue was needed (see Table 9-1). So many of the Bowling Green voters were familiar with the specifics that a smaller proportion, one-third, responded with general expressions of commitment to education; one-fifth expressed concern for the welfare of their own children.[4]

Opposition to the levies by (302) negative voters in Washington was based on a complex of reasons:

1. The most popular reason was that "taxes are too high." (110)

2. Schools are wasting money, spending too much, exercising poor money management.(69)

3. Criticism of the school administration—policies, inability to communicate, lying, and the curriculum—too many frills. (67)

4. Criticism of the levy system or this specific levy. (31)

5. Criticism of physical plant—improper use, no standardized floor plans, high architect fees, and, in some districts, location of schools. (25)[5]

Naturally there is more variety in the explanations of the negative than the affirmative voters, since the possible particularistic dissatisfactions are legion, and the inventories will not be identical for all elections. The most frequently mentioned specific dissatisfaction in Austintown was the school superintendent; whereas at Bowling Green there were more frequent mentions of intense displeasure about the forced merger of school districts and the length of bus routes in the vast new district—potent reasons for parents in the annexed area to vote No. In Washington there were specific dissatisfactions anent curriculum frills and access to information. As one voter stated pithily, "Scarce amount of information given to the voters. Also honesty in presenting the information asked."[6]

These inventories demonstrate that taxes are not the exclusive concerns of naysayers, but they also confirm that taxes are their paramount concern in operating levy elections, although not necessarily so in bond elections. Taxes were the *stated* reasons of 40 percent of the antilevy voters in Austintown, of 47 percent in Washington, and 50 percent in Bowling Green—most naysayers are "economic men." Seventy to 80 percent of the stated reasons for negative voting related to money—taxes, frills, fiscal management, and the need to economize. The distributions of the expressed reasons were remarkably alike in the Ohio and Washington school districts.

Perceptions are another form of self-report which may provide clues about the genesis of voting decisions. Two of the surveys provide such data. Austintown voters were asked "who?" supported and opposed the levy. The voters in the eighteen Washington districts were asked to rate their teachers, administrators, and school boards, their salaries, and the accessibility of information from the school system. The supporters and opponents of school levies are as significantly different in their perceptions of their school systems as they are in backgrounds. The yeasayers were nearly unanimous in their favorable ratings of school officials and teachers, especially the teachers. They regarded the salaries of teachers as about right or too low. A fourth did agree with the naysayers about those fat salaries of administrators. Only half of the naysayers evaluated their school boards and administrators favorably. There was less disagreement about the quality of teachers, but only 35 percent of the naysayers rated the teachers as "good."

Two other contrasts are noteworthy. The *acknowledged* information of

Table 9-3
Contrasting Perceptions of Yes and No Voters in Washington (Percent)

	Yes Voters	No Voters
Teacher salaries are		
Too much	4	20
About right	65	64
Too little	28	7
Don't know	3	9
Rating of Teachers		
Good	59	35
Somewhat good	33	42
Bad	6	14
Don't know	2	9
Rating of School Board		
Good	50	21
Somewhat good	35	34
Bad	10	30
Don't know	6	16
(N)	(385)	(280)
Administrator salaries are		
Too much	26	53
About right	54	27
Too little	10	1
Don't know	11	19
Rating of Administrators		
Good	52	18
Somewhat good	34	34
Bad	11	37
Don't know	3	12
Information obtained		
Very easily	30	17
Easily	48	34
With difficulty	16	33
Much difficulty	4	13
Don't know	2	4

Table 9-4

Contrasting Perceptions of Voters in Austintown

PERCEPTIONS OF WHO SUPPORTED THE LEVY

By the Pros	Mentions	By the Cons	Mentions
Parents of school children	60	School personnel	63
Churches, civic leaders, & responsible people	54	Parents of school children	35
		Nontaxpayers	38
School personnel	39	Rich, upper class	21
Business and industry	26	Churches	15
Others	17	Others	25

PERCEPTIONS OF WHO OPPOSED THE LEVY

By the Pros	Mentions	By the Cons	Mentions
Retirees, fixed incomes	47	Homeowners & taxpayers	105
Homeowners & taxpayers	29	Retirees, fixed incomes	39
Have no school children	22	Workingmen	31
Workingmen	18	Angry at schools	12
Others	43	Others	34

the naysayers is distinctly less—10 to 20 percent did not even hazard a response to the survey questions. Obviously "when in doubt vote no," is not an idle phrase. Nearly half of the naysayers say it is difficult to secure information; many state that school officials withhold information and are not always candid. The fact that a fifth of the yeasayers agree, suggests that not all the naysayers are engaging in rationalization. Evidently, say the authors of the Washington survey,

A sizeable proportion of the electorate feel alienated from the school system, unable to get information easily from it, or to influence its decisions. Under these circumstances the levy offers an opportunity not only to vote on school expenditures but also to exercise control (in an indirect way) over the activities of teachers, administrators and school boards.[7]

The association of perceptions and voting is obvious in Table 9-3. Indubitably these associations are to an appreciable extent the result of post hoc rationalizations on the voter's part, but to the investigators they seemed "at least partially causitive of the voting patterns."[8]

Austintown voters were asked: "What people or groups do you think were *for* the levy?" "What people or groups were *against* the levy?" The responses were a clear-cut demonstration of social distance and the self-other relationship, in addition to further evidence of economics. Who were the supporters? "Parents" was the most frequent reply of the yeasayers, but the naysayers more frequently saw teachers and school employees after more money. Who were the opponents? Here was even greater incongruence of images. "Homeowners and taxpayers," replied the

naysayers, but the yeasayers more frequently saw the opposition as retired, elderly people and others on fixed incomes.

Social psychology furnishes an explanation for this perceptual incongruence. Social distance is a concomitant of sharply conflictual situations,
like the series of elections in Austintown. Most of the effective communication occurs among like-minded voters. Therefore, common images of reality develop among the pro voters and among the con voters, and inevitably
the images are not congruent. The result is a self-other relationship pattern.
When the pros were describing levy supporters they were describing themselves, and the nonsupporters were the others, and vice versa. The pattern
may be elucidated by a matrix.

SELF-OTHER RELATIONSHIP MATRIX

*Perceptions of Those Who Favored and Opposed the Levy, by
Respondent's Position on the Levy*

	Self	*Others*
Proponents	parents	elderly, retirees, persons on fixed incomes
Opponents	homeowners & taxpayers	teachers & school personnel

Again one sees the primacy of economics for naysayers. They did not
perceive themselves as opposing the welfare of children. They were
homeowners resisting burdensome taxes, protecting their homes against
the teachers and school employees after more money, and also defending
the interests of retirees and the working man. They saw their opposition as
including nontaxpayers and the "filthy rich." The yeasayers perceived
their position to be that of the churches, business and civic leaders, professionals and other educated and responsible people; but, of course, it also
was the side of the parents of school children, whose votes were not
entirely manifestations of enlightenment and altruism. The images of the
Austintown voters lend impressive support to the self-interest theory of
school referenda voting.

Attitudes: Alienation

The theory that voting decisions are linked to external stimuli by attitudes
which mediate the impact of perceptions, social influences, and demographic variables[9] has some applicability to this species of voting. Three
attitudes have been noted as particularly apropos to fiscal referenda, and
the authors have observed some others. Wilson and Banfield infer that the

decisions of numerous voters derive from the antithetical attitudes of public or private-regardingness. The authors have observed a similar pair of attitudes: that public services and expenditures are "good" or that taxes are "bad" per se. There may be some additional attitudes operating in school referenda, as there were in Austintown and Youngstown, which are described in Chapter Ten. Political alienation, which has been observed in fluoridation, metropolitan charter, and open housing plebiscites, has been seen in fiscal referenda and has been posited as an explanation of negative voting.

The Corning and Ithaca surveys were an investigation of the hypothesis that naysaying may be more than a rejection of the specific public service or facility listed on the ballot; "it may be, in addition, an expression of general distrust on the part of the politically alienated." The hypothesis rests on evidence that the perspectives of the powerless members of society "are especially relevant to their political behavior insofar as they are likely to project their personal fears and discontents into politics," and the "perspectives which color the political action of the powerless are of a particular negative character, negative at least in terms of the norms of the dominant powers."[10] The characteristics of the Corning and Ithaca school bond campaigns displayed evidence of alienation. Each campaign was pervaded by an atmosphere of controversy generalized beyond the specific issues and directed against experts and local leaders; the opposition leaders professed to be championing the interests of "the people." In each community there were conspicuous symbols of power—the company and the university—on which to attach general discontents. Application of a political alienation index to voter samples produced striking evidence of the association of alienation and negative voting, an association that was not spurious since it shows when socioeconomic variables are controlled. Significantly, in both instances alienation was far more potent than property ownership.

Alienation was also important at the repeat levy election in Austintown. It was manifested frequently in the meetings conducted by the school authorities, letters to the newspaper, radio talk shows, and the interpersonal communication networks. It also was evident during the survey interviews.[11] A fifth of the sample (actual voters) scored high on an alienation scale; and four-fifths of those scoring high voted No, compared to one-fifth of those scoring low on the alienation scale.[12] However, the writers on alienation seem to overstate the alienated-voter theory of referenda voting, since seventy percent of the naysayers were not alienates. Referenda voting, like most social processes, is a complex field of forces containing numerous interests and attitudes. Two other pertinent attitudes are political liberalism and sense of political efficacy; both were strongly associated with the voting in Austintown.

Table 9-5

Political Alienation and Voting on School Bonds in Ithaca and Corning (percent favorable)

	University Town		Company Town	
	Alienated	Not A.	Alienated	Not A.
Socioeconomic Status				
High status	45	68	0	72
Middle status	50	68	7	44
Low status	26	51	13	46
Occupation				
Prof. or managerial	57	76	17	63
White collar	57	61	47	37
Labor, farm, service	24	48	6	53
Education				
College	46	74	23	66
Less than college	32	48	12	43
Property ownership				
Taxpayers	30	82	16	63
Non-taxpayers	55	81	26	43
(N)	(70)	(135)	(101)	(96)

Table 9-6

Association of Three Attitudes and School Levy Voting in Austintown (percent favorable)

	Low	Inter-mediate	High
Political alienation scale	79	42	19
(N)	(67)	(211)	(75)
Political efficacy scale	21	31	60
(N)	(48)	(135)	(173)
Political liberalism scale	28	46	58
(N)	(78)	(223)	(52)

Alienation was evident in six of the nine cases reviewed here; it was responsible for the defeats in Corning, Ithaca, and Bowling Green; and it was strong in Okemos, Youngstown, and Austintown.

Political alienation is described in social science literature as a diffuse attitude built up by accretion over considerable time rather than the product of a momentary event like a referendum, which merely furnishes an outlet for acting out the pre-existent attitude. That, however, is likely not to be an accurate explanation of alienation in referendum voting. Much of the alienation may be specific to the referendum. The alienation which tipped the scales in Bowling Green was not only accumulated discontents with property and federal taxes and whatever; it also was the legacy of a bitter redistricting controversy in which a rural area was compelled by state school standards to merge with an urban district. Loss of community identity, rural-urban sentiments, and coercion by state officials—"they" —inevitably evoked intense alienation attitudes.

Some negative voting from alienation appears to be a structural component of referenda, since the proposal emanates from officials and is publicly supported by community elites. The scenario is made to order for the evocation of images of conspiracy and tyranny in the eyes of persons with underdog and powerlessness feelings, who of course are not privy to the planning of the proposal, and also in the eyes of foes of taxation and everyone with any species of dissatisfaction with local officials, other elites, "the government," or "they." If alienation is not miniscule, self-appointed leaders may emerge to voice alienation themes and confirm the perceptions of the alienates. Fluoridation and open housing referenda offer maximal scope for the opposition to exploit alienation sentiment, but there is ample opportunity also in school referenda. Perhaps no other formal structure of our political system furnishes an equivalent opportunity—so visible, convenient, and direct—for alienates to resist policies they perceive to be elite schemes injurious to their interests. That the structure is used seems evident by the numerous instances in which elite visions of civic monuments, school budgets and building plans, fluoridation, open housing, and metropolitan government schemes have foundered at the polls. It is attested by the survey data.

Alienation probably is endemic and to some extent omnipresent in school elections, since referenda furnish what our other political structures deny alienates, a convenient, direct opportunity to project their distrust, fears and discontents, to strike back at "they" and resist the policy plans of elites. "This is the only time when I can say No!" The impact of alienation varies tremendously and may even fluctuate sharply between school elections a brief period apart in the same community, as in Bowling Green. Although these surveys indicate that alienation is likely to be a significant factor in intensely contested elections, it is easy to exaggerate its significance. It may be only an emotional reinforcement of voting decisions. At Bowling Green, a mature farmer with no children but a large property tax, living in the area that had been legally compelled to join an urban district, and one with a much higher tax rate to boot, indubitably was alienated; but he did not lack unemotional reasons for voting No. Indeed, alienation usually is a reinforcement of other predispositions against voting for fiscal proposals, because both alienation and naysaying correlate highly with social status. Half of the Austintown voters that scored high on the alienation scale were low on a socioeconomic index. Only 4 percent of the high SES voters were alienates.[13]

The Political Ethos Theory

The political ethos theory has been the subject of considerable interest and controversy since it was propounded by Wilson and Banfield. They asserted that two distinct and opposing orientations towards politics "have decisively influenced attitudes toward both issues and governmental structures," an Anglo-Saxon Protestant public-regarding ethos and an immigrant private-regarding ethos.[14] Subsequently, apparently in response to criticism of the validity and invidious appearance of those terms,[15] they have relabeled those syndromes as the unitary and the individualist ethos, which they describe thusly:

The middle-class Anglo-Saxon Protestant ethos, we said, conceived politics as a cooperative search for the implications of an "interest of the whole"; accordingly it stressed the obligation of the individual to participate disinterestedly in public affairs, the desirability of rule by the "best qualified" (meaning "experts" or those otherwise specially equipped by training or character to perform the essentially technical operation of discovering the interest of the whole), and the ideal of "good government" (meaning especially honesty, impartiality, and efficiency). The logically implied (but not always achieved) institutional expression of this ethos were at-large representation, nonpartisanship, a strong executive (especially the council-manager form), master planning, and strict impartial enforcement of laws. The other ethos, we said, was characteristic of the immigrant—and, therefore of the lower- and working-class—life; it emphasized family needs and personal loyalties and took no account of the larger community; it conceived of politics as competition among individual (that is, family or parochial) interests. The institutional forms that expressed it were ward politics, the boss, and the machine.[16]

The validity of those syndromes has been investigated by ecological analysis with contradictory results.[17] Substantial support for the ethos theory is, however, furnished by some surveys of referenda voting on metropolitan government proposals.[18] School referenda surveys offer an ideal opportunity to investigate it, but that has occurred only once. The levy election in Austintown, a heavily ethnic community, affords an opportunity to investigate the ethos theory directly with survey data in a situation where public- and private-regardingness is extraordinarily relevant. The American public school system is the greatest monument to the unitary ethos, and school district government is the epitome of its structural prescriptions.

The hypothesis that some categorical groups are more public-regarding than others has been challenged vigorously. "Such upper status people may not be more public-regarding; they only appear to be, because they can afford to vote for public expenditures," says Thomas Flinn.[19] Occasionally the diminishing utility of money is mentioned. The strong association of voting with the voter's tax/income ratio in Table 8-11 confirms that there is considerable basis for the challenge. Most of the upper-status other-

Table 9-7
Voting on Austintown School Levy (percent voting Yes)

| | By Ethnicity and Social Class[a] | | By Ethnicity and Parental Status | | |
	Working Class	Middle Class	Parents[b]	Others	Total (N)
British	49 (35)	66 (44)	64 (42)	51 (37)	58 (79)
German	26 (27)	52 (44)	54 (37)	29 (34)	42 (71)
Italian	47 (34)	30 (27)	50 (24)	32 (37)	39 (61)
Slavic	17 (34)	37 (32)	29 (31)	26 (35)	27 (66)
Total	32 (130)	49 (147)	51 (134)	35 (143)	43 (277)
	$p < .03$	$p < .02$	$p < .03$	$p < .10$	$p < .01$
British	49 (35)	66 (44)	64 (42)	51 (37)	58 (79)
Others	31 (95)	42 (103)	45 (92)	29 (106)	36 (198)
	$p < .06$	$p < .01$	$p < .05$	$p < .02$	$p < .001$

[a]Self classification.
[b]Of children in public schools.

regarding voters, particularly those without school children, had a favorable or very favorable tax/income ratio. This analysis does not negate the ethos theory at all, but it demonstrates that acting out their unitary ethos by generous support of public expenditures entails slight strain for most upper status voters.

It is European ethnicity that is important for the ethos theory; the syndromes are ascribed respectively to Anglo-Saxon Protestants and European Catholics (specifically) the Irish, Italians, and Slavs). Do survey data confirm the voting behavior which ecological analysis indicates? If so, what are the quantitative differences, and is the association authentic or only epiphenomenal? Unfortunately the big-city studies report only black-white voting rates. The Youngstown study notes that the least support for the school levy was among European ethnic voters, but provides no measurements.[20] The Austintown survey made a special effort to gather ethnicity data, which are presented in Table 9-7 with parental status and social class controlled.

The voting of ethnic groups in Austintown matches the Chicago and Cleveland gross data patterns and the ethos theory in every respect.[21] The affirmative vote of the British ancestry respondents was 58 percent compared to 36 percent by the European ethnic groups. The correlation is not spurious. When controlled by each of the other two most potent influences on the voting, social class and parental status, the association is undiminished.[22] Ethnicity was distinctly more potent than social class or parentage.

Table 9-8
Voting by Occupation and Income on Austintown School Levy (percent voting Yes)

	Below 10000 (N)	10-14999	15000 up	Total (N)
Manual	35 (112)	27 (52)	56 (18)	33 (182)
Clerical	18 (34)	60 (15)	67 (3)	33 (52)
Managerial	47 (19)	54 (28)	48 (23)	50 (70)
Professional	83 (12)	92 (24)	73 (11)	85 (47)
Total	36 (177)	50 (119)	56 (55)	44 (351)
	$p < .05$	$p < .001$	ns	$p < .001$

An interesting aspect of this case is the voting of the German segment. The Germans and Scandinavians are never mentioned by Wilson and Banfield, perhaps because they are not Catholic (or do not reside in Boston).[23] The voting of the Germans also fits; their support rate should be, and was, between the Anglos and the Catholic Europeans, but closer to the "immigrant ethos" than the Anglo-Saxon. In an open housing plebiscite, however, the German affirmative vote was equal to the British rate and double the Polish.[24]

The Importance of Occupation

Occupation is the neglected variable in political ethos research. Wilson and Banfield's correlations of referenda voting treated income, home ownership, and ethnicity; their subsequent study adds schooling and religion, but again omits occupation. It also is neglected in the other studies, perhaps because it is less amenable to the ecological method. How important is occupation for defining the subcultures of the unitary or individualist ethos? We have observed (Table 8-4) the consistent and strong association of occupation and voting in strongly contested school referenda; it was even stronger than parentage in the Austintown and Bowling Green cases.

The Austintown data afford a test of the relative importance of occupation and income. Cross-tabulation of those variables demonstrates that occupation is far more significant. The range between occupational categories within the income classes is substantially greater than the range between income intervals. Income had only a modest effect on professionals and businessmen, but it did affect the decisions of clerical and manual workers. The least enthusiasm for expenditures and taxes was among low-income white collar and middle-income blue collar workers. Middle-income clerical workers displayed public-regardingness, but that was manifested by only those manual workers with high family incomes.[25]

The primacy of occupation also was evident in the partial correlations of the socioeconomic and demographic variables in the Bowling Green election (Table 8-14). Under controls, both income and education faded and occupation remained as the strongest correlate except urban or rural residence, even stronger than parental status and property tax payments in an election where taxes were of extraordinary concern. Evidently political ethos not only is more accurately defined by occupation than income, but occupation also is the principal generator.[26]

The subcultures of each ethos are "definable in ethnic and income terms," said Wilson and Banfield. The latter appears to be erroneous, and the former is not very relevant to school referenda in many communities. European ethnicity was of some consequence in only three of the school election surveys. If the political ethos theory currently has much significance throughout America, political ethos must be an element of class subculture. The school referenda surveys unanimously attest that it is —and substantially so. Hence occupation, because of its contribution to the class structure, is of singular importance as a conduit of both the unitary and the individualist ethos.

School referenda are the most logical occasions for public- and private-regardingness to be the value premises of voting, as that is the inescapable choice that confronts a majority of the voters. For most voters, other than school employees or parents of children enrolled in the system, the question is whether to augment their contributions to the welfare of other people. Theodore Lowi's policy taxonomy is extraordinarily apropos. Distributive policies, he notes, are more numerous and popular than regulatory or redistributive policies, because they have the appearance of generating costless benefits—the costs being so dispersed, obscure, and ambiguous.[27] A school referendum is the polar opposite—a redistributive policy in so stark a form that everyone perceives that it is redistributive and, unlike most other fiscal referenda, the identities of the beneficiaries and the payers are not ambiguous. Indeed, it is that very rare situation where the payers are told precisely the cost, e.g., 5 mills or 3 mills for twenty years for a bond issue. (A voter may be less certain of his cost for a bond issue not accompanied by a special levy, but in that case it will not look small.)

To our knowledge, there has been no effort to ascertain the parameters of private- and public-regardingness voting, which could not be done by ecological analysis. The preceding data, notably Tables 8-11 and 9-7, demonstrate incontrovertibly that there are large quantities of both in school plebiscites, which should afford an ideal situation for measurement, as the identities of the beneficiaries and payers are so evident. However, the parameters cannot be fully measured, because parents and school employees are simultaneously payers and beneficiaries. One may reasona-

Table 9-9
Private- and Public-Regardingness Voting in Twenty Narrowly Defeated School Levy Elections

	Austintown	Bowling Green	Washington*	Total	Pct.
Voters against tax levy					
Parents of school children	84	54	99	237	
Other voters	118	107	191	416	
Private-regarding votes	202	161	290	653	48
Public-regarding votes					
Nonparents voting Yes	64	80	167	311	23
Either one or both					
Parents voting Yes	92	81	220	393	29
Total votes	358	322	677	1357	100
Voting of Nonparents					
Percent Yes	35	41	47		

*A 60 percent majority is required in Washington.

bly infer that nearly all No votes by parents are private-regarding decisions that the certain tangible costs exceed the uncertain intangible benefits. An astonishing fraction of parents read the scales that way in all these surveys except the Detroit and Birmingham cases—nearly half of the Austintown parents.

Manifestly the proportion of private- and public-regarding votes varies with the object of expenditure on the ballot and even among school referenda—the bulk of "nonparents" voted affirmatively in the Birmingham and Detroit cases. Hence, Table 9-9 is the set of elections that are the most comparable.[28] It is indicative of a distinct class: strongly contested and narrowly defeated operating levy referenda. Evidently private-regardingness was the premise of at least half of the votes, and public-regardingness was the basis of at least a fourth. Perhaps the voting of "nonparents" is a rough index of public-regardingness voting. On the one hand it has an inflating factor, since it contains some school employees, but on the other hand the incidence of public-regardingness should be higher among parents than nonparents, since the latter category has all the senior citizens. Hence the yeasaying of "nonparents" would seem to be a conservative index of the volume of public-regarding voting. It follows that the proportion of public-regarding voting in those twenty school levy referenda ranged between 35 and 47 percent.

The foregoing is impressive evidence for the political ethos theory, unless school levy voting fluctuates wildly and is not based on stable attitudes. The consistency of the patterns of Table 9-9 and of the correlates data in the preceding chapter demonstrate beyond peradventure that school referenda voting is based on quite stable attitudes. The stability of voting was measured by the Washington survey, which asked the voters how they had voted in the last previous election and whether they had ever voted for a levy. In a state with annual levy elections, a fourth of the naysayers said they had never voted for a levy. Nine-tenths of the respondents had voted the same way in the last two elections. Ninety-six percent of the yeasayers had voted yea in the previous one. "The best indicator of how a person will vote in a levy election is his vote in preceding levy elections."[29]

The substantial volume of public-regarding voting requires considerable qualification of Sigel's theory of school referenda voting, but by no means negates it, since the only votes inconsistent with self-interest, narrowly conceived, are those of Yes votes by "nonparents." Hence three-fourths of the votes in Bowling Green were consistent with self-interest and four-fifths of those in Austintown and the Washington districts.

Other Attitudes

Despite the space allocated here to alienation and public-regardingness, they are not the only general attitudes that are significant for school election voting. Apparently the paramount attitude in the Austintown election was the voter's feeling about the local property tax rate, as too high or about right (Table 8-10). Austintown voting also was strongly associated with two other general attitudes, political liberalism and sense of political efficacy.

Overlapping the ethos theory pair of attitudes, and also feelings about the local tax rate, are a pair of attitudes noticed by interviewers at Bowling Green; i.e., that public services and expenditures are "good" things or that taxes are "bad" *per se*. That impression was confirmed by the patterns of voting on the four simultaneous fiscal propositions. A majority of the sample voted a "straight ticket," either all Yes or all No. Over 40 percent of the electorate voted for three or all propositions, indicative of a predisposition in favor of public services and a willingness to pay for them; whereas about 40 percent had the opposite predisposition. The presence of those attitudes in Austintown is reflected in the association of political liberalism with yeasaying. A subsequent survey of an election with five nonschool propositions disclosed an even higher rate of straight ticket voting.[30] These widespread predispositions toward public expenditures and taxation may be closer to the reality of fiscal referenda voting than Wilson and Banfield's congruent concepts. They also may be the principal devices used by voters for simplifying the problem, i.e., for coping with the information problem and reducing the decision-making burden.

Table 9-10

Attitudes re Public Expenditures: Straight-Ticket Voting in Bowling Green on Four Fiscal Propositions (percent)

"Split tickets"		
Voted for one only	17	
BG School and others	15	
Other combinations	15	
Total "Split"		47
Straight No		21
Straight Yes		32

The preceding attitudes are pertinent to all fiscal referenda, but two are of exclusive significance for school elections. The survey data confirm that education is most highly valued by those people who have the most of it, notably professionals. In some communities, however, voting may be affected more by attitudes toward *public* education, as in Austintown and Detroit, where there are numerous adherents of parochial schools. In Austintown, this unfavorable attitude prevailed even in the voting of parents with children enrolled in the public schools. Not infrequently they have children in both systems and are, as they say, subject to "double taxation."

Inferences from Voting Correlates

At the large end of the funnel of causation of voting decisions are the attributes, associations, and perceptions that give rise to the voter's attitudes. Hence one method of investigating the genesis of voting decisions is by inference from voting correlates, the data of the preceding chapter. It may be a less satisfying method than self-report or use of attitudinal scales, and it is fraught with pitfalls; but it furnishes the most comprehensive picture of the influences on voting, and is the most widely used method of voting research. Thus, the partial correlation coefficients are the best indicators of the influences on voting at Bowling Green (Table 8-14). Now we will examine the correlates data for Austintown.

Table 9-11 is a convenient way of summarizing correlates data in a standardized form, expressing each in terms of its predictive value, i.e., the percentage of votes that could be "predicted" (actually postdiction) by knowledge of the respective attribute for each voter. Thus, 67 percent of the Austintown votes could be predicted correctly by knowing each voter's occupation (the strongest correlate in all the surveys except place of residence in Bowling Green and Okemos and alienation in Corning). In-

Table 9-11
Predictive Value of Demographic Variables, Attiudinal Scales, and SES Index: Austintown School Levy Election

Single Variables		Attitudinal Scales	
Occupation	67	Alienation	67
Education	62	Political efficacy	67
Tax/income	61	Political Liberalism	58
Ancestry	61		
Income	59	*Three-factor Index*	
Property tax	57	Socioeconomic status	66
Age	57		
Religion	56		
Parental status	56		

Table 9-12
Index of Austintown School Levy Support: SES, Parental Status, and Religious Preference (percent voting Yes)

	Parents[a]		Nonparents	
SES	Protestants	Catholics	Protestants	Catholics
High	84 (25)[b]	80 (28)	60 (25)	54 (26)
Middle	61 (31)	36 (28)	40 (25)	30 (30)
Low	40 (35)	33 (36)	18 (34)	24 (32)

[a]Of children in Austintown public schools.
[b](N).

deed, occupation is a slightly better predictor than a three-factor SES scale combining occupation, education, and income. The intercorrelation of occupation and social status with alienation and sense of political efficacy is shown by the fact that those attitude scales had equal predictive values.

The exceptionally strong influence of a few demographic variables, i.e., voter attributes, on the voting in Austintown, the relative strength of those attributes, and the remarkable consistency of their impact is shown by the three-variable matrix of Table 9-12. The matrix is arranged with the variables operating in the same direction in order to measure their cumulative influence. If the variables are independent of each other and linear, the maximum levy support rate should be in the upper left cell, and the values should diminish step wise from left to right and top to bottom. These variables definitely are linear, independent, and potent. The monotonicity is amazing; there is only one deviant cell in the matrix. The cell values constitute an Index of Levy Support that ranges from 18 to 84.

Status was the preeminent influence of the set, with an average range of forty points. The simple correlation of voting with religion was equal that of parental status, but this matrix, by controlling, discloses that parental status was the stronger influence. The average difference between parents and nonparents of the same religion and SES is sixteen points; whereas the average difference for religion is only ten points. A reader may notice other messages, such as, that the endorsement of the levy by Catholic leaders influenced upper-status Catholics but not lower-status Catholics.

Voting in school referenda is not will-o'-the-wisp; it is not unstructured—nor inscrutable. It displays a high order of rationality, perhaps more than in most elections.

Notes

1. Roberta Sigel, *Election with an Issue* (unpublished), p. 21.

2. James Q. Wilson and Edward C. Banfield, "Public-Regardingness as a Value Premise in Voting Behavior," *American Political Science Review* 58 (December 1964), p. 885.

3. Temporary Special Levy Study Commission, *Summary Report and Research Reports* (Olympia: Washington Legislature, 1971), vol. 1, p. 337.

4. Howard D. Hamilton and Byron Marlowe, "Survey of Voting on Tax Levies in Bowling Green" (unpublished); and Sylvan H. Cohen, *Voting Behavior in School Referenda* (dissertation, Kent State University, 1971).

5. Washington Special Levy Study Commission, op. cit., pp. 337-338.

6. Ibid., p. 333.

7. Ibid., p. 335.

8. Ibid., p. 336. Such a super cautious generalization is not very helpful, but we are in no position to second guess the Washington investigators.

9. Cf. Angus Campbell et al., *The American Voter* (New York: Wiley, 1960), ch. 8.

10. John E. Horton and Wayne E. Thompson, "Powerlessness and Political Negativism: A Study of Defeated Referendums," *American Journal of Sociology* 67 (1962), pp. 486-488.

11. "We don't want to be bothered by any —— from the schools." "After establishing that we wanted their opinion because we valued it, in most cases we were able to complete the interview. Somewhere along the way when a particular attitudinal statement provided a stimulus, we would get this response: 'It's about time they asked people like us about that.' After thanking *us* for the interview, they sometimes would add, 'Be sure you tell those —— what I said.'" Cohen, op cit., p. 211.

12. The scales were divided into thirds numerically, which results in a distribution approximating a normal curve.

13. Cohen, op. cit., p. 214.

14. James Q. Wilson and Edward C. Banfield, *City Politics* (Cambridge: Harvard University Press), esp. chaps. 3, 16.

15. Cf. Timothy M. Hennessy, "Problems in Concept Formation: The Ethos 'Theory' and the Study of Urban Politics," *Midwest Political Science Journal* 14 (November 1970), pp. 537-564; Thomas Flinn, *Analyzing Decision-Making Systems: Local Government and Politics* (Glenview, Ill.: Scott Foresman, 1970), pp. 48-52; Dennis S. Ippolito and Martin L. Levin, "Public Regardingness, Race, and Social Class: The Case of a Rapid Transit Referendum," *Social Science Quarterly* 51 (December 1970), p. 633.

16. James Q. Wilson and Edward C. Banfield, "Political Ethos Revisited," *American Political Science Review* 65 (December 1971), p. 1048.

17. Cf. Raymond E. Wolfinger and John Osgood Field, "Political Ethos and the Structure of City Government," *American Political Science Review* 60 (June 1966), pp. 306-326; Robert Lineberry and Edmund P. Fowler, "Reformism and Public Policies in American Cities," *American Political Science Review* 61 (September 1967), pp. 701-716; Robert R. Alford and Harry M. Scoble, "Political and Socioeconomic Characteristics of American Cities," *The Municipal Yearbook, 1965* (Chicago: International City Managers' Association, 1965), pp. 82-97; Daniel N. Gordon, "Immigrants and Urban Governmental Form in American Cities, 1933-60," *American Journal of Sociology* 74 (September 1968), pp. 158-171.

18. Cf. James A. Norton, "Referenda Voting in Metropolitan Areas," *Western Political Quarterly,* 7 (March 1962), pp. 195-212; Henry J. Schmandt, Robert J. Steinbacher, and George D. Wendel, *Metropolitan Reform in St. Louis* (New York: Holt, Rinehart, and Winston, 1961); Richard A. Watson and John H. Romani, "Metropolitan Government for Metropolitan Cleveland: An Analysis of the Voting Record," *Midwest Journal of Political Science* 5 (November 1961), pp. 365-380; Scott Greer, *Metropolitics* (New York: Wiley, 1963), pp. 165-167.

19. Flinn, op. cit., p. 49.

20. J. Kiriazis and S. Hotchkiss, *Community Attitudinal Survey* (unpublished).

21. J. Q. Wilson and E. C. Banfield, "Public-Regardingness," *American Political Science Review* 58 (December 1964), pp. 876-887.

22. We have used subjective social class ("What social class would you say you belong to, the middle class, the working class, or the lower class?")

because it is more appropriate for political ethos, but the results were the same using an objective SES scale, a composite of education, income, and occupation. Religion was the other significant variable, but it would be inappropriate to control for religion, because it is an element of Wilson and Banfield's definition of the ethos.

23. Public-regardingness is the most prominent component in the description of the Norwegian political culture in Harry Eckstein, *Division and Cohesion in Democracy* (Princeton, N.J.: Princeton University Press, 1966). Has the public-regardingness of Scandinavians gone unrecognized because they did not locate close to Harvard?

24. The Toledo referendum, September 1967, the only survey of open housing voting with European ethnic data. H. D. Hamilton, "Voting in Open Housing Referenda," *Social Science Quarterly,* 51 (December 1970), p. 718.

25. These data are not contaminated seriously by renters, as Austintown is "a community of homeowners."

26. It would be anomalous if occupation were not a leading determinant, in view of the ways that, in a specialized society, occupation hooks the individual into the social structure. An explanation of why income is of lesser importance is in Eshref Shevky and Wendell Bell, *Social Area Analysis* (Stanford: Stanford University Press, 1955).

27. Theodore J. Lowi, "American Business, Public Policy, Case Studies, and Political Theory," *World Politics* 16 (July 1964), pp. 677-715.

28. The total column of Table 9-9 is unweighted intentionally, because weighting would make the data reflective of only Washington, which has the 60 percent rule.

29. Washington Special Levy Study Commission, *Report,* p. 337.

30. John H. Bowden and Howard D. Hamilton, "Some Notes on Metropolitics," in Jack Gargan and James Coke, eds., *Political Behavior and Public Issues in Ohio* (Kent: Kent University Press, 1973), pp. 274-293.

10

Discovering an Electorate's Attitudinal Configurations by Q Factor Analysis

In the two preceding chapters we tried to penetrate the mystery of the voting patterns in school referenda and the voter's decision-making process. In both instances our data base has been largely the different correlates of voting. From those correlates we have constructed attitudes and explanations that are linked to the direction of individual votes. Implicitly, we have conceptualized the sum of those individual votes as the collective political decision of an electorate. Thus, through understanding individual decisions we have assumed that the collective decision of a given electorate (or even of generalized electorates with like voters) could be comprehended.[1] That is a common approach, one that parallels the ground-breaking Erie County study of voting, *The People's Choice*.[2] And like that seminal study, we have also based our case on an approximation of the contention that in the main "social characteristics determine political preference."[3]

In this chapter, however, we depart from the time-honored tradition of collecting social and demographic data for a large sample of individual voters from which attitudes and explanations are inferred. Rather, we try to discover such attitudes and explanations more "directly" through a small-sample technique, Q factor analysis, a method hitherto unused in voting behavior research.[4] Through Q analysis we hope to expand our understanding of the *why* of voting.

The colossal volume of voting research since the Erie County study has not succeeded in fully dispelling the mystery of the *why* of voting after thirty years of using such research methods as self-report, attitudinal scaling, and voting correlates. Archives now bulge with punch cards and computer tapes containing voluminous aggregate voting records and mountains of data from surveys by academic and commercial pollsters. The data have been manipulated on computers to a fare thee well, employing the most sophisticated wrinkles—regression, correlation, and factoring—and a web of esoteric, prepossessing theories have been spun by the frenetic voting research fraternity. But the intractable *why* remains. Likewise, there are some genuine doubts, as one member of that fraternity has observed: "At this point one must face a very central problem: To what extent are the findings of the voting studies "real"?"[5] We claim no ultimate answer to that question. Nevertheless, the query was uppermost in our minds when we chose a research technique to get at the "real" attitudes that help to explain the dynamics of a school fiscal referendum.

The burden of this chapter is that a research "tool," Q analysis, hitherto ignored by voting researchers, has great potential for penetrating this mystery of *why*. It appears to be quite useful for studying voting behavior in local elections, the characteristics of which are so varied and usually so markedly different from presidential elections, which have been the preoccupation of voting research.[6]

The utility of Q analysis should be maximal for illuminating referenda voting, since referenda are the least standardized elections, being both subject specific and, to some extent, place specific. The beauty of Q analysis is its versatility; it is equally useful for any referendum subject at any location, because—in contrast to the scales used in survey research —this technique does not require that the situation contain some anticipated set of attitudes and cognitions appropriate to the instrument. It is our contention, then, that Q analysis ferrets out the principal cognitive and attitudinal configurations that actually exist in a specific situation—any situation. Indeed, with Q, we share the sentiments of Peter Rossi, that "The diversity of nonpresidential elections. . . need not be looked upon as a source of bafflement."[7]

The absence in Q analysis of constraining assumptions about the electoral (or any conflictive) situation can be interpreted as the basis of both its felicitous versatility and its most serious limitation for the *typical* generalizing objective of the social sciences. One can never be certain that the factors Q discloses as being significant determinants of voting in one election at one location will ever recur. For persons interested in the dynamics of a particular election, that is irrelevant.[8] It may not be irrelevant for social scientists whose only or major concern is generalizing about *the* determinants of voting, in this case for *all* school referenda. Clarifying the distinction between those two perspectives is one objective of this chapter.

There is an article of faith that is subscribed to by Q analysis:[9]

Measurement is not quite the *sine qua non* of a developing science of behavior that American psychology has long supposed it to be. Nor are large numbers of persons necessary for our studies. In principle, one may work scientifically for a life time with a single case, X. What is essential is a good theory and faith that there are plenty more cases where X came from.

Our X is a single referendum. The assumption is that there are plenty more referenda like it "where X came from," an assumption that is supported by the data of the preceding chapters, which demonstrate that referenda on the same subject—and most certainly school referenda—are not idiosyncratic. Consequently, one might expect the cognitive and attitudinal configurations found in one school election to recur frequently. If so, Q analysis may contribute to science. We have done a test of this matter with gratifying results.[10]

Functional Explanation of Q Analysis

Q analysis is a method of discovering the principal configurations of "feelings, attitudes, opinions, thinking, fantasy, and all else of a subjective nature"[11] that exist in a specific community of any size at an instant in time relative to a specific event, such as the pending bond election, a teachers' strike, a school busing program, the new school dress code, or even the Mai Lai massacre and Lieutenant William Calley.[12] Although Q employs questions (in the form of statements) similar to those of survey research, it is not a public opinion poll since it does not count opinions. Q discloses the broader configurations or perspectives that are the foundation of opinions,[13] but the frequency of the ascertained perspectives among the small sample of subjects is not an index of their frequency in the community. Q is not a counting technique; it does not tally the frequency distribution of attitudes in a given population.

The principal perspectives are discovered by devising a set of statements—mixtures of perceptions, values, and opinions—about a controversy, for instance, drawn from the discourse in a community. The statements, called the Q sample, are selected to cover the full range, if possible, of the discourse. A small group of community residents, fifteen to twenty may suffice, are selected as the subjects, called the P set, to sort the statements on the basis of each subject's degree of agreement or disagreement with those statements.[14] "Sorting" the statements is a rank-ordering procedure according to a forced distribution that will be explained presently. The subjects are not a random nor a representative sample of the community as in more familiar research techniques. Rather, the P set may be chosen for many reasons; the most usual purpose is to represent known interests in the event under study.[15]

In the Q sorting, the subject assigns each statement a rank-order value ranging from -5 to $+5$ or in effect from 1 to 11.[16] This is a convenient way of ranking statements from "least liked" to "most liked." The rankings by each subject are correlated with the rankings of each other subject, and the resulting matrix of correlation coefficients is factor analyzed by a "canned" computer program that discloses clusters of persons who ranked the statements similarly. Thus each cluster is a separate attitudinal system —one perspective of the controversy under study—called a factor. Frequently three to five strong factors appear. Occasionally a person is a distinct factor, and there are likely to be some subjects who " do not load highly on any factor," i.e., who simply do not fit any of the principal perspectives.

Then one looks at how each cluster scored the statements. A convenient way is to array the scores for each factor for the respective statements. (Actually this is the average scoring of the statement by the persons in the cluster.) Thus, in the example below factor 1 people strongly disagreed with statement one, factor 2 people were neutral, and factors 3 and 4 agreed with it somewhat.

Statement	Factor Scores			
	1	2	3	4
1. The people would have voted for the school levy if the Board of Education and the school system had explained it better.	−5	0	+2	+2

Interpreting the factors requires thorough knowledge of the community controversy; experience also helps. What follows is a nontechnical description of our Q analysis of the perspectives during the Youngstown school crisis. A brief technical supplement is provided in Appendix A.

Design of the Youngstown Experiment

Our investigation of the Youngstown school crisis began after the fifth consecutive levy defeat.[17] In that special election the school forces had not campaigned vigorously. Indeed, as far as the general community was concerned, they did not campaign at all. Instead, with the apparent cooperation of the local communications media, they counted on a low-profile election to shrink the number of naysayers from the fourth defeat of the previous month, while holding the yeasayers reasonably constant. The ranks of the naysayers were thinned out by about 10 percent. But there was a minor problem: the strategy reduced the yeasayers by over 25 percent.

In the five referendum setbacks not a single meeting was held by antilevy forces, at least not of record. Not a pamphlet, brochure, or flyer was published attacking the schools and their attempt to raise funds. Not an advertisement appeared against them. There just was no organized opposition. In fact, the most reasonable explanation of these defeats seemed, at the time, to be that more people were regularly against the school levy than for it. The popular name for that situation in this community was "a taxpayers' rebellion." This seemed to be an ideal subject for Q analysis.

The P Set

This consists of the subjects who rank the statements that attempt to model the discourse of the event studied, in this case the Youngstown school fiscal crisis. Normally, the discussion of an experimental design for Q analysis begins with those statements, because it is the theories embodied in those statements that are "sampled," not the sorters (subjects). However, we first conceptualized an ideal P set.[18] This, in turn, guided the design for and the choice of our statements.

The dialogue that attended this series of school referenda suggested that voters in those elections could be placed somewhere on three separate continua: (A) their trust in the school system, (B) their attitude toward self-taxation, and (C) their personal stake in the continued operation of the public schools. It was assumed that individuals would tend to gravitate toward one or the other end of each continuum. We conceived of "self-taxability" as have Wilson and Banfield—an independent variable, with the direction of referenda voting as the dependent variable.[19] "Personal stake" in the schools was taken to be more inclusive than the most obvious interest, parentage of school children. Our view of salience here exceeded demographic correlates; and our ideal set extended to include grandparents, those with children soon to enter school, even childless couples with close friends in any of the above situations, or who had had a good school experience of their own.

Table 10-1 illustrates the logic of the dichotomization of the three continua: (A) trust, (B) self-taxability, and (C) salience. For example, A_1 presumes that the voter ranks relatively high in trusting the school system and A_2 presumes the reverse. Using these continua, the ideal P set would contain eight ideal types of voters, the eight possible combinations of these three variables.[20]

It is important to note that, although the above representation may provide some grounds for differentiation among the public, there was no hypothesis about how the respondents chosen must operate (sort) in order to achieve statistical representativeness. That kind of representativeness does not exist in Q analysis. The P set only serves as a rough control of the effects and it supplies a technique for repeating the experiment.[21] Too much stress should not be placed on the logic that we have used in structuring the P set.

The Q Sample

In assembling a Q sample (the statements to be sorted), one can use a factorial design such as was used to select the P set, or one may opt for an unstructured, random selection of statements.[22] The current trend in Q studies is to build into the statements a formal theoretical design that comprehensively covers theories or a theory relevant to the situation studied.[23]

Our effort does not have a sophisticated theoretical framework. The Q sample found in the appendix was created with a loose design as a guide, aided by: (1) knowledge of the conflict situation as a participant observer and (2) imagining the sorting process not by a "real" P set but by the ideal one posited above. Thus, we conceived the persons who would rank-order

Table 10-1
Factorial Design P Set for a School Referendum

Effects	Levels		N
A. Trust	A_1 high	A_2 low	2
B. Self-taxability	B_1 high	B_2 low	2
C. Salience	C_1 high	C_2 low	2

Possible combinations: $2 \times 2 \times 2 = 8$ $(A_1B_1C_1 \ldots A_2B_2C_2)$

statements, and then set about designing statements that would stimulate their ego-involvement in the process and that they could comfortably sort into the forced distribution pattern we shall describe subsequently.

In constructing a population of measures that might conceivably accommodate eight *potentially* different perspectives, it is well to keep in mind that the subject of this discourse was a school referendum without the convenience of candidate and party and other cues that usually go with nonreferenda elections. It was hypothesized that this would place unusual stress upon communication. It was necessary, then, to find other symbols that would provide potent forms for the transmission of ideas and feelings. Lasswell and his associates influenced our statement design with their discussion of "key symbols," which they describe as the "focal points for the crystallization of sentiment."[24]

They classify key symbols as *identification*, *demand*, or *expectations*.[25] Random statements culled from letters to the editor, local talk shows, news accounts, and the like seemed to be readily adaptable to those three categories. For example, identification statements can be recognized by their attempt to supply the convenience of "groups" as symbols: Catholics, Blacks, families-without-children-in-school. Demand covers general and specific value demands; e.g., that the state of Ohio should support the local school systems, that the school system should live within its budget, that the Board of Education should have figured out a tax credit for families with children in parochial schools. Expectations read as follows: if they had passed this levy, if the schools close, etc.

Key symbols were combined with "cognitions" to construct the Q sample. We borrowed Lasswell's concept of "climate" to discern two levels of cognition: image and mood. These levels, in turn, distinguish among subjective events according to explicitness of reference; e.g., image refers to "patterns of relatively specific reference," while mood designates "highly generalized reference."[26] This attempt to combine symbols and cognitions can be illustrated in a simple factorial arrangement, as in Table 10-2, where we have added a sample statement, with the score of each factor. Note the self-referent character of the statement; one can preface

Table 10-2
The Youngstown Q Sample Design

Main Effects	Levels	N
Symbols	(a) identities (b) demands (c) expectations	3
Cognitions	(d) image (e) mood	2

Possible combinations: $3 \times 2 = 6(ad, ae, bd, be, cd, ce)$
Replicated 9 times: $N = 54$ statements

5. (cd) If the students bought their own textbooks, like in the good old days, they would take better care of them. Free textbooks is probably another give-away deal to satisfy certain minority groups.	Factor Scores			
	1	2	3	4
	−5	+4	+1	+4

each statement with "I believe that. . . ." The "factor scores" indicate how different clusters "believed."

The Q sample is designed to provide comprehensive coverage and a formula for repeating any set of statements; it is not intended to "test" respondents, or, for that matter, to test *specified* hypotheses.[27] Respondents are not aware of the structure of the Q sample when they sort statements. Even the factorial arrangement that is used to collect statements is pretty much subjective to the researcher. Thus, it is not a point of contention from the standpoint of the sorter, the creator of the Q sample, or even a critic thereof, where in that factorial design, any statement is placed.[28] The design is only a guide because the statements are not matters of fact, but matters of opinion that cannot be judged by true-false criteria. They are synthetic statements which lack an either/or quality; consequently one can never be absolutely certain that any given statement belongs either in one cell or another.[29] That prior "uncertainty" about the meaning of the statements of the Q sample is central to Q factor analysis. However, some of the uncertainty is alleviated through the process of Q sorting, using the forced distribution of statements which is imposed upon respondents.

Sorting

In most research, it is customary for researchers to supply the logic by which respondents' behavior is measured. In Q analysis, however, the process is reversed. Respondents behave (sort) and *they* thereby supply the logic which is synonymous with their behavior. As one Q enthusiast has observed:

Data to be analyzed by Q method are S's operations in Q sorting, not scores to items or scales of predetermined meaning. Therefore, what an item [statement] is logically defined to mean is not necessarily related to what S actually does with that item.[30]

Through sorting, i.e., assigning priorities of positive, negative, and neutral affect toward the statements of the Q sample, respondents assign their *own* meanings to those statements. Through a rank-ordering procedure, respondents model their subjective grasp of the event studied, in this instance the Youngstown school referendum.

In the Youngstown investigation, respondents evaluated a number of stimuli (the 54 statements of the Q sample) along a value scale.[31] The population of stimuli were expressions of symbols and cognitions derived from monitoring local press, radio, and conversations following the fifth referendum. These were fashioned into statements, after the factorial design of Table 10-2 and typed on cards randomly numbered from 1 to 54. Respondents were first requested to place statements into three piles: disagree, neutral, and agree. Then they were asked to sort statements into eleven ranks, designated from −5 (most disagree) through 0 (neutrality or ambiguity) to +5 (most agree). Instructions advised respondents how to proceed with this task, working from the extremes of feeling (−5 and +5, then −4 and +4, etc.) toward the midpoint of the continuum, placing a *fixed* number of statements under each increment of the scale.

This sorting process is illustrated by the tabulation below.

Placing:	−5	−4	−3	−2	−1	0	+1	+2	+3	+4	+5
Ordered metric:	1	2	3	4	5	6	7	8	9	10	11
Tied ranks:	4	4	5	5	6	6	6	5	5	4	4

"Placing" is the scale of discrimination, the evaluation of the Q sample items from −5 through +5. "Ordered metric" assumes intervality for that scale, i.e., assigned values from 1 through 11, in which it is possible to rank the size of differences between elements of the scale.[32] "Tied ranks" is the forced choice upon which the postulates of Q technique are predicated.[33]. Respondents were not free to assign any number of statements to any interval of the scale; instead, they were required to follow the pattern prescribed under "tied ranks."

The forced-choice method described above requires subjects to compare all statements with one another. This cannot be done in survey research, wherein respondents can be naysayers or yeasayers without indicating preferences among nays and yeas, or they can opt for an "I don't know" response as often as they like.[34] In Q technique, subjects cannot escape the responsibility of assigning priorities to their choices according to the ubiquitous "scarcity principle." This way intensity is rarely abstract, since choices are made across the entire array of statements of the Q sample. And very practically, subjects can set their own pace for sorting, go back and review the situation, and adjust, if necessary, initial responses. This may be possible in survey research; but it is an unlikely possibility.[35]

Q sorting is behavior; using forced choice, that behavior approximates reality, wherein choice is not free, but constrained. If a relevant and comprehensive Q sample and P set are used, the process of sorting is a measurable operation by which structures of attitudes can be ascertained. Let us look at the perspectives uncovered in Youngstown through the use of Q analysis, and consider their applicability for referenda in general.

Identifying the Q Perspectives for Youngstown

In the Youngstown investigation, the Q sample was used with three different P sets under three somewhat different circumstances; four almost identical ways of sorting the statements appeared each time. The first P set were adults, chosen according to the factorial design of Table 10-1, following the fifth levy defeat. A similar set of adults was chosen just prior to the sixth election; however, some of the categories of the eight ideal types of voters were unavailable. Still, the four ways of sorting the statements remained remarkably stable.[36] At that point in the investigation, some alternatives were available: study could have been turned inward toward intensive measurement of the respondents,[37] or a survey tool could have been fashioned to measure the proportion of each of these perspectives in the Youngstown community, with an eye to correlating perspectives with direction of voting. Instead one more P set was used, university students, to test the effects of political socialization vis-a-vis this referendum conflict.

The four ways of sorting the Q sample were referred to earlier as "factors," i.e., hypothetical entities.[38] However, it is important to note that these are empirically based constructs derived from the sorting process, and that the four factors considered here comprise an empirical typology, as distinguished from one that is deductively created. Certainly, there are grounds for disagreement over the interpretation of each factor and even more so over the possible contribution of this typology toward understanding the conflict situation. But Q analysis does preserve the integrity of each sorter and each perspective produced by the clustering of sorters. Consequently, the conflict situation is observed from the position of the actors, not of the researchers. This is one advantage of Q analysis, its capacity to meet Herbert Blumer's test of valuable social research:

Since action is forged by the actor out of what he perceives, interprets, and judges, one would have to see the operating situation as the actor sees it, perceive objects as the actor perceives them, ascertain their meanings in terms of the meanings they have for the actor and follow the actor's line of conduct as the actor organizes it—in short, one would have to take the role of the actor and see the world from his standpoint.[39]

Thus, the four perspectives discovered in Youngstown, have been fashioned from the behavior of each actor. The goal of Q analysis is to find out what the actor (sorter) means in his action.[40]

But there are moments of doubt, when investigators using Q analysis view the Q sample itself as a closed universe, one in which you get out what you put in. Typically, the question is raised, "What if we had used 54 different statements?" There is no answer to that question except to point out that if the statements of the Q sample are matters of opinion, not fact, no one can guess what has been "put in" to this Q sample—or a substitute one, for that matter. The statements have no provable or disprovable meanings, nor do they have any meanings whatsoever until they are sorted in an identifiable way. On that basis, the universe is remarkably "open." The perspectives that follow are identifiable ways of organizing this open universe of discourse.

Factor One: Good Citizens

This construct may be one crucial element of all contested school tax elections and, for that matter, all contested referenda that are proposed by what has been popularly designated of late as "the establishment." Factor one embraces the "good citizens," who identify very closely with the school establishment. The name has been borrowed from a cross-cultural study that singled out this kind of citizen as one who feels strongly obligated to participate in civic activity, who shares with others like him a sense of civic competence.[41] Another study has identified this perspective as "civic responsibility" or "community identification," ascribing it to relatively high-status groups within the community that feel they have a stake in the outcome of community elections.[42] Scales have been developed to measure this sense of *citizen duty* and research has shown a positive relationship between being high on this scale and high on political participation, with income, education, and occupation highly related to this feeling of civic obligation.[43] Although the data of the Q sort do not directly measure socioeconomic status variables or political participation, the relationship is helpful as a guide. (This was tested directly in Austintown.) In scanning the factor array for the "good citizen" construct, it is well to keep in mind that the most obvious distinguishing characteristics of this behavior are support for the school authorities and for public education, and the obligation to be "responsible." A less obvious, but equally important, characteristic is a strong sense of distrust for the "other kinds of voters" or possibly for voting itself on matters that are best left to experts.

The content of the "good citizen" attitude is revealed by the sample of factor one statements below, which shows those statements that evoked strong positive or negative response by the good citizens and thus differentiate their perception from the other three.

Statement	Factor Scores			
	1	2	3	4
1. The people would have voted for the school levy if the Board of Education and the school system had explained it better.	−5	0	2	2
5. If the students bought their own textbooks, like in the good old days, they would take better care of them. Free textbooks is probably another give-away deal to satisfy certain minority groups.	−5	4	1	4
14. The authorities have tried reasonably hard and the local communications media have cooperated but it seems to be very difficult to communicate with voters. When it comes to school levies, more often than not, the voters react emotionally, without checking the facts carefully.	4	−5	−4	−1
15. A six mill levy probably would have been passed in May, 1968 in the primary elections. The school system goofed up when it got grandiose ideas.	−3	3	0	5
20. Since the local community has not faced up to the responsibility of taxing itself, at least at a rate comparable to that of the trend of inflation, our school system has deteriorated in Youngstown. Not passing five consecutive school levies may have "helped" the voters, but it darn well has hurt the students.	5	−3	−3	−3
24. It seems as if a barely adequate local school system costs more than the Youngstown voters are willing to pay.	3	−2	−4	−4
29. The financial plight of our local schools is quite real. It's every bit as bad as the Board of Education and schools have said it is. It's really amazing that the levy failed.	3	−4	−4	−1
34. Possibly the most important contribution to America's greatness has been its system of public schools. Rather than weaken this important institution, voters should support the school system through self-taxation, even if it hurts.	4	−2	3	2
50. With a large Catholic population such as Youngstown	−4	0	1	0

	1	2	3	4

has, there ought to be more Catholics on the Board of Education. Catholics support two school systems but what happens in the public school system affects the parochial system as well. Therefore more Catholics on the Board of Education will also help the passage of local school levies.

51. School teachers and school administrators in the Youngstown public schools tend to give Negro children somewhat favored treatment, often times even overly favorable treatment.   −5   2   −2   −3

The "good citizens" are the school loyalists; they defended the communications effort of the school authorities; rejected a possible anti-public-school and racial slur; distrusted ill-informed, emotional voters; defended the school system, disregarding the possibility of compromise; worried that local education had deteriorated; castigated the niggardliness of the voters; backed up the claim of the authorities of "financial plight;" reaffirmed their faith in the institution of public schools and the reciprocal responsibility of self-taxation; did not agree that there should be more Catholics on the school board; and righteously denied that the schools were showing favoritism to Negroes. Factor one might be called the "liberal" one; however its liberality may be that of an upper socioeconomic group that can afford to indulge its tastes in fiscal referenda and does not feel threatened by the changing composition of the schools.

In the context of that controversy, the good citizens' responses to items 50 and 51 are noteworthy. They were the only factor group that rejected the complaint that Catholics were underrepresented on the school board and they were the most emphatic in denying the charge that the schools were showing favoritism to Negroes. These righteous responses appear to be examples of the power of symbolic language. Any disadvantaged group is likely to receive some extra help, and in fact such effort by the Youngstown schools had been well publicized, but good citizens would not acknowledge "favored treatment."

Four of the distinguishing statements display the good citizens' critical view of the other voters. That is a significant clue to the nature of the levy controversy in Youngstown, where the good citizens' mental set pervaded all the communication from the schools and their supporters. The good citizens approve of the decisional outputs of the one-party system that is characteristic of school districts, and they accept the assumption of educationists that "people are either 'right thinking' or ill informed."[44] Consequently, the good citizens of the sample coupled their ardent support of the school authorities with a denial of the legitimacy of the other three perspectives in the sample and the controversy, because the other voters had failed to "support our schools." That denial of the legitimacy of the views of the opposition was manifest in the conduct and communication of the good citizens during the protracted controversy. If for any force there is a counter-force in politics as well as mechanics, the existence of the good-citizen perspective may be one reason for the stable existence of the other three perspectives of the P set, which may, in part, be reaction to such an unabashed, sometimes insensitive, display of civic virtue. The factor two group reacted strongly to it.

The good citizens, after five levy defeats, were caught on the horns of a dilemma, one which has been termed "An American political dilemma."[45] This is the rather schizophrenic belief in *both* town-hall democracy and mass participation, on one hand, and rule by the better qualified and responsible few, on the other. This is an acute dilemma for the good citizens, because they have the strongest commitment to the "civic culture" and also the strongest belief that discussions should be based on the judgments of technical "experts," in this instance the school authorities. What is one to do when, in the words of item 24, a "barely adequate" school system costs more than "the voters are willing to pay"? Which is to say, what do you do when the electorate repeatedly fails to ratify the judgment of the school establishment? Not surprisingly, the responses of the good citizens intimate a preference to remove politics from decision making, i.e., politics that disrupt the one-party system of educational decision making. Ideology serves practical ends.

Factor Two: Alienation

In the Q-sorting investigation, this emerged as a complex construct, as has the construct of alienation in recent literature. This is one of the most vague concepts used by contemporary social scientists.[46] Perhaps both popularity and vagueness stem from the proliferation of dimensions that have been added to the phenomenon; thus it may be popular because alienation can be used to explain so much in the way of behavior and yet it may be vague because the domain has become unmanageable as a single concept. To the perceived lack of power in community affairs and distrust of those who hold power, there has been added interpersonal distrust (Do you trust people?) and personal inefficacy (Do you feel personally ineffective?).[47] These additional sources of alienation seem to be especially significant for referenda, where the so-called alienated voter can be *politically* efficacious, and was for six consecutive elections in Youngstown. He may however, have felt ineffacacious for many reasons, including the inability to influence the school authorities to stem the tide of repeat elections. Further, his distrust of people may have extended to more than only school authorities. Those possibilities seem to be reflected in the Q responses.

One of the most conspicuous aspects of the items that distinguish factor two (see below) is their strong negative correlation with factor one. The distinguishing items of factor two contain nearly all of the elements of alienation—parochialism, ethnocentrism, local chauvinism, aggressiveness, mistrust of authority, suspiciousness, and a persecution complex. Factor two was the only group opposed to integration of the schools.

Statement	Factor Scores			
	2	1	3	4
2. The graduates of Youngstown city schools do as well or better in college than graduates of school systems of comparable size communities in Ohio.	4	0	0	2
7. Aside from the fact that busing students is impractical, artificial schemes designed to force integration violate the traditional concepts of the neighborhood as well as the civil rights of the taxpayers who don't want artificial integration.	5	−3	−1	−3
16. Whenever the school levy fails, people secretly blame the Catholics. This is one of the worst forms of discrimination and intolerance that I can imagine. And it just isn't one bit true!	5	−1	−2	0
25. The fact that they brought in some high salaried out-of-towners for high paying, high status jobs, basically has nothing to do with the real reasons for the failure of the levy. You want the best man for the job even if he isn't a local man.	−5	5	−1	−1
30. People don't like to talk about it openly, but most of the opposition to the levy is due to the obvious fact that the people who are costing the schools the most money and causing these levies to be higher in millage and to come more often—these same people are contributing little or nothing toward maintaining the school system.	5	−2	4	2
32. If they had passed this levy, it's a good guess that they would have been around again in another two years or so asking for another one. From time to time it may be necessary to let them know that the little guy isn't going to be pushed around that easily.	3	−4	−3	2
46. Although this is not the reason to vote against the school levy, I still say, even though the levy has failed the Youngstown schools will continue to provide an education well above the average of schools in Northern Ohio of similar size.	3	−4	−3	0
48. Let's be honest, even if it isn't pleasant—as you increase the number of Negro students in a school district you decrease the chances for passing a school levy.	3	−3	2	−3

Our Q analysis also revealed another element of alienation, i.e., populism, thus confirming an association noted by the historian, Richard Hofstadter.[48] Factor two people defended the voter and his right to second guess the authorities on every occasion presented (six items) and attacked the authorities at every opportunity (five items). Like the Populist movement, factor two people were rebellious and projected their feelings on to blacks, the notable practice of Southern Populism.

Factor Three: Ambivalent and Cautious

This factor was difficult to interpret. It had the fewest number of statements that distinguished it from the other factors; therefore it was something of a composite of the other perspectives. This, perhaps, reflects the complexity of school referenda, the cross pressures that electorates face in controverted situations. Factor three people sorted the Q sample in a pattern that suggests that they saw the situation in Youngstown, in part, from all of the perspectives uncovered in the Q analysis. The label appended to this factor comes from statement 39; ambivalency is a natural response to a prismatic view of the referenda controversy, obviously a view not shared by the other factors.

In contrast to the good citizens, factor three people did not agree that the financial situation was "as bad as the Board of Education said." On the other hand, their responses to three statements (13, 28, and 54) show that they shared with the good citizens a strong attachment to the public school concept, and they were concerned that it not be jeopardized by trifling with the separation of church and state or by voting decisions based on emotions about race.

Statement	Factor Scores			
	3	1	2	4
13. If private enterprise could take over the management of the school system, in the long run it would be cheaper for the taxpayer, more democratic in terms of sharing the cost, and quality of education would no doubt improve dramatically.	−5	−5	0	−2
28. The Board of Education could have figured out some sort of a tax credit for families with children in parochial schools. This would not have violated the concept of the separation of church and state, nor would it have undermined the tradition of American public schools.	−5	−2	1	−1
39. When it came right down to voting "yes" or "no" on the school levy, it was a tough decision to make. Either way there were reasons that seemed logical.	5	0	−1	1

	3	1	2	4
44. Even though it may mean that a levy is defeated now and then, the electorate should never give up voting directly on taxation for school levies and school bonds. In fact the voter ought to vote directly on more issues in our democracy.	3	0	2	3
53. Some people say that if you raise taxes on real estate you drive away businesses that would normally move into Youngstown. Other people say if you don't raise taxes the schools will deteriorate and businesses won't move into Youngstown. It's impossible problems such as this that discourage voters and keep them away from the polls altogether.	−5	−2	−3	−2
54. In the last two school levy elections entirely too many voters based their decision on the emotional aspects of racial tension and the racial composition of our schools.	3	−2	−5	−2

The length of the Youngstown crisis, and the closing down of the schools for a month, led some people to question the wisdom of tax levy plebiscites. That question was presented in statement 44, admittedly and deliberately with a slanted phasing. This item distinguished the ambivalents from the good citizens, who had become uncertain about the merits of direct democracy for school policy making, while the ambivalents continued to favor participatory democracy, notwithstanding some school levy defeats. On the other hand the ambivalents objected to voting on the basis of emotion about a race and emphatically rejected a statement that a levy defeat may be "necessary to let them know that the little guy isn't going to be pushed around," counsels of caution.

The perspective of factor three subjects is somewhat obscure, but they certainly were not alienates nor good citizens nor caretakers (the fourth factor). They shared with the good citizens an attachment to the public schools, but they were not school loyalists. They shared with the other groups an attachment to plebiscitary democracy. They had their particular dilemma and "it was a tough decision." The cloudiness of factor three derives from the inability of the ambivalents to simplify motivation as readily as did the other groups. The other three approach the clarity of stereotypes; the responses of the ambivalent and cautious voters have a refreshing air of confused realism. That perspective is a reminder that school referenda may not be morality plays for some people.

Factor Four: Caretakers

The sorting of the statements by the factor four group revealed them to be caretakers, that is, they favored the maintenance of only traditional services in as economical a way as possible, because of their intense concern for economizing. Supporting that policy preference was a high valuation of self-reliance, manifested in their endorsement of two statements: that students would take better care of their books if they had to buy them, and that "if the students want to learn, they'll learn even if there are two more in the room than last year."

For the caretakers, the school levy elections were a matter of economics—taxes and economy. Hence they agreed strongly with these statements: that children should buy their books, the school tax should not "soak the rich," the tax should be based on the number of children in school, and the school levy would have passed if it had been only six mills. They disagreed emphatically with the proposition that families without children should be taxed. The caretakers were positive that the schools did not need more revenue; observe their ranking of statement 45, a comprehensive expression of the caretakers viewpoint.

The caretakers and the alienates agreed on numerous items; in fact there was a +.52 correlation between their sorts. The obvious explanation for the extensive agreement is that both groups were intensely anti-levy. Hence they concurred in their ranking of statements that contained either criticism of the school authorities or approval of the decisions made by the voters. The appearance of extensive similarity between the two factors is facilitated by the compound nature of many of the statements of the Q sample, an inevitable result of using statements drawn from actual discourse.

It does not follow, however, that the two groups are essentially the same. They arrived at the same anti-levy position by different reasoning, starting from different concerns, i.e., their perspectives were different. A study of school budget elections in Oregon, published subsequent to the Youngstown Q study, identified two perspectives, antibudget and antiadministration, which correspond roughly to our caretakers and alienated factors. These were distinct orientations, since each exerted an independent effect on voting decisions.[49] Some of the Q statements also furnish unambiguous evidence of this distinction, for example, the contrast in the factor-two and factor-four scores for statements 10 and 31.[50]

Statement	Factor Scores			
	4	1	2	3
10. Basically the school levy didn't fail because of the Board of Education or the school system or even the fact that property taxes may be unfair. The real reason for the present financial mess is that the schools have become responsible for all kinds of programs such as health services, psychological testing, counseling, special programs for physically handicapped children, behaviorally disturbed students, etc., etc.	5	−1	5	−3

	4	1	2	3

31. The School Board hasn't always been representative of the real common man in Youngstown and that is one key reason why the school levies have been defeated.

                            −5   −1   2   −1

45. I'm not that worked up about the defeat of the school levy. If the school administrators are any good they'll use their ingenuity and manage to live within their means and provide good education. If the teachers are sincere, they'll teach because they want to teach and because the good Lord gave them this calling. And if the students want to learn, they'll even learn if there are two students more in the room than last year.

                             5   −1   5   −3

For the caretakers, the issue was economics, and hence they rejected with maximum intensity any alternative explanation of the levy defeats. The extensive communality of factors two and four derive from the fact that caretakers and the alienated, having made the same antilevy decision, offered the same rationalizations for rejecting the prevailing norm of the primacy of education. This suggests that alienation may be a reinforcement for some caretakers.

The Four Perspectives

Q factor analysis uncovered four distinct and different "versions" of the Youngstown school referendum crisis, as represented by good citizens, alienates, the ambivalent and cautious, and caretakers. Taken together, these factors advance our understanding of this complex event at least one step beyond such dichotomous classifications as proponents and opponents, school supporters and nonsupporters, public-regarding voters and private-regarding ones, etc. Each of the factors extracted is characterized by a recognizable and believable logic. That is to say, the arrays of each of the four factors exhibit an internal consistency of response (behavior), so that each factor can be "given a name." It is important to point out, too, the sequence by which these names were arrived at, because this is typical of Q research and is one of the crucial advantages of the Q approach: First, an "ideal" P set relevant to that situation was conceived. A collection of statements, the Q sample, was then created, comprehensive and balanced, so that each respondent in the ideal P set could comfortably sort them along an opinion continuum from −5 to +5 with a point of neutrality that approximated 0 for each sorter. At that stage of the investigation we did not know how many or what kind of factors would emerge from the sorting process. The research sequence, then, is that of an observed phenomenon (sorting), followed by giving the phenomenon a concept, i.e., "naming" it. This reverses the procedure of large-sample surveys which typically originate with an operationalized concept and a tool that measures aspects, properties, or characteristics of that concept. For example, an investigator may define a concept in terms of an attitudinal scale, which is then used in the field or the laboratory in search of phenomena that match the concept so defined.[51] Using this approach, investigators find or do not find what they are looking for. By contrast, Q analysis—unfettered by prior operational definitions—may uncover unexpected phenomena related to a generalized situation under study without limiting the breadth of possible discoveries.

A review of the factor arrays suggests that the four factors extracted in the Q study can be conceptualized as patterns of activity rather than only as clusters of people with like points of view. As patterns of activity, these factors can contribute toward understanding school fiscal referenda as a class of events. Thus, the "good citizenship" reported in other referenda accounts can be seen, not as the *opposite* of "bad citizenship," but as a *different* pattern of activity, nor can either be subsumed accurately under such simplified categories as referendum "supporters" and "opponents".

The writers are aware that the preceding inference drawn from the Youngstown Q analysis involved some unverified assumptions. There is the explicit assumption that the results of the Q investigation were an authentic mirror of some significant dynamics in the Youngstown controversy. The implicit assumption is that the findings also are relevant to school referenda in other communities—that our findings are more than an interesting but idiosyncratic snapshot. A host of questions suggest themselves. Are the extracted factors real or an artifact of similar P sets and some fortuitous coincidences in sorting? Do the factors provide insights for the Youngstown situation or only for understanding the patterns of activity uncovered? Do these patterns of activity recur in other referenda? If so, what is the incidence? Finally, how much bearing do they have on voters' decisions? That is, how useful are they for the explanation of the *why* of voting? We cannot offer definitive answers to these questions, but the opportunity to make a small beginning in that direction became available through a study of the nearby community of Austintown, Ohio, undertaken approximately two years after the Q investigation of Youngstown, Ohio.

Testing the "Validity" of Q Analysis in Voting Research

In December of 1970, a survey was conducted in Austintown immediately following the second defeat in five weeks of a 5-mill operating levy. One section of the interview schedule was made up of questions derived from the Q investigations of the school tax situation in Youngstown. Those questions were converted from the six most distinguishing statements from the Q sample for each of the four factors uncovered in the Youngstown research. An example of one such conversion for each factor follows showing the Q statement first, then the revised survey question:

Statement	*Response*

Good Citizens

1. The people would have voted for the school levy if the Board of Education and the school system had explained it better. — −5

C50. The people would vote more favorably for school levies if schools would explain things better. — strongly disagree

Alienates

16. Whenever the school levy fails, people secretly blame the Catholics. This is one of the worst forms of discrimination and intolerance that I can imagine. And it just isn't one bit true! — +5

C52. Whenever a school levy fails, people secretly blame the Catholics. — strongly agree

Ambivalent and Cautious

39. When it comes right down to voting "yes" or "no" on the school levy, it was a tough decision to make. Either way there were reasons that seemed logical. — +5

C26. Voting on the 5-mill levy was a tough decision. — strongly agree

Caretakers

15. A six mill levy probably would have been passed in May, 1968 in the primary elections. The school system goofed up when it got grandiose ideas. — +5

C29. In view of the times, 5 mills probably was too much to ask for.[52] — strongly agree

Twenty-four survey questions (six per factor) were used to construct scales, on the assumption that these scales measured aspects, properties and/or characteristics of the patterns of activity that each of these factors represented. There are several leaps of faith in that assumption. First, it is obvious that the converted questions to not retain all of the excess meaning of the original Q statements. Second, unless the questions are rank ordered as in Q, there is no basis for expecting that there would be any correspondence between response to a Q sample and response to twenty-four "important" questions derived from a Q sample. Third, and this is related to the previous consideration, without a forced distribution as in Q, differences between factors that shared statement response would be washed out even further, once priorities of intensity were not at issue. Basically, all three "problems" with the conversion process are closely related to differences between the two methodological approaches: Q factor analysis and survey research. Those problems were not resolved; however, a compromise was achieved through the use of *summated scales* to measure the attitudes of the respondents in Austintown on the four dimensions suggested by the Q research. The goal was to correlate this scaled response with the voting position of respondents and with a wide range of other response, including social and demographic data.

The so-called attitude scale is the most widely used and the most carefully designed and tested method for the measurement of attitudes, for which several types of scales have been developed.[53] Regardless of differences, all attitude scales consist of a number of items (stimuli) and a scale of response to these that sorts out respondents along a continuum of valence toward the object measured. In this method of scaling, all of the statements are equal. Hence, the scale is not built into the statements as such; instead, it is the end-product of the response to the series of statements in question. However, the respondent can register an intensity of response to each item, because there is a provision for a five-point continuum: (1) Strongly agree, (2) Somewhat agree, (3) Neutral, (4) Somewhat disagree, (5) Strongly disagree. It should be noted that the numerical values assigned to the response did not appear on the interview schedule; they are only for the purpose of scoring response, to find out where the respondent was located on the scales that purported to measure the four factors of the Youngstown Q investigation. An attempt was made to proceed from the Q−analysis focus on "how" the attitudes were sorted to the survey-research concern for "how many," i.e., for the frequency distribution of these factors in a given electorate. The data of the Austintown survey furnish a partial answer to the question of "how many?" Table 10-3 is a distribution of Q−analysis factors, based on response to the scales used in Austintown.

One additional difference in the methodologies is highlighted in Table 10-3; respondents are located on every scale using survey research. That counters the underlying assumption of Q, the independence of factors unless they are bi-polar. We infer, however, that respondents who scored high on a given scale are distinct instances of that factor, since the cutting points were set as thirds of the range of scores rather than thirds of the sample.

In a different community, and two years after the Q analysis, most of the Austintown respondents had attitudes that corresponded to one or another of the attitudinal configurations disclosed by the Q analysis in Youngstown—certainly evidence that contested school referenda are not

Table 10-3

Distribution of the Austintown Sample on Attitudinal Scales Constucted from Q Analysis Factors

Scale Interval	"Good Citizens"	Ambivalent & Cautious	Caretakers	Alienation
High	51	66	120	90
Intermediate	211	246	194	210
Low	94	43	42	55

Table 10-4

Association of Attitudes and Voting: Percent Voting for the Austintown Tax Levy

Scale Interval	"Good Citizens"	Ambivalent & Cautious	Caretakers	Alienation
High	88	35	12	8
Intermediate	47	43	53	49
Low	12	65	93	82

unstructured; there are behavior patterns. Some respondents were high on both the caretaker and alienation scales, which confirms the evidence of the Q analysis of the compatibility of those factors and that a caretaker policy preference may be reinforced by alienation sentiment.

In Austintown, "caretakers" were the most numerous, "good citizens" were the least numerous, and a fourth of the electorate was strongly alienated from the school system. A crushing defeat for school levies was in the cards—unless these attitudes are insignificant for voting. Table 10-4 furnishes the answer.

Table 10-4 demonstrates the strong association between scaled attitudes and the direction of the vote. In Austintown, knowing whether a respondent was a good citizen, caretaker, or an alienated individual was more valuable information for determining the direction of the vote than were the typical demographic variables employed by most voting research. It seems reasonable to conclude that the Youngstown Q factors were present in the Austintown referendum and had a potent impact on that event.

On the basis of this limited research, the Q factors appear to be "real." They are relevant attitudes. As one astute observer, noting that political behavior is the manifestation of political attitudes, has written: "Ultimately all political events are the resultants of the attitudes of individuals."[54] In Austintown, attitudes that approximated the factors of caretaking and alienation, and to a lesser extent, ambivalence and caution, in opposition to and reaction to good citizenship, were contributing factors of some significance to the making of this political event. Q enthusiasts would probably go one step beyond that conclusion: the subjective attitudes of the participants *were* the event.[55]

The Potential of Q Analysis

The general function of Q factor analysis is to uncover the principal perspectives in a specific controversy. Through the factor arrays, the content of each perspective is disclosed *in depth*: the values, and the opinions that distinguish the different ways of viewing a situation. This can be valuable, because the two-sided statement of most controversies—especially referenda—tends to obscure some of the important and informing differences among conflicting perspectives, and beclouds the mechanics of the situation, the structure of the conflict. The task of Q researchers is to "read" the attitudes of each configuration for clues concerning dimensions of the conflict situation that may or may not be guessed at. The Youngstown research provides an example of such potential benefits.

In Youngstown, a number of different logics were discovered by which four positions on a school referendum were perceived. Look from factor one, "good citizens," toward the other factors; but this time posit the factors as the electorate, but engaging in the activity suggested by each of the separate factor arrays. It is reasonable to assume that the other factors were aware of factor one and were generally "opposed" to the activity associated with that factor. After the results of the sorting by the first P set, we postulated a communication model for the results of that sorting based on the Table of Distinguishing Statements for each factor. Using the table for factor one, out of the eight statements that separated this factor from the rest—these are the perceptions, values, and opinions that mattered most for this factor—each one was on the opposite side of the opinion continuum from all of the other factors. And it is well to recall that at the time of the sorting for five consecutive elections the good citizens were as isolated in the objective election returns as in the subjective sorting! Indeed, the good citizens who controlled the school board, the communications media, and the symbols of status in Youngstown tried to hold the fifth election quietly without public notice because they felt the need to hide their activities from the "bad" and silent majority. Their misperception of reality was made undeniably clear by the crushing defeat in that "sleeper" election.

The silent majority was not only perplexing but more complex than the good citizens realized. It was not outside of the channels of communication; rather, it perceived the situation differently than those good citizens did. Each group that made up the silent majority responded on the basis of its own logic vis-a-vis this event. As a footnote, the final victory in this troubled community was won with the good citizens well in the background. Hortatory communication from on high, directed *at* the electorate, was traded for house-to-house canvassing by parents of average and below average socioeconomic status. In addition, appeals were made for consideration of the practical economics of school management; and the support of the hitherto inactive majority political party, with its broad base of membership, was solicited successfully. We are suggesting that Q factor analysis has a practical function for school authorities in providing possible insights on which campaign strategy may be based. Short of that, Q analysis should help school officials to understand and to show more understanding to competing logics in resdistributive and conflictive situations. At least they will escape the pitfalls of stereotyping *the* opposition as a single "they" and accept the fact that the oppositions are also individually logical.

Q analysis can also be used by voting researchers to uncover the dynamics of an election suggested by the various community perspectives. In fact, it may be employed in lieu of a survey, particularly when time and resources are lacking. However, Q has further utility as a means for devising appropriate questions and attitudinal scales for an election survey. This is not so unusual as our study may make it seem. Careful voting researchers typically interview community people when preparing survey schedules; they even "test" these schedules out into the field. We submit, however, that Q analysis is a more systematic approach to validating a survey instrument, to finding out what indeed is worth counting.[56] Indubitably, the Q investigation of Youngstown informed the survey research in Austintown.

Q analysis has some advantages that recommend it as an intelligence tool for schoolmen, researchers, or anyone for that matter. (1) Q analysis discloses the *actual* perspectives in a specific election situation as opposed to trying to dope them out by the scrutiny of voting correlates. It is a more direct route to attitudinal configurations and, as it has been noted, that route begins with behavior—the observed phenomenon, then an explanatory construct—the concept. (2) Q analysis, if successful, is characterized by depth and wholeness. It reveals the full perspectives, not the isolated bits that surveys are likely to pick up. Q factors are complex, but the *gestalt* of each factor is generally preserved, yet penetrable. (3) Q analysis is a versatile tool. It can be used for *any* election, for any conflictive situation, and is ideal for the mosaic of local elections and referenda. It does not require that *special* variables or characteristics be present in the situation under study; rather the situation, as it is, becomes the basis for the Q sample; never the other way around. (4) Q analysis is unusual as an administrative convenience. It is wonderfully inexpensive and speedy. It is suitable for amateurs; in every respect it is a do-it-yourself tool. And it rarely fails to uncover some insights of potential value. (5) Q analysis sensitizes its users to the variety of logics that often make up a complex situation. Q enthusiasts learn to keep their "logical" view of a situation from preventing their recognition and appreciation of other logical explanations of the same situation. Admittedly, one does not need Q to develop this skill, but it is a typical by-product of experimentation with this versatile research tool.

Regarding what are seen as limitations to Q analysis, there is first the fact that if a frequency distribution of the factors in the community is wanted, Q must be supplemented by a poll—but Q is not supposed to measure "how many," it is supposed to illuminate "how." In the same view, the P sets of Q analysis are not random samples of the "population" of people involved in the situation under study, anymore than a mentally disturbed individual studied by a psychoanalyst is a random sample of all mentally disturbed individuals or of all of the individuals in a community. Thus, there are limitations that are traceable to any P set selected, if one does not understand that Q is a small-sample technique in which specific theories in the form of statements are sampled, not respondents. One obvious limitation of the Q sample relates to comprehensiveness. How can the investigator blanket a complex situation in a limited number of statements? It cannot be done, but then the Q sample can be structured so that an investigator does not leave the statements to chance (randomization) but proceeds according to a plan that satisfies the research needs of the investigator, and that is where all research originates and should originate.

Perhaps, as Q enthusiasts, we have been overly enthusiastic about this research tool. However, it appeals to us as an alternative framework for gaining insights into the myraid of conflicts involving, for example, the schools. Q factor analysis is one way, certainly not the only way, of looking at things. It is also a way to find out the different ways that other people are looking at things.

Notes

1. V. O. Key, Jr., and Frank Munger, "Social Determinism and Electoral Decision: The Case of Indiana," in William J. Crotty, ed., *Public Opinion and Politics* (New York: Holt, Rinehart and Winston, Inc., 1970), p. 251. This is a paraphrase of the author's criticism of the micro approach to explaining voting behavior.

2. P. F. Lazarsfeld; B. R. Berelson; and Hazel Gaudet, *The People's Choice*, 2nd ed. (New York: Columbia University Press, 1948).

3. The criticism of *The People's Choice*, according to Key and Munger, op. cit., p. 250.

4. For an extensive explication of Q factor analysis, see: William Stephenson, *The Study of Behavior: Q-Technique and Its Methodology* (Chicago: The University of Chicago Press, 1953).

5. Eugene Burdick, "Political Theory and Voting Studies," in Eugene Burdick and Arthur J. Brodbeck, eds., *American Voting Behavior* (Glencoe, Illinois: The Free Press, 1959), p. 137.

6. See: Peter H. Rossi, "Four Landmarks in Voting Research," in Burdick and Brodbeck, op. cit., p. 51, on the exclusive attention to presidential elections and the value of studying nonpresidential elections to provide "a set of comparative frames which may illuminate processes which cannot be studied in the presidential contests."

7. Ibid.

8. It is irrelevant, too, to serious students of Q technique and its supporting methodology, who are well aware that this approach is not concerned with generalizing "from one to all."

9. Stephenson, op. cit., p. 343.

10. Sylvan H. Cohen, "Voting Behavior in School Referenda: An Investigation of Attitudes and Other Determinants by Q Technique and Survey Research" (Kent State University, unpublished dissertation). One phase of this research was testing the methodological utility of joining small-sample technique in one referendum to large-sample method in another in a different community. This will be discussed subsequently.

11. William Stephenson, *The Play Theory of Mass Communication* (Chicago: The University of Chicago Press, 1967), p. 11.

12. For a condensed explanation of Q methodology that covers the basic propositions with research seamples, see Stephenson, op. cit., pp. 13-32.

13. William Stephenson, "Definition of Opinion, Attitude, and Belief," *Psychological Record*, 15 (April 1965), pp. 281-288.

14. Cohen, op. cit., p. 75 suggests the use of *P* set rather than Stephenson's terminology, *P* sample. The reason here is that "sample" in this methodology refers to the statements. In the usual sense of survey research, people are not sampled; theories are. Those theories are embodied in the sample of statements, the Q sample.

15. Stephenson, *Play Theory*, op. cit., pp. 20-21. For example, if we were selecting a P set to execute a Q sort on "women's liberation," we might choose 5 men who favored it, 5 who opposed it, and 5 women who favored it, 5 who opposed it. That is not to say that they are represented in the population in that proportion or, what is more, that they have to

respond in an anticipated way to be valid representatives of their particular "interest."

16. This range is referred to as "placing," the discriminating or evaluating function of Q. To relieve the reader's anxiety as to how that "looks" and to make the exposition that follows more intelligible, it is perhaps advisable to actually set out the range as follows: $-5, -4, -3, -2, -1, 0, +1, +2, +3, +4,$ and $+5$.

17. See: Sylvan H. Cohen and Richard W. Taylor, "An Experimental Study of the Public Mind: An Application of Q-methodology to a Local Referendum Situation," *Experimental Study of Politics* 1 (July 1971), pp. 82-117 for a parallel account. We are indebted to Richard W. Taylor for his assistance during this research and to Steven R. Brown, a student of William Stephenson, the founder of Q methodology.

18. This was our first experimentation with Q factor analysis and we were no doubt unduly influenced by our greater familiarity with survey research.

19. James Q. Wilson and Edward C. Banfield, "Public-Regardingness as a Value Premise in Voting Behavior," *American Political Science Review* 58 (December 1964), pp. 876-887.

20. Cohen and Taylor, op. cit., pp. 89-91. According to this structuring of the P set, there could be the following eight kinds of voters (respondents): $A_1B_1C_1$, $A_1B_1C_2$, $A_1B_2C_1$, $A_1B_2C_2$, $A_2B_1C_1$, $A_2B_2C_1$, $A_2B_1C_2$ and $A_2B_2C_2$. In assembling the real P set that sorted the statements the first time, we searched out 2 respondents for each type of the ideal P set, with an extra $A_1B_1C_1$ and $A_2B_2C_2$. This gave us 18 sorters chosen on the presumed orientation of $A_1B_1C_1 \ldots A_2B_2C_2$.

21. Stephenson, *Play Theory*, op. cit., pp. 20-21.

22. Stephenson, *Study of Behavior*, op. cit., p. 74. In his words: "It would be a mistake to suppose that we are to recommend that all samples in Q-studies should be structured ones; on the contrary, some of the best work possible can proceed without them."

23. Fred N. Kerlinger, *Foundations of Behavioral Research: Educational and Psychological Inquiry* (New York: Holt, Rinehard and Winston, Inc., 1964), p. 593.

24. Harold D. Lasswell, Daniel Lerner, and Ithiel de Sola Pool, *The Comparative Study of Symbols* (Stanford, California: Stanford University Press, 1952), p. 14.

25. Ibid., p. 15.

26. Harold D. Lasswell, "The Climate of International Action," in Herbert C. Kelman, ed., *International Behavior* (New York: Holt, Rinehart and Winston, Inc., 1965), p. 341.

27. Stephenson, *Play Theory*, op. cit., pp. 19-20.

28. Stephenson, *Study of Behavior*, op. cit., p. 75.

29. Steven R. Brown, "On the Use of Variance Designs in Q Methodology," *The Psychological Record* 20 (1970), p. 183. Brown acknowledges his debt for this important distinction between synthetic and analytic statements to D. W. Hamlyn, "Analytic and Synthetic Statements," *The Encyclopedia of Philosophy*, Vol. 1 (New York: Macmillan, 1967).

30. Ibid., p. 184.

31. Fred N. Kerlinger, "Q Methodology and the Testing of Theory," New York University, 1958 (mimeographed) p. 7.

32. Ibid., p. 8.

33. Stephenson, *Study of Behavior*, op. cit., pp. 59-61.

34. For the confirmation of the utility of Q sorting to eliminate much of the bias of yes or no response set, see: Everett F. Cataldo, Richard M. Johnson, Lyman A. Kellstadt, and Lester W. Milbrath, "Card Sorting a Technique for Survey Interviewing," *Public Opinion Quarterly* 34 (Summer 1970), pp. 211-214.

35. Ibid.

36. Cohen, op. cit., pp. 85-86 for a discussion of the minor changes in factors, none of which altered the perspectives noticeably.

37. For an example of this genre of research, see: Steven R. Brown and John Ellithorp, "Emotional Experience in Political Groups: The Case of the McCarthy Phenomenon," *American Political Science Review* 64 (June 1970), pp. 349-366.

38. Kerlinger, *Foundations of Behavioral Research*, op. cit., p. 659.

39. Herbert Blumer, "Sociological Implications of the Thought of George Herbert Mead," *American Journal of Sociology* 71 (March 1966), p. 542.

40. Derek L. Phillips, *Knowledge From What? Theories and Methods in Social Research* (Chicago: Rand McNally & Company, 1971), p. 134, explaining Max Weber's concept of *verstehen* as applied to research from the perspective of the social actor.

41. Gabriel A. Almond and Sidney Verba, *The Civic Culture* (Boston: Little, Brown & Company, Inc. 1965), pp. 117-121.

42. Alvin Boskoff and Harmon Zeigler, *Voting Patterns in a Local Election* (Philadelphia: J. B. Lippincott Company, 1964), p. 19.

43. Angus Campbell, Gerald Gurin, and Warren E. Miller, *The Voter Decides* (Evanston, Illinois: Row, Peterson, 1954) pp. 194-199.

44. Robert E. Agger and Marshall N. Goldstein, *Who Will Rule The*

Schools? A Cultural Class Crisis (Belmont, Calif.: Wadsworth Publishing Company, Inc., 1971) p. 96.

45. Ibid., p. 1.

46. Joel D. Aberbach, "Alienation and Political Behavior," *American Political Science Review* 63 (March 1969), p. 86.

47. Ibid., p. 90.

48. Richard Hofstadter, *The Age of Reform* (New York: Vintage Books, Inc., 1960), p. 5: "I believe that Populist thinking has survived in our own time, partly as an undercurrent of provincial resentments, popular and 'democratic' rebelliousness and suspiciousness, and nativism."

49. Agger and Goldstein, op. cit., p. 150.

50. Using the computer printout which shows the difference of Z scores between pairs of factors, the following represent descending differences between factors two and four:

Item	Statement Description	2	4	Difference
7	Busing bad	1.682	−0.971	2.652
31	Board against little guy	0.542	−1.643	2.185
48	Negro students defeat levy	0.787	−0.971	1.757
16	People blame Catholics	1.725	0.037	1.688

51. Brown, "On the Use of Variance," op. cit., pp. 183-184.

52. This pairing (15 and C29) may confuse the reader because of the millage on the ballots of the two separate communities. In the Youngstown context, 6 mills was a compromise because 12 mills was requested. However, in Austintown 5 mills was requested; thus, the 5 mills in question C29 could not be interpreted as a compromise millage.

53. David Krech, Richard S. Crutchfield, and Edgerton L. Ballachey, *Individual in Society* (New York: McGraw-Hill Book Company, Inc., 1962), p. 147.

54. Rossi, op. cit., p. 9.

55. Cf. Stephenson, *Play Theory*, op. cit.

56. Fred N. Kerlinger and Esin Kaya, "The Construction and Factor Analytic Validation of Scales to Measure Attitudes Toward Education," in Gene F. Summers, ed., *Attitude Measurement* (Chicago: Rand McNally & Company, 1970), pp. 254-264.

11

The Efficacy of the Referendum as a Public-Policy Decision-Making Instrument

Although it is rather unfashionable in political science since the behavioral revolution to engage in evaluation of political institutions, we are venturing to engage in some normative discussion of school referenda. We have marshalled a formidable volume of data on the subject during the past six years and we have engaged in some reflection. Readers outside the political science guild may expect some evaluation; they may expect political science research to have, as college students say, some relevance. Three distinct and important considerations or reference points for evaluating school referenda are the effect on community conflict, the effects on public finance and administration, and the efficacy of the referendum as a public-policy decision-making instrument. The latter is the topic of this chapter. We have considered community conflict in a preceding chapter; the effects on public finance and administration will be considered in the next chapter.

Decision-Making Models

Some prominent analytical decision-making models furnish perspectives for appraising the efficacy of plebiscitary democracy in the formulation of public policy. Some models are particularly apropos to fiscal referenda. Therefore, we suggest a comparative analysis of the referendum process, which we label the Populist model and perceive its structure by reference to a Rationalist or technocratic model, an Economics model, and a Pluralist model.

Each model posits different standards for the policy process. Critics of direct democracy traditionally have based their case on the premise that the paramount goal should be "sound policy," gestated by the mature deliberation of an enlightened representative or unrepresentative body. Latter-day enthusiasts of expertise, the sovereignty of facts, and information systems assert that rational decisions are not achievable by even the most perspicacious laymen without extensive tutelage by experts—a Rational-Technocratic model. Participation and representativeness are the supreme values for Populists. These are maximized by the referendum, which is regarded as the key to sound policy because the populace thereby can correct any errors of judgment or venality of officialdom.

Both of those polar models are ridiculed as simplistic by the Pluralist model exponents, the currently dominant school of academic political science. These realists, or elitists, are not distressed by the hard data exposures of the Populist political-man fallacy or of the limits of rationality in politics, because democracy, they say, really requires only a modicum of participation by Everyman, indeed is more stable and effective thereby, and policy is, and ought to be, made by "political elites" responding to the forces of group politics. Sociologists are likely to hold the paramount requirement of policy making to be effective accommodation and resolution of conflict. That standard also is congenial to the Pluralists, who are confident that their divine hand of providence model maximizes social harmony as well as the public interest. Economists, the latest entrants on the stage of democratic and decision theory, inform us that politics is really their bag, because it is the allocation of utilities. Consequently, sound policy requires their particular decisional model in order to optimize the allocation of scarce resources.[1]

The Populist Model

Proponents of direct democracy have not based their case as much on the claim that a plebiscite is a superior decision-making institution as on the claim that it is the authentic register of the popular will, the intrinsic values of popular participation, and numerous attendant values: increased public education and reporting by officials, a keener sense of responsibility by officialdom, and the opportunity of the electorate to correct any derelictions or misperceptions of the general will. Populism is the bearer of what Walker designates as the principal orienting value of classical democratic theory, the emphasis on individual participation as the grand agency of human development.[2]

For classical democratic theorists, such as Mill, the policy products of democracy were only a secondary concern, but that has never been true of American populism.[3] The Progressives were mightily concerned about policy and also asserted that popular legislation, when occasionally exercised, would be superior to the quality of the decisions of officials.[4] Fiscal referenda, both state and local, originated from explicit and intense concern about the substance of policy, were not intended to be neutral institutions, and have not operated in neutral fashion. There could be no clearer demonstration of the axiom that budgetary procedures are not neutral.[5] Therefore, a legitimate test of the referendum is its decisional efficacy, which has always been the target of its critics.

The argument for the efficacy of the referendum as a decisional mechanism rests on the legitimacy claim, as the guarantee that legislation is a correct embodiment of the general will. Significantly, opponents, perhaps not wishing to appear antidemocratic, have directed little fire toward that proposition. Indubitably, a plebiscite has a higher probability of assuring congruence of majority perferences and legislation than does representative democracy, but the premise that it is an accurate register of the general will is vulnerable for three distinct reasons: the frequency of low turnouts, the system's disregard of the "intensity problem,"[6] and the legal exclusion of a large part of the populace. The potential of low-turnout plebiscites to be an inaccurate or even an erroneous reading of the general will is confirmed by the evidence of the bearing of turnout rates on outcomes of fluoridation and school referenda, and by the difference observed in the views of nonvoters and voters in an open housing referendum.[7]

The most vulnerable aspect of the referendum's legitimacy claim is its postulate that the general will is a tally of the unweighted preferences of the electorate. That postulate is incontrovertible only if the preferences of all voters are of equal intensity—palpably false—or if the distribution of intensities among yeasayers matches that among naysayers. That implicit assumption of public opinion polls has been widely challenged; it surely is challengeable for referenda. The disregard of intensity has been cited as a principal defect of plebiscitary decision making.[8] It weakens the legitimacy claim and also the efficacy of the referendum as an agency of conflict resolution. Legislators are responsive to intensity, but voters are less disposed or able to make such calculations.

Can one assume that turnout fluctuations compensate for ballot equality by providing an automatic adjustment for intensity? A virtue of the Pluralist model, according to Dahl, is that the intensity problem is solved automatically by the varying amounts of effort by protagonists,[9] a proposition that has elicited some skepticism. We have observed no evidence that turnout fluctuations fortuitously compensate for intensity differences, and the evidence of an open housing referendum indicated that low turnout had the opposite effect.[10] In statistical terms, the legitimacy claim of direct legislation rests on a set of probability assumptions: that excluded persons either have no preferences or their preferences are irrelevant, that the distribution of preferences is the same among voters and the usually more numerous nonvoters, and that the distribution of intensities among Yes voters matches that among No voters.

The Rationalist Model

The Rationalist decision-making model has been employed by critics of direct democracy from Madison to the present day. The burden of the attack usually is not a bald heresy that members of the electorate are intellectually deficient for the legislative role nor that they are animated by prejudice rather than pursuit of the commonweal, but that they are compelled to make decisions on the basis of inadequate information and that plebiscites omit a *sine qua non* of the legislative process: mature, collective deliberation. The information charge has been most frequently mooted, but the deliberation theme is probably the more trenchant and least rebuttable. Palpably a plebiscite is not a town meeting. A referendum surmounts the physical impediments to only one form of participation—and not even that for numerous nonvoters. It maximizes one component of classical democratic theory only by a very considerable trade-off of the deliberative component. True, the referendum usually, and fiscal referenda nearly always, follows the deliberation of a representative organ, and need not constrict the volume of deliberation a whit. It merely transfers the decision from deliberators to the nondeliberators!

Furthermore, the deliberative phase may be adversely affected by the availability of a referendum. Protagonists may resist compromise because of confidence of victory in a referendum, or conversely the official body may not make a thorough effort to negotiate a viable compromise.[11] Consequently, advocates of the Rationalist model assert, the referendum entails a critical loss of "legislative values"; it truncates the legislative process. There is no opportunity for negotiation and compromise once a referendum campaign begins; only a yes-or-no, all-or-nothing outcome is possible.[12]

Several of the darts of Rationalist partisans are irrelevant to fiscal referenda (defective drafting, cluttering the ballot, blurring the distinction between statute and constitution) and some are less apropos (e.g., that direct legislation is only a tool of "special interests"), but the contention that voters lack information is fully pertinent. In view of the importance and antiquity of this debate, one is impressed by the paucity of data. Opponents point to instances of the electorate's foolishness (easily found), which defenders parry: "Every example of ineptitude in popular lawmaking may be matched by a similar instance of legislative bungling."[13] Lacking data, some scholars have dealt with the question inferentially by assaying the judgment of the electorates of selected states, but those generally favorable appraisals establish only a prima facie case that electorates are knowledgeable in local fiscal referenda.[14]

Mueller employed an ingenious method of investigating the rationality of referenda voting by analyzing a sample of absentee ballots in a California election with numerous candidates and nineteen propositions. There was evidence of both reason and caprice, and some voter confusion.[15] The data indicate that even in California plebiscites are not entirely roulette and voters may exhibit rationality despite the burden of a bedsheet ballot. The data do not, however, measure the adequacy of the voters' information. The charge of Rationalists is not that voters are boobs, but that their information is inadequate and unlikely to approach that of the legislature whose judgment they supersede.

There has been scant direct measurement of the electorate's knowledge of fiscal referenda. In the low-interest DeKalb bond referenda, measurements of information sources and influence demonstrated that few voters exerted themselves to secure information and any deliberation was mostly internal—only 44 percent of the sample had discussed the matter with anyone. County officials issued brochures and conducted sixty meetings, but their penetration was slight. The brochures were the principal source of information for only 10 percent of the voters and even fewer attended any meetings. Few voters were aware of the positions and activities of civic organizations. The "basic thread" was the "extensive immunity to argument, information, or persuasion. Both sets of voters followed their own preconceived notions of their own and the county's needs."[16]

As one would expect, exposure and, hopefully, information are functions of the intensity of a controversy.[17] In a populous jurisdiction, even a strong campaign on an important issue may not produce high levels of exposure. Several measurements of information in a city open housing referendum showed that most of the public paid little attention to the campaign and that the electorate's knowledge of significant aspects of the issue, of the candidates, and their positions was meager.[18] In a plebiscite on a metropolitan government plan, only 10 percent of the voters had roughly correct notions of the three most important provisions of the plan, and only 20 percent could state any of those provisions correctly. "Thus the ordinary voters were not even voting on the plan; nobody knows what they were voting on."[19]

Probably there is less of a knowledge deficit in school elections than in most other referenda, since schools are so familiar; approximately a third of the electorate has children attending schools and/or other contacts; and school plebiscites usually attract more attention and generate more literature, more media coverage, and more discussion. The information level in the Bowling Green elections was distinctly higher than the few measurements reported for plebiscites on other subjects. However conditions were optimal in Bowling Green; and recall that Professor Sigel attributed the influence of the Detroit press to the voters' sense of inadequacy. The Austintown survey demonstrates that selective exposure and selective perception are formidable barriers to the acquisition of knowledge. Essentially half of the voters did not know, or refused to believe, that teacher salaries were lower in Austintown, and two-thirds of the naysayers had seen no leaflets although literature was distributed to every door.

Whether one deems the preceding inconclusive soundings as tending to support or refute the Rationalist critique depends on what order of information one regards as requisite for legislating. One might contend that fiscal measures inherently require considerable information for an intelligent decision. Consider, for example, the information that was germane to one of the Bowling Green tax levies, a disarmingly simple proposal of a new county home: How an imminent expressway would affect the existing home, the maintenance costs of a century-old structure, the operating costs of an obsolete facility, the length of the waiting list, the cost of keeping the overflow elsewhere, population projections, the relative merits of single floor and multifloor structures, the changes in the functions of a county home wrought by prolongation of life and gerontology. These and other considerations were pondered by the county commissioners, who visited other facilities and sought the counsel of authorities. Did the voters traverse that ground? And simultaneously do their homework on the three other issues?[20] Possibly there is some truth in Laski's aphorism, "In any political system, trust must reside somewhere."

One may detect evidence in the case studies that numerous voters make their decisions on the basis of limited knowledge; and some are conscious of it, by their decisional methods. Appropriations committees have methods for coping with uncertainty and for simplifying complexity to manageable scale,[21] and referendum voters have their methods. Two are the Yeasayer's touchstone that public expenditures are good and the Naysayer's assumption that taxes are bad. Another is faith in esteemed others, particularly the officials whose fiscal plans are at issue. "I know three members of the board, and if they say . . .." Some other voters, the DeKalb study found, make the obverse deduction.

The vintage thesis of critics of direct democracy that the populace is likely to be poorly informed, and hence a referendum is an asinine arrangement of the ignorant second-guessing the decisions of the knowledgeable, recently has received support from two quarters: voting behavior literature documenting the selective perception and the low levels of interest and information among the electorate with reference to national elections,[22] and Anthony Downs' economic theory of information costs. Nonvoting, little information, and use of simple methods for balloting decisions are rational behaviors, because the cost of acquiring information exceeds the stakes of the election for many people.[23]

The case studies also demonstrate that fiscal referenda may fall short of the Rationalist ideal in another important way, by the intrusion of extraneous and nonrational forces: general alienation (Corning and Ithaca), lingering passions from prior controversies (Bowling Green), personal distrust and animosity toward officials (DeKalb), or antagonism between neighborhoods (Okemos).

It is paradoxical that fiscal policy, the paramount category of local referenda, is the very thing which frequently is excluded from the ambit of state referenda. Most initiative and referendum articles in state constitutions exclude tax and appropriation statutes from the referendum. The conjunction of this exclusion with that for emergency legislation indicates that the Progressives did not presume that fiscal matters per se were inappropriate for popular legislation, but that referenda on fiscal statutes might generate instability, a prediction that has been confirmed abundantly by subsequent local experience.

The Pluralist Model

Exponents of the Pluralist model largely concur with Rationalist strictures of homo politicus and other postulates of Populism, and also concur with the latter's critique of Rationalist postulates, debunking the Rationalist notions of an objective "public interest" and an immaculate conception of public policy by pure ratiocination. However, Pluralist specifications of the "real" model of the policy process display some discrepancies about the quantum of rationality in policy making and the degree to which decision-makers do or ought to respond to endogenous as well as exogenous forces. The discovery of Bentley led some Pluralists to an unqualified embrace of his group politics theorem, a Newtonian mechanics model in which public policy is the resultant vector of group forces in the political arena, as diagrammed in Figure 11-1. E.g., Hagan and LaPalombara said, "there never does exist general welfare but only particular group welfares. . . . At any given moment, policy which is being put into motion will be that supported by the interest groups which are currently dominant."[24] But for Dahl the virtue of the Pluralist model is its balanced output of numerous values, consensus and stability as well as political equality and popular sovereignty, and its decisions entail "rational choices" derived from debate, deliberation, reflection, and technical knowledge.[25] Dahl's beatific model has a closer kinship to Rationalism than to Bentleyism.

Our diagram of an application of the Pluralist model to local fiscal policy making does not specify the proportions of the three classes of inputs —technical data and expertise, the preferences and judgments of the decision makers, and external forces—because the mix certainly is not a constant, but for this purpose we accept the Pluralists propositions that external forces, including norms and other elements of community ideology, comprise the paramount class of inputs and that policy is largely the resultant vector of the forces impinging on the decision makers. We also accept, *arguendo*, the Pluralist propositions that the political system is open and that group competition is the most effective process possible for determining whose preferences shall prevail in order to maximize societal income, and hence the resultant vector is the best indicator and the closest possible definition of the "public interest" in a society of persons with an

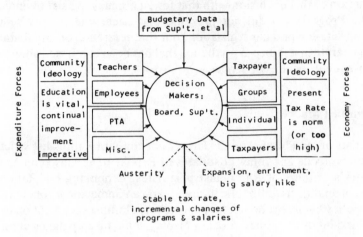

The Field of Forces of School Budgeting

Figure 11-1. Pluralist Politics Model of Policy Making

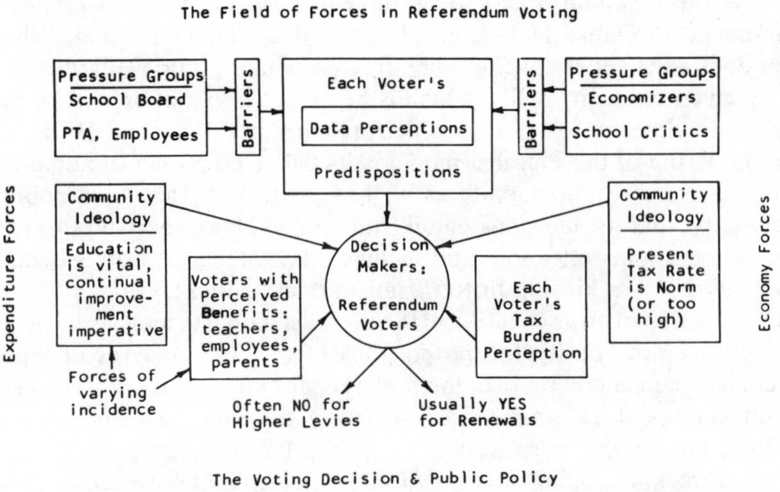

The Field of Forces in Referendum Voting

The Voting Decision & Public Policy

Figure 11-2. Populist Model of Policy Making

infinite variety of utility functions and lacking any normative theory of budgeting.

Assuming that the Pluralist model is the appropriate description of the policy process preceding a referendum, one may explore the significance of systemic change by juxtaposing the diagram of the Populist model (Figure 11-2). The plot and cast are the same for the second act, but the scene is shifted from the council chamber to the voting booth and members of the cast switch roles as the sovereign voters replace officialdom as decision makers and the displaced officials are thrust into the interest group ranks.

To adherents of the Rationalist model, the consequences of the system switch may seem painfully obvious. ''In the Pluralist model, according to the Pluralists' own doctrine, rationality is subordinated to the vagaries of self-serving pressure groups; in the Populist model it is annihilated.'' A Populist, of course, makes the obverse evaluation of the systems from his definition of rationality as folk wisdom. But if rationality be defined as informed, objective, and deliberative judgment, only a Populist true believer could fail to observe that the referendum has more hazards and barriers to rationality than the Pluralist model.[26] Depending upon the proportions of the classes of inputs, which is to say the extent that it is elitist, it probably entails some trade-off of rationality in exchange for other values. The Populist model may trade-off a substantial amount of rationality in favor of the values of participatory democracy. ''The people have the right to make their own mistakes.''

Is the referendum conceptually sound or defective when measured by the Pluralist claim of maximizing societal income? That there may be some bearing of systems on outcomes is intimated by the frequency of fiscal referenda defeats and even more so by the results of open housing plebiscites.[27] Are the divergences of outcomes only random, perhaps occasional instances of the malfunctioning of Pluralism? For fiscal referenda the divergences appear to have some systemic origin. The obscure forces impinging on the individualized decision making (Figure 11-2) surely are unstandardized, if not kaleidoscopic, and for numerous voters are likely to bear scant resemblance to the force field that enveloped the preceding collective decision making of officialdom (Figure 11-1). The force field of few voters will approach the comprehensiveness and symmetry of the field of the official body's deliberations, and is likely to tilt in one direction or the other, depending upon which forces surmount communication barriers and penetrate the screen of each voter's predispositions. Officials are likely to be sensible of all pertinent elements of community ideology, but many voters will have differential perceptions. Technical premises can hardly have the same strength for many voters as for officials. Potent forces are added to the field by the referendum, personal costs and benefits, which are likely to be the dominant ones for numerous voters, tilting their fields decisively. Such extraneous forces as personal antagonisms or alienation may be added. The Pluralist claim to superiority, that it is the surest route to the public interest, is explicitly bottomed on the conditions that all forces are present and none is excluded or unduly handicapped. It does not seem that those conditions fully obtain in the Populist model, and to that extent it is deficient per Pluralist logic.

In view of the character of the changes in the composition of the forces with a switch to Populist decision making, frequent rejections of the policy output of the Pluralist model are not mysterious; the aggregate net effect is distinctly directional. A potent economy force, tax burden, is added for most voters concurrently with some diminution of strength of expenditure forces vis-a-vis numerous voters. The referendum tilts the field of forces. The Pluralist model, however, also is unlikely to be neutral, because the predispositions of officials normally are somewhat oriented in favor of expenditures. We expect officials to have some identification with their programs. Each system has its structural bias, the Pluralist toward and the Populist against expenditures; the choice of system is a choice of policy.[28]

There is an additional reason why the Pluralist system is more hospitable to expenditures than the Populist. Steiner observes that within legislatures expenditure proponents may exploit that venerable device of coalition building, logrolling; whereas in a referendum the proposal must carry without logrolling support.[29] Single-purpose expenditures, therefore, are likely to be rejected unless the proposal displays benefits to an extraordinarily large fraction of the electorate.[30]

Logrolling and game theory suggest another contrast between Pluralist and Populist decision making that seems pertinent to their utility for conflict resolution. Immemorially, it has been thought that representative democracy is superior, because solons are third parties who can cheerfully compromise other people's interests. Logrolling points to possibly another virtue of the "legislative way." May one postulate that the measure of legislative genius, like a labor mediator, is artfulness in contriving positive-sum solutions for zero-sum conflicts?[31] If so, a congenital weakness of the referendum may be that for numerous voters the ballot has the appearance of a zero-sum proposition, e.g., open housing or a school levy to a retiree.

The Economics Model

The economists' cost/benefit decision-making model is strikingly apropos. No policy process is more distinctly and literally a cost/benefit calculation, and it appears to be a remarkably simple decisional situation. One is not obliged to compute numerous ratios, to grapple with nebulous incommensurables, or ponder uncertainty; and there is no Arrow problem. The fiscal referendum appears to be rather an ideal situation, and the decision requires only the determination of whether the benefit/cost relationship of the ballot proposition is greater or less than unity. As Herbert Simon phrased it, in offering this as a general purpose decision making model some time before the economists became the high priests of decision making, what is the value of Efficiency = Output/Input?[32]

Although the economics model is the current vogue in the political arena, the economists themselves have made scant application of their tool in this particular sector of public finance. One conspicuous exception is James Buchanan who essays to establish public finance on new foundations by developing a theory of demand for collective goods as rational individual behavior, a "utility-maximizing model of individual choice." Fiscal decisions are the rational behavior of the individual "citizen-taxpayer-beneficiary" voting his choices, as best he can amid the vicissitudes of uncertainty, numerous fiscal illusions, and high information costs. It follows that the norm for fiscal institutions is ye auld marketplace, and policy structures will approach an optimum allocation of resources to the extent that they correspond to it.[33]

Although Buchanan regards his ideal model as laid up in heaven with Plato's, "collective decisions are not made in this manner,"[34] local referenda are a remarkable equivalent of market choice for collective public goods and afford nearly optimal conditions for the voter-taxpayer-beneficiary to engage in utility maximizing by ballot.[35] But some observers, even some economists, are skeptical that voter-consumer sovereignty optimizes the allocation of resources of a community.

Appraisal of Buchanan's thesis that individual utility-maximizing decisions optimize the "purchase" of public goods, as they operate in local referenda (only),[36] entails two levels of analysis, empirical and logical. Do referenda voters engage in individual maximizing behavior and are the conditions favorable for rational "individual-collective" choice? If so, how reliable a mechanism for optimizing is this Smithian invisible hand decisional method? Is it more likely to achieve the public interest than that more relaxed version of providence, Bentleyan Pluralism, or than Elitist Pluralism? Patently, validity of the thesis, which explicitly embodies the foundation premises of the fiscal referendum, requires affirmative answers at both levels.

Local tax and bond referenda fulfill admirably the conditions requisite for individual utility-maximizing in the polling station, except for renters who may be misled by one of our classical fiscal illusions. The distortion from that factor is not great in most plebiscites because of the low ratio of renters and the tax incidence sophistication of an indeterminate but substantial fraction of them. Conversely, state fiscal referenda usually handicap individual utility decisions variously by the package strategy, by partitioning the budgetary process, and by deliberate cultivation of fiscal illusions.

Wilson and Banfield speculate that few voters consciously engage in utility-maximizing. Psychoanalysis is unnecessary, however, because the germane question vis-a-vis Buchanan's thesis is: what proportion of votes are consistent with economic self-interest? A consistent vote fulfills the economic logic for optimizing the allocation of resources, irrespective of the voter's thoughts. An inconsistent one does not, even though it fulfills a voter's noneconomic preference. For this purpose, voter utility function must be defined narrowly as only economic, because we are considering an economic model which postulates that self-interest does and altruism does not optimize the allocation of resources.

The Wilson-Banfield correlation analysis demonstrates that a substantial amount of voting contradicts the economic man hypothesis.[37] The survey data of the case studies reported here also display contradictions: the support of school levies by nonparents, the potency of alienation in some referenda, and the influence of neighborhood or organizational membership in others. However, the case studies also have abundant evidence of economic behavior: the association of voting with age, income, property ownership, and parentage in school referenda.

The Bowling Green voting study made the most distinct measurements of the quantum of economic behavior. There was a strong association of amount of property tax and support of the levy and an even stronger association with the tax/income ratios of the voters. A school referendum furnishes the best conditions for ascertaining whether a vote is consistent with economic self-interest; and at least four-fifths were in that plebiscite.

The individual utility-maximizing model appears to be the best single explanation of voting behavior in fiscal referenda. There is little point in quibbling about the parameters of categories of "errors" or noting that voter perceptions of the public interest often coincide conveniently with perceptions of private interest, because the critical question is the validity of the proposition that the model optimizes, i.e., that the majority of unweighted individual decisions of personal advantage *ipso facto* is the correct policy decision for a community. The issue is not the pertinence of the economic model but how do we apply it. What values belong in the $E = O/I$ formula, the personal costs and benefits of each voter or appraisals of aggregate community costs and benefits? The Pluralist model uses aggregate community costs and benefits and weighs intensities; the Populist model permits—even implies—the use of personal costs and benefits, and the evidence is incontrovertible that numerous voters do so. Indeed they could hardly do otherwise, because the situation furnishes the information for the personal calculus, whereas the voter is likely to lack information for a judgment of whether community benefits are commensurate with the cost, and effort to acquire such information is likely to seem superfluous and be uneconomical behavior. Why should a voter labor to acquire information when the decision making system indicates that he already posses- ses the touchstones for public policy, his preferences and his wisdom?

To the extent, evidently considerable, that referenda ballots are state- ments of private preferences rather than judgments of the community interest, a plebiscite is a sound decisional mechanism if the majority of private preferences fortuitously coincides with or inherently is the public interest—Buchanan's explicit postulate and the premise of Populism and much interest group literature. Now we reach bedrock, the classical public interest argument. Rationalists and Elitist Pluralists "know" there is a public interest to be divined by their respective decisional models. Bent- leyans chide us to put away belief in spooks, because there are only particular interests. And economists never weary of telling us that there are only private interests, and we need not fret about the public interest, because "Thus God made the universal frame, and bade self love and social be the same." Here is the root of the long standing encounter of economics and politics. Many of our political institutions and most of the content of our statute books attest to an extensive nonconfidence in the invisible hand.

Interestingly, the thesis that individual maximizing will automatically maximize community welfare has been rejected cogently by an economist who agrees that "voters will fairly consistently act in their own self-interest rather narrowly conceived." Says Roland N. McKean:

We must recognize that ordinarily there are serious discrepancies between the self-interest of the individual voter, employee, or official and the interest of the whole group. That is, there are important divergences between the costs and gains felt by each individual alone and the total effects that cost-benefit analysis seeks to measure. Discrepancies between individual and total costs or gains in the private sector of the economy have been discussed for years. . . .

We must not forget that analagous phenomena are present in the public sector of the economy. It is probably even harder there to bring self-interest into line with community interest. . . . the governing process is shot through and through with discrepancies between self-interests, other group interests, and total community interest.[38]

If individual cost-benefit calculus is not synonymously community cost-benefit calculus, what are the odds that the majority of private prefer- ences unweighted will coincide fortuitously with the public interest? This possibility has face validity for a few referenda, e.g., to legalize colored margarine. It would be plausible for any referendum where the incidence of costs and benefits is fairly evenly distributed—but patently most fiscal plebiscites are characterized by pronounced disparities.

Even if one agrees that the invisible hand operates in referenda, because of individual maximizing decisions, to optimize resource allocation for the community, it does not follow that every outcome is the public interest from the standpoint of conflict resolution, not to mention a possible divergence of short- and long-range community welfare. For those of little faith, skeptical that providence guarantees the identity of the public interest with any simple majority of private interests, the legislative function remains essential. If so, when the electorate, itself a representative body rather than "the people," supersedes the legislature, it acquires the concomitant responsibilities of the acquisition of knowledge, consideration of intensities, deliberation, and an earnest quest for the public interest. These are formidable tasks even for some very local referenda.

Conclusion

On theoretical grounds, the referendum does not seem to be a superior decision making institution unless one is wedded to either the Populist premise that the highest form of rationality is folk wisdom or the premise of Buchanan's particular Economic model, that individual utility-maximizing decisions in the booth automatically optimize the allocation of a community's resources. We have indicated reasons why we view the theory as fallacious, as do some economists, and noted that not all voters presume that self-interest and public interest are identical decisions. Observation of actual allocations of community resources by plebiscite does not strengthen one's faith in the invisible hand. Furthermore, the disparities of the incidence of costs and benefits among the electorate, plus the volume of nonvoting and the volume of exclusion, furnish little basis for assuming that there is a high probability that the majority of the unweighted preferences among those voting will fortuitously coincide with the community interest, immediate or long range.

In fine, we are unconvinced that the legislative function is superfluous, and we have noted that even for apparently simple local referenda questions adequate discharge of the legislative function may be quite a chore. All voters are not Athenians, it would be uneconomical for them to be, and the plebiscite doctrine suggests to the voter that his function is to vote his private preference. Indeed we suspect that the system's optimizing success is, above all, a function of the electorate's confidence in its legislature, and that the system is tolerable only because a large portion of the electorate is influenced in some degree by confidence in the wisdom of the prior decision of the legislative organ.[39]

Notes

1. Exponents of each model naturally do not state their cases without

qualifications, but our concern here is with the principal and distinctive features of each model.

2. Jack L. Walker, "A Critique of the Elitist Theory of Democracy," *American Political Science Review* 60 (June 1968), pp. 285-295.

3. ". . . the most important point of excellence which any form of government can possess is to promote the virtue and excellence of the people themselves. The first question in respect to any political institution is how far they tend to foster in the members of the community the various desirable . . . moral, intellectual, and active." J. S. Mill, *Considerations on Representative Government* (New York 1862), p. 39.

4. Joseph G. LaPalombara and Charles B. Hagan, "Direct Legislation: An Appraisal and a Suggestion," *American Political Science Review* 45 (June 1951), p. 400.

5. The leitmotif of Aaron Wildavsky, *The Politics of the Budgetary Process* (Boston: Little, Brown, 1964).

6. Cf. Wilmoore Kendall and George W. Carey, "The 'Intensity' Problem and Democratic Theory," *American Political Science Review* 62 (January 1968), pp. 5-24.

7. Howard D. Hamilton, "Direct Legislation: Some Implications of Open Housing Referenda," *American Political Science Review* 64 (March 1970), pp. 128-129.

8. Raymond E. Wolfinger and Fred I. Greenstein, "The Repeal of Open Housing in California: An Analysis of Referendum Voting." *American Political Science Review* 62 (December 1968), p. 768.

9. Robert A. Dahl, *A Preface to Democratic Theory* (Chicago: University of Chicago, 1956), pp. 134-135.

10. Hamilton, ibid.

11. An instance of this is reported by Louis H. Masotti, *Education in Suburbia* (Western Reserve University Press, 1967), pp. 122-123.

12. Cf. Stanley Scott and Harriet Nathan, "Bay Area Regional Organization: The Case against a Referendum" (mimeo., Institute of Governmental Studies, University of California, 1969). Significantly, the authors were opposing submission of any Bay Area metropolitan government plan to a referendum.

13. John Mabry Mathews, *American State Government* (New York, 1934), p. 205.

14. James K. Pollock, *The Initiative and Referendum in Michigan* (Ann Arbor, 1940), pp. 66-70, concluded that the judgment of the Michigan electorate was at least as good as the legislature's. Claudius O. Johnson found that "Few, if any, absurd or freakish laws have been enacted in Washington through the initiative, and few obviously beneficial bills have

been defeated by use of the referendum." "The Initiative and Referendum in Washington," *Pacific Northwest Quarterly* 36 (1945), p. 41. LaPalombara and Hagan evaluated the evidence of five states as all "pointing in the same direction" and generally refuting the dire consequences that opponents had predicted of direct legislation. They assumed that "Over the long period, the electorate is not likely to do anything more foolish than the legislature is likely to do." Op. cit., p. 414.

15. Reason was reflected in self-interest patterns, in evidence that some voters had read the state election booklet, and the greater support of bond issues and open housing by Democrats than Republicans. Caprice was reflected by the influence of ballot order and by yeasaying and naysaying patterns on noncontroversial items. Confusion occurred on two mutually contradictory proposals. John E. Mueller, "Voting on the Propositions: Ballot Patterns and Historical Trends in California," *American Political Science Review* 63 (December 1969), pp. 1197-1212.

16. Alvin Boskoff and Harmon Zeigler, *Voting Patterns in a Local Election* (Philadelphia: Lippincott, 1964), ch. 4.

17. Exposure rates were high in the close Bowling Green, Ohio referenda with 80 percent turnout. Three-fifths of the populace discussed the topic and read leaflets as well as the newspaper. But some significant information was missed by numerous voters: a fourth were unaware of the level of teacher salaries, half of the newspaper's endorsement of the four propositions, and as many were unsure of the purpose of the one levy that passed. Howard D. Hamilton and Byron Marlow, "The Bowling Green Tax and Bond Referenda (unpublished, 1967).

18. Hamilton, op. cit., pp. 131-133.

19. Scott Greer, *Governing the Metropolis* (New York: Wiley, 1962), p. 125.

20. Hamilton and Marlowe, op. cit. In rebuttal, one might observe that there was one other germane consideration which the commissioners misjudged (the first time) and for which the electorate has superior competence: whether the community wishes to buy a new home. "He who wears the shoe is the best judge of its fit." And the rejoinder: Who really is wearing the shoe, the electorate or the commissioners or the senior citizens? Should the purchase decision be made without close examination of the object? And should it be made on the basis of a voter's personal cost-benefit calculation? (The next election that was the only expenditure proposal and passed.)

21. Wildavsky, op. cit., pp. 6-16, 47-62.

22. Angus Campbell et al., *The American Voter* (New York: Wiley, 1960); Paul Lazarsfeld et al., *The People's Choice* (New York: Columbia

University Press, 1944); Bernard R. Berelson et al., *Voting* (Chicago: Chicago University Press, 1954).

23. *An Economic Theory of Democracy* (New York: Harper & Row, 1957), pp. 207-276.

24. LaPalombara and Hagan, op. cit., p. 416.

25. Dahl, op. cit., p. 57.

26. Whether individual behavior or a political system is rational depends on the postulated definition of rationality, as Michael J. Shapiro has pointed out. "The evaluation of any particular criterion above others such that choices are considered rational to the extent to which they are designed to maximize it, usually involves the pre-selection of some notion of collective rationality." "Rational Political Man: A Synthesis of Economic and Social-Psychological Perspectives," *American Political Science Review* 63 (December 1969), p. 1118.

27. Open housing laws were repealed in six of seven referenda, and blocked by another, prior to enactment of the national open housing statute. Subsequently, open housing has won in three of five plebiscites, only in Michigan cities. Howard D. Hamilton, "Voting Behavior in Open Housing Referenda," *Social Science Quarterly* 51 (December 1970), p. 716.

28. A large-scale demonstration of the bearing of the two systems on taxation and expenditures occurred recently in Ohio. By initiative, the Ohio Education Association in 1966 offered the electorate the opportunity to augment school revenue by raising the state sales tax. Despite a tremendous campaign and neutrality by state officials, the OEA lost by a two to one margin. The next legislature did raise the sales tax rate and support of schools.

29. Gilbert Y. Steiner, "Municipal Tax Referenda and the Political Process," *Current Economic Comment* 15 (February 1953), pp. 3-16.

30. The "Ohio Bond Commission" bond proposal, 1967, was a blanket authorization of bonds for any state or local activity, but to be sure that no interest group would fail to see its stick of candy, the proposition enumerated a hundred activities. That package failed, however, because of a tactical *faux pas*. So, in 1968, the electorate received, and approved, a smaller package which required 1,700 words to enumerate all the goodies. See Ohio Constitution, Art. VIII, Sec. 2i.

31. That logrolling is a device for transforming zero-sum conflict into a positive-sum solution has been observed and extolled by economists James Buchanan and Gordon Tullock. Political theorists, they say, err by habitually conceiving conflict in zero-sum terms and by moralizing against logrolling, a species of vote trading which resembles a market transaction in which all participants gain. They also noted that the referendum is one of

the rare institutional situations in which logrolling is unlikely to occur. *The Calculus of Consent* (University of Michigan, 1962), pp. 133-145, 253-255, 265-281.

32. Herbert Simon, *Administrative Behavior* (New York: Macmillan, 1947), ch. 8.

33. James Buchanan, *Public Finance and Democratic Process: Fiscal Institutions and Individual Choice* (Chapel Hill: University of North Carolina Press, 1967).

34. Ibid., p. 144.

35. He votes on a single issue rather than a general fund bundle; the "tax price" is explicit, and the tax incidence is clear for all but renters; the proferred benefits are explicit; information costs are lower than usual; he is not snared by fiscal illusions; and here *mirable dictu* the budgetary process is not bifurcated; present is that *sine qua non* of fiscal rationality, a one-to-one nexus of costs and benefits.

36. This is not a general appraisal of Buchanan's ambitious and laudable body of theory; merely of its validity in this particular and clearest instance of "individual-collective" choice. Political scientists would not quarrel with many of Buchanan's deductions, although a few are sharply at variance with the author's observations anent state fiscal administration. To this limited extent we are glad to respond to Buchanan's request for empirical examination of his proposition.

37. Wilson and Banfield find that Anglo-Saxon and Jewish upper-income homeowners are habitual yeasayers even though they will pay relatively more and derive relatively less benefit from the expenditures they support. James Q. Wilson and Edward C. Banfield, "Public Regardingness as a Value Premise in Voting Behavior," *American Political Science Review* 58 (December 1964), p. 885.

38. "Costs and Benefits from Different Viewpoints," in Howard G. Schaller (ed.), *Public Expenditure Decisions in the Urban Community* (Resources for the Future, 1963), p. 151.

39. This position parallels that of Theodore J. Lowi, *The End of Liberalism* (New York: NOrton, 1969).

12 Posting the Ledger: An Appraisal

Another reference point for evaluating plebiscitary democracy is its effects on public administration and finance. The effects are regarded as very significant by school officials and teacher associations, a view shared by public finance scholars. Recent events, notably the frequency of school crises, have dramatized the importance of this benchmark. The high passage rate of bond issues and operating levies during the 1950s conveyed the impression that referenda were largely ritualistic, but the volume of defeats since 1965 attest that they are more than symbolic. By 1968, the rate of budget and levy defeats was alarming to school officials in several states, and efforts were launched in some states to modify or abolish the referendum system. Demands for change mounted from antithetical sources, from property taxpayers urging "tax reform" and from schoolmen urging legislatures to develop "a better system of financing public education."

Effects on Administration

The consequences of fiscal referenda have been treated extensively in public finance literature under the rubric of "tax and debt limitations." The initial effect of the enactment of tax limitation schemes was acute dislocation of local fiscal systems, catastrophic in some states.[1] Public finance scholars are highly critical of tax limitation laws and also of the local debt limitation laws. Numerous articles and monographs have described the deleterious effects of legal limitations in various states;[2] their alleged futility and unwisdom is a refrain of textbooks. This "Chinese footbinding" approach is "not sound in theory and practice" and "the results have been disappointing and at times disastrous."[3]

The resulting desperate financial condition of local governments was alleviated by a revolution in state and local revenue structures—state relinquishment of the property tax, enactment of sales and income taxes, and extensive state grants and tax sharing arrangements—and by permitting local governments to exceed the legal debt and tax limitations when authorized by a referendum. A recent inventory by the Advisory Commission on Intergovernmental Relations found the referendum option available to all or some local governments (particularly school districts) in thirty-one of the thirty-five states with legal tax limitations[4] and in all but two of the states with debt limitations.[5]

Surely these referenda were expected to occur only occasionally, affording necessary flexibility and some deference to the tradition of local self-government; but it turned out otherwise. Referenda became "a way of life," and have largely nullified the anachronistic limitation laws, which, except in a few states, no longer fix firm tax or debt ceilings, and have become merely obstructions and depressants of public expenditures. All the evidence indicates that the purposes of the tax and debt limitation schemes were largely unachieved, but there were numerous unintended results, both temporary and enduring, of which the foremost was the institution of plebiscitary democracy in school districts.

An extensive study in 1962 by the Advisory Commission on Intergovernmental Relations documented a long list of the deleterious effects of legal limitation schemes on public administration: that they have aggravated the proliferation of local governments, necessitated recourse to short-term financing to cover operating deficits, encouraged long-term borrowing for activities that might better be financed out of current revenue, necessitated quantities of special legislation, undermined the integrity of property assessment, imposed onerous burdens on administrative agencies, and impaired the ability of local officials to budget effectively.

The Commission, the agency established by Congress for sustained monitoring of intergovernmental relations, "recommends the lifting of constitutional and statutory limitations on local powers to raise property tax revenues." The ACIR's paramount argument is that tax limitation schemes impair the vitality of local governments.[6]

The case against State imposed restrictions on the taxing powers of local governments is that they are incompatible with responsible local government responsive to the needs of a rapidly growing, constantly changing, mobile community. If the case against property tax limitations on the basis of their crippling effect on local revenue is not compelling, it is all the stronger on the basis of universally accepted principles of sound public administration and the essential ingredients of our federal system of government.

Although the Commission did not mention it, a recommendation to repeal property tax limitation laws is a proposal to discontinue tax levy referenda.

A parallel ACIR investigation of local debt limitations produced parallel findings and recommendations.[7]

. . . the Commission believes that the maze of constitutional and statutory restrictions upon local government borrowing constitutes a serious impediment to effective local government in the United States. These restrictions handicap self-reliance of local communities and governments, and impel them toward increased financial dependence on State or Federal Government resources. In many States, present provisions have contributed to complexity and deviousness in local debt operations.

In this instance, the Commission took cognizance of the referendum system and recommended its partial retention. Local governments should have unfettered discretion to issue bonds, "subject to a permissive referendum only, on petition" with the result determined by simple majority vote. That proposal embodies one of the classical justifications of direct democracy, "the shotgun behind the door." The frequency of bond referenda under such an arrangment would depend on the stringency of the petition requirement.

The overarching effect of the referendum system on public administration is evident in, but not explicated by, the ACIR's indictment: the uncertainty and instability of school finance and operation. Surely it is not mere coincidence that most of the school crises and all the school "closings" have occurred in referenda states. It is an erratic feast-or-famine system, and disruptive even when conditions do not reach a crisis level or precipitate teacher strikes or acute community conflict. The disruptive effects were stated succinctly by the Michigan superintendent of public instruction in a plea for "a better system":

Last year in the wake of millage defeats, some districts had to reduce the length of the school day, some curtailed transportation, some felt compelled to leave new buildings idle, and some eliminated educational programs. This year several districts are giving notice to teachers that they do not have the funds to continue to employ them.[8]

The uncertainty and disruption were the principal concerns of the Washington Temporary Levy Study Commission. "The special levy is one of the most unreliable and unstable possible sources of school funding."[9] To one who has resided in a state without school referenda, it does seem to be "a poor way to run a railroad," and one can understand the discomfiture of school officials who note that "No other important public service is subject to a referendum of this kind."[10] Educators assert that more is involved than the vicissitudes of officials or teacher salaries. In the words of the Michigan superintendent, "Children are the victims when local school millage votes fail."[11]

There is substantial variation among states in the amount of uncertainty and disruption created by the referendum system. Stability of school revenue is related to the term of voted levies—annual, short-term, or permanent; the proportion of school revenue supplied by state appropriations; the tax rates that school boards may levy without a plebiscite, i.e., the proportions of "within" and "outside" millage; local assessment ratios; the tax rates mandated by state law either directly or indirectly by state grant qualifications; and the voting rule, whether by a simple or a supramajority. A precise ordering of the state referendum systems on a revenue stability-instability scale might be difficult, but some systems cluster near each end of the scale. At one pole are systems well designed to assure revenue stability, notably those of Colorado, Kansas, and Oklahoma. Near the other pole are systems with provisions that assure instability—in states where the property tax is the principal source of school revenue, most of the school tax is voted millage, and authorizations are annual or for a few years, as in Michigan, Ohio, Oregon, and Washington. The latter state also has the 60 percent supramajority rule. Missouri moved away from the instability pole in 1970 by revising its system.

Thus, there are ways of reducing the uncertainty and disruptive effects of referenda, although nearly all entail some attenuation of direct democracy. One specious way is the solution trumpeted by antitax forces in Ohio: "Pass a law against school closing." The Ohio legislature's response was to require that any temporary suspension of operation must be preceded by a state audit of the school district's accounts, certifying that the treasury is empty. Ohio has taken most of the other steps to mitigate the dysfunctional fruits of fiscal plebiscites: abandoning supramajorities for referenda at primaries and special elections, authorizing indefinite period levies (subject to a backdoor referendum), raising the millage qualification for the equalization grant, and augmenting state support.

The most logical and straightforward way would be to base the "legal rate" on true value, either by market-value assessment or by applying the appropriate multiplier to the assessed value of each local jurisdiction. Most of the archaic tax limitations would not be implausible but for the underassessment game. With 15 mills, the modal legal ceiling, applied to true value, there would be few extramillage elections. Apparently the combination of vested interests and mythology (fiscal illusions, as the economists say) makes the direct route the least feasible for legislatures.

The preceding enumeration of the elements of referenda systems which affect school revenue stability can be subsumed in a simple proposition. The amount of uncertainty and disruption is a function of the scope and authenticity of direct democracy. All of the ways of fostering revenue stability require some trade-off of direct democracy. The New York and New Jersey systems achieve stability by permitting school boards in *extremis* to adopt budgets disapproved by electorates. Colorado and Kansas achieve stability by conducting referenda only for budget increments in excess of 5 or 6 percent. Oklahoma has taken a devious route to revenue stability, one that maintains the forms of direct democracy without the substance. Nature requires her price.

Effects on School Revenue

The short-run effects of the referendum system in specific communities are quite evident, but the long-range impact on aggregate school revenue is murky. The ACIR commented that "Revenue trends suggest that the long-run effect of the limitations has not been substantial."[12] That judgment was not a specific reference to schools, but if it is a valid generalization it must have some applicability to school districts, since they have the largest budgets, rely most on the property tax, and have the most referenda.

The sample of bond elections in Chapter 5 and other evidence indicate that bond referenda have not had a profound effect on the aggregate volume of capital expenditures in most states. There have been delay and numerous elections in some states, but California and West Virginia seem to be the only states where the system has had a substantial aggregate effect. We have surmised that the enrollment boom of the postwar era was an important factor, furnishing an incontrovertible case for many ballot propositions. With stable enrollment, henceforth the impact of the system may be greater.

Perhaps referenda exert more constraint on operating than on capital expenditures, but the amount is difficult to determine. Some inhibition occurs, since the effect of the system is monodirectional; in particular communities the constraint may be substantial for periods of a few years when levies are defeated repeatedly. It also may be substantial in districts with no levy defeats, if school boards choose austerity in preference to predictable electoral defeat. This is one of the several formidable impediments to ascertaining the effect on referenda on revenue. Nonevents are difficult to measure.

There is considerable evidence that in some states the referendum system has had more than localized and ephemeral effects. We have observed that in West Virginia, the state with the most rigorous tax limitation system, thirty-two of the forty-five counties in 1972 were levying the maximum additional millage permitted by the provisions of the state constitution, and recall the facts in *Gordon* v. *Lance*, the lawsuit challenging the supramajority vote requirement. Missouri's requirement of a two-thirds majority for rates above 37½ mills appears to be a not inconsequential constraint, since thirty-nine districts were at that rate in 1972 and numerous efforts by suburban and large city districts to break through the ceiling have failed. Indubitably the disruptive effects of referenda have been greatest in Ohio, and school officials would say that the system has been a profound constraint on aggregate revenue. They would cite teacher salaries and the relatively low per pupil expenditures for many years, with emphasis on the low ratio of school expenditures to personal income.

It would seem reasonable to expect that the referendum also is a significant constraint on aggregate revenue in California, Michigan, and Washington, states where voted millage is an exceptionally large fraction of sehool revenue, where there are so many levy elections and so many defeats, and where the system has evoked intense concern and strenuous efforts to abolish it. The comparative statistics of Table 12-1, however, do not verify that hypothesis. In fact, despite all the levy defeats and alarm, the revenue of Michigan schools is near the top of the nation. The data do suggest that plebiscitary democracy exerts some constraint on aggregate revenue in California and Washington, whose school revenues are somewhat less than comparable industrial states with equivalent personal income levels. By some measures, their schools do not fare as well as do Oregon schools on the annual budget election system.

One might suppose that the magnitude of the effects of referenda could be ascertained easily by comparison of the referenda states with other states, but such comparative data defy confident judgments. One complication is the choice of revenue and expenditure yardsticks. Observe the differences in ranks of the states on the four measures in Table 12-1. By one measure, per pupil expenditure, Ohio ranks higher than Indiana, a state with no referenda. Michigan expenditures exceed those of all three adjacent nonreferendum states. (The number of referenda in Minnesota to date has been negligible.) West Virginia school expenditures are essentially equal to those of Tennessee, a nonreferendum state. Such interstate comparison can not illuminate the revenue effect of referenda, because their effects are not segregated from those of other variables: personal income, the amount of state grants, and the amount of millage required to qualify for state grants. The potency of those variables is demonstrated by the contrast of Ohio expenditure in 1971 and 1973, produced by raising the millage qualification for the foundation program and a leap in state aid following enactment of a state income tax. Table 12-1 indicates that two of the most significant influences on school revenues are the level of personal income and regional patterns. Expenditure levels of most state functions, schools above all, are influenced strongly by regional norms. Legislators, other officials, and teacher organizations constantly compare their state with neighbors in the region. Expenditure/income ratios (school operating expenditure/personal income), the measure of "effort," indicate that more effort occurs in some states than others, and the amount of effort does not correlate with the presence or absence or type of referendum system.

The potential impact of referenda on aggregate school revenue is circumscribed severely by powerful countervailing forces. One limiting factor is the influence of the teacher organizations, lobbying at state capitols for educational standards and expenditures and bargaining with school boards for salaries. The teachers have been lobbying vigorously for two or three generations; the state codes and appropriation laws attest to their considerable success. Recent studies of lobbying report that the "education lobby"—the teachers allied with the PTA, administrators, and school

Table 12-1
School Operating Expenditures—Selected States

Region State	Per Pupil Expenditures 1971	Per Pupil Expenditures 1973	1973 Expenditure Per Capita	1973 Expenditure Expend./ Income	Average Teacher Salary
Appalachia					
Kentucky	$ 621	$ 707	$159	.044	$ 7,825
Tennessee	601	730	173	.048	8,305
West Va.	624	703	182	.051	8,183
Great Lakes					
Illinois	937	1235	265	.052	11,200
Indiana	770	812	232	.053	9,856
Michigan	937	1271	326	.068	11,950
Minnesota	1021	1179	321	.074	10,526
Ohio	778	946	217	.048	9,300
Wisconsin	977	1134	281	.060	10,423
Pacific					
California	879	1000	281	.056	11,760
Oregon	935	1155	253	.059	9,567
Washington	873	953	271	.061	10,852

Sources: *Digest of Educational Statistics, 1971; Statistical Abstract, 1973.*

boards—is one of the strongest in numerous legislatures.[13] Three other limiting factors are products of that assiduous lobbying: the steady expansion of state funding of school districts, the imposition of millage qualifications for state aid, and a host of statutory school standards. Local electorates may be free to vote for as much school taxes as they please, but they are not free to vote for as little as they please.

The Views of School Officials

In light of the inherent burden and hazards of referenda for school officials and the alarming number of levy and bond defeats recently in some states, it is not surprising that some officials and leaders of teacher organizations are intensely critical of plebiscites. One of the most vehement critics is the Michigan superintendent of public instruction, who has waged a vigorous campaign against the system, which he characterizes as "inadequate, unfair, and unrealistic."[14] An official in another state quipped, "The Viet Nam war and perhaps space exploration and some other matters should be financed by voted levies."

The burden of referenda on school boards is another count of the indictment. Frequent millage campaigns, says the Michigan superintendent, are "an enormous drain of time and ability which should instead be devoted to seeking improvements in curriculum and in fulfilling the basic role of the board."[15] The Washington Levy Study Commission also emphasized the "cost in educator and layman energies" diverted from other concerns by levy campaigns.[16].

One should not infer, however, that all or even most schoolmen are intensely critical of referenda and bent on liberation. There is a paucity of information. The critical statements that appear in the press are not a representative sample, since they usually are from those states where the frequency of referenda and/or defeats have generated acute distress. Our solicitation of information from state officials produced only fragmentary data. Some officials (properly) are not eager to issue analytical or evaluative statements.

Information gleaned from documents, correspondence, and the press permits a few tentative generalizations. (1) Evidently few schoolmen favor referenda in principle. None of the state education officials offered an endorsement. The systems did not originate by choice of schoolmen and they are well aware that schools are unique in their dependence on plebiscites. (2) Their views perhaps and their concern definitely are a function of the pinch of the shoe, since there is so much difference in the hazards and burdens of the various state systems. The absence of overt criticism and opposition may not be indicative of attitudes; it may be only a decision not to tilt with windmills. (3) Substantial hostility and vigorous efforts to abolish referenda exist currently in only a few states. There is dissatisfaction in other states; but more frequently the concern of schoolmen is to achieve specific modifications, e.g., elimination of supramajority rules, reform of assessment practices, increases in the amount of millage that may be voted or that may be levied without a plebiscite, or indefinite-period levies. (4) Bond referenda logically should be more palatable to school officials than budget and operating levy referenda. That was the finding of a survey in one state, and it is consistent with the scant amount of visible opposition. Schoolmen did not challenge bond referenda per se in the lawsuits noted in Chapter 3.

The views of a sample of Ohio local officials were inventoried by interviews in 1970.[17] Perhaps their responses are representative of schoolmen in those states that have experienced the most acute difficulties with referenda and where the system is the object of the most controversy. City and county officials also were interviewed, as fiscal referenda are important in all local governments of Ohio. Referenda were approved in principle by most of the county officials, disapproved by most of the city officials, and almost unanimously disapproved by the school officials. The opposition of the latter arises from a natural esteem of their own function and an acute sense of inadequate revenue. A majority, however, did approve of bond referenda.

They advanced a variety of arguments for abolition of levy referenda.

Some spoke to the fundamental issue, questioning the competence of the public to make critical decisions of school budgeting. The professional viewpoint was stated pithily by one respondent. "Going to school is the only thing each of us has in common. Because he has been a part of the educational process, each person feels he is qualified to judge the needs of the school system. And that is just not true."[18]

Schoolmen are not congenital elitists. Some agreed that over the long run voters display good judgment; but in the short run, they said, voters may be affected by "emotional issues" and make disastrous mistakes. One of the emotional issues was cited by officials in two metropolises: that some people are "voting race." Some whites, they said, are saying "no" in referenda to black demands for busing, integration, and curriculum changes; simultaneously some blacks are voting "no" because of insufficient busing, integration, and curriculum change.

Another objection was perceptible during the interviews, an aversion to levy campaigning. Only one official explicitly stated that he did not like to "beg" for money, but the interviews indicated that campaigns are begging in the eyes of many schoolmen and that is one significant reason for their dislike of the system. The foremost objection of nonmetropolitan officials was the difficulty of securing adequate revenue by plebiscite.

The Credit Side of the Ledger

The school fiscal referendum has been appraised in the preceding pages by reference to three standards: the effects on public administration and finance, its efficacy for avoidance and resolution of community conflict, and its logic as a decision-making process for making some of a community's major fiscal decisions. Although some of the revenue effects are hazy and there is wide variation among the state systems in the magnitude of the detrimental effects on administration, direct democracy in school districts does not score high marks by any of these standards. For each standard, the logic and the evidence appear to be preponderantly on the debit side of the ledger.

There are certainly other pertinent standards to which some observers may attach higher priority. Perhaps the paramount merit of the institution is the opportunity provided for civic participation. "The act of voting for or against," say Wirt and Kirst, "relates the individual citizen to his schools in an intimate fashion unknown to other major political structures."[19] That observation is incontrovertible, since in most states school districts are the only polities with any substantial amount of plebiscitary democracy. School referenda furnish abundant opportunity for meaningful participation in the making of significant decisions of the community; the issues are not trivial and popular sovereignty is authentic. Here is the fulfillment of Aristotle's idea that every citizen should hold some office if only juryman and Mill's ideally best form of government with "every citizen not only having a voice in the exercise of that ultimate sovereignty, but being, at least occasionally, called on to take an actual part in the government, by the personal discharge of some public functions."[20]

Referenda foster other important democratic values. Despite the frequency of low turnouts, the augmentation of the public's interest in and knowledge of the schools surely is not negligible. Officialdom is obliged to do extensive reporting and to make strenuous efforts occasionally. Some campaigns are tremendous mobilizations in which officials and volunteers labor mightily to "explain" the propositions. Except for perfunctory renewals, substantial quantities of information about school operations and finance are disseminated in the media and campaign literature. Major campaigns entail, and often are preceded by, concentrated reporting to community influentials, a process in which the aspirations and judgments of officials are exposed to some scrutiny and appraisal—the price of co-option.

Accountability was the fervent concern of the Progressives and their rationale for direct democracy; state "I and R" were expected to provide effective "control" of officialdom. School budget and tax referenda did not originate for that purpose, and it should be noticed that they are not the control mechanism which the Progressives proposed. Instead of providing electorates with "a shotgun behind the door" available for occasional use to countermand decisions of officialdom, the school referenda systems transferred the legislative function to the electorate in a measure never contemplated by the Progressives.

Nevertheless, school referenda are control instruments and evidently that is the *raison d'etre* in the eyes of most citizens, including many who are not passionate about property taxes. That is attested by the failures of efforts by school forces in some states to eliminate or modify the systems and by the absence of any challenge in other states. If the frequency of proposition defeats is a valid index, school referenda currently are remarkably important instruments of control.

Accountability is far more than raw control; there are subtle dimensions. One is "anticipated reactions," that pervasive influence on the decisions and behavior of officialdom. Patently school referenda are vehicles for the operation of that "law" abundantly. There are various other ways that referenda may foster accountability: by augmented reporting, the necessity to justify proposals to the electorate as well as to community elites, and the consequent incentive to formulate carefully proposals that can be "sold." In those instances where officials misjudge anticipated reactions, control is exerted by the electorate. The referendum system may oblige officials to be more accountable to some segments of the community than they might be otherwise. One can list the potential contributions to accountability and notice occasional visible instances of each, but that is about all. How much referenda actually contribute to accountability is unknown. The processes are difficult to observe and intractable for measurement.

More entries could be posted on the credit side of the ledger, but most of them would be facets of the ones which have been considered or alternative phrasings. We have not posted details, such as the sheer cost of special elections, which are not small in some communities. The important merits of school referenda appear to be some augmentation of the public's interest in and knowledge of schools, the fostering of accountability, and the *opportunity* for participation. Those certainly are not negligible values in this age of organization and alienation, although the citizens of some states evidently do not think they require referenda.

The next step would be to draw a balance sheet, but we are not disposed to try it. The parameters of most of the entries are hazy, particularly the credits. Furthermore, the weights to be assigned to each entry require value judgments. So let it be every man his own philosopher. Perhaps most people are less concerned about the net balance than about the policy results of the alternative decision-making systems.

The Future of School Referenda?

There have been modifications of details but slight change in the scope of direct democracy in the school districts since the tax limitation wave of the early 1930s. That will not continue another forty years, and changes may be sweeping, sudden, and soon. Bond referenda may survive indefinitely, but the future of operating levy and budget elections is very uncertain, because of the opposition of school forces in some states, the property tax ferment, taxpayer resistance, and now the drive by education and civil rights groups to knock out the property tax entirely by litigation.

The criticisms of the legal debt limitation schemes by scholars, the ACIR, and other champions of local government "revitalization" have had no effect; no one is listening. The strictures are heard by few of the officials who would have to initiate action and not at all by the electorates which would have to endorse repeal proposals. Hence, evaluation of the debt limitations is not on the agenda; and bond referenda may continue, sustained by inertia and the illusion that they are profound inhibitions of capital expenditures, extravagance, and taxes. Thus, when the Washington legislature in 1973 proposed, by nearly unanimous vote, to discontinue the 40 percent turnout requirement (not the 60 percent majority rule), its modest proposal was defeated at the polls by the cry of "higher taxes" and the theme that "it is wrong to encourage lesser participation in public affairs."[21] Although school boards are affected the most by the debt limitation laws, they can not complain of discrimination since those restrictions apply with equal frequency to municipalities and counties.[22]

The efforts of school forces in some states to abolish referenda continue despite the scant success to date. Missouri teachers make repeated efforts to eliminate the millage ceilings and the supramajority rule. Within a period of four years, 1969-1972, the Michigan Education Association made two futile assaults, proposing two plans to supplant tax plebiscites by full state financing of the schools. Both were declined by the legislature and the second one by the state electorate. In Oregon, a plan to replace the property tax and budget elections by nearly full state financing has been endorsed by the legislature and is scheduled for consideration by the electorate in May, 1974.[23]

Washington education groups hold the record for strike-outs. Four efforts during the 1960s to remove the tax limitation provision of the state constitution failed, as did litigation against the supramajority rule. In 1973, they turned to the state-funding-property-tax-abolition strategy, which enabled them to build a broad coalition "Against Unfair Taxes and for Property Tax Relief."[24] The legislature helped prepare the way by the reports of Temporary Special Levy Study Commission. Nevertheless the proposal of property tax abolition, full state financing, and a graduated income tax lost by a three to one landslide. Evidently opposition to "high property taxes" may be simply opposition to taxes, and property tax "relief" has less lustre when coupled with substitute taxes. Significantly, the arguments in the official voter information pamphlet contain not a word about the wisdom and virtues of direct democracy.

Fabian strategies may be employed by education forces in some states. Ohio schoolmen have not ventured an open attack on the sacred cow, the "right" of the people to vote on taxes, but they have provided an example of what can be done by indirect methods.

The foremost change agent is the current attack on the property tax, not by the traditional antitaxers, but by civil rights and education organizations in order to attain total state financing of the schools. The attack has exploded like a roman candle in legislatures and courts across the nation. Since few legislatures initially were receptive to proposals for revolutionizing school finance, the proponents resorted to litigation. In a wave of lawsuits it was argued that supporting schools by property taxes inexorably produces differences in per pupil financial support of a magnitude that constitute a contradiction of the equal protection of the laws standard of the Fourteenth Amendment. That proposition was accepted by the state courts of California in 1971 and New Jersey in 1973, although the latter rested its decision on a text of the state constitution.[25]

The ostensible objective of the litigation and lobbying is equalization of per pupil revenue, but that could be achieved very considerably without a property tax *coup de grace*. The plaintiffs evidently have other fish to try. Attacking the property tax by litigation is a propitious strategy, one that eludes the legislatures and the electorates, capitalizes on antiproperty tax sentiment, achieves an anomalous informal alliance with the traditional opponents, and avoids beautifully the issue of how to provide alternative revenue. Elimination of the property tax, of course, also eliminates several other things including referenda, although that is never mentioned. When the Supreme Court on March 21, 1973 ruled on the constitutionality of the use of the property tax as a school revenue in Texas, school referenda survived by a five to four vote.[26]

Few school referenda systems owe their genesis to the winsomeness of direct democracy. They were not established by a deliberate assessment of the efficacy of the plebiscite as a policy-making process or by consideration of the abstract virtues of participatory democracy. Most of the state systems were unanticipated by-products of agitation against taxes and schemes to clamp lids on expenditures. Although overt attempts to abolish them have been conspicuously unsuccessful, they seem not to have deep intrinsic appeal. Consequently the future of school referenda, now in dire jeopardy, hinges not on the merits but on what happens to the venerable property tax.

Notes

1. Cf. Simeon Leland, *Property Tax Limitation Laws* (Chicago: Public Administration Service, 1936); James W. Thompson, "Effects of Property Tax Limitation in West Virginia", *National Tax Journal* 4 (1951), p. 131; and Advisory Commission on Intergovernmental Relations, *State Constitutional and Statutory Restrictions on Local Taxing Powers* (Washington: The Commission, 1962), ch. 3—hereafter cited as ACIR, *Tax Limitations*.

2. Ibid.

3. Merlin Hunter, *Outline of Public Finance* (New York: Harper & Brothers, 1926), pp. 271-272. The same theme is to be found in *1938 Proceedings of the National Tax Association*, pp. 788-804, and in the textbooks of William H. Anderson, Harold M. Groves, Harley L. Lutz, Philip E. Taylor, and William Watkins.

4. ACIR, *Tax Limitations*, Appendix A.

5. Advisory Commission on Intergovernmental Relations, *State Constitutional and Statutory Restrictions on Local Government Debt*

278

(Washington: The Commission, 1961), Appendix A—hereafter cited as ACIR, *Debt Limitations*.

6. ACIR, *Tax Limitations*, p. 5.

7. ACIR, *Debt Limitations*, p. 4.

8. Michigan superintendent of public instruction, *The Blade*, Toledo, Ohio, April 23, 1969, p. 65.

9. *Summary Report and Research Reports*, vol. 1, p. 8.

10. *The Blade*, Toledo, Ohio, September 25, 1968, p. 38.

11. Ibid.

12. ACIR, *Tax Limitations*, p. 2.

13. Cf. Harmon Zeigler and Michael Baer, *Lobbying: Interaction and Influence in American State Legislatures* (Belmont, California: Wadsworth, 1969), p. 32-33.

14. *The Blade*, Toledo, Ohio, September 25, 1968, p. 38.

15. Ibid.

16. Op. cit., p. 8.

17. James S. Ginocchio, *Local Tax and Bond Referenda in Ohio* (Thesis, Bowling Green State University, 1971), pp.83-87.

18. Ibid., p. 85.

19. Frederick M. Wirt and Michael W. Kirst, *The Political Web of American Schools* (Boston: Little, Brown, 1973), p. 97.

20. *Representative Government*, ch. III.

21. *Official Voters Pamphlet, General Election Tuesday, November 6, 1973*, p. 19.

22. ACIR, *Debt Limitations*, Appendix A.

23. *National Civic Review*, September 1973, p. 452.

24. *Official Voters Pamphlet*, p. 16.

25. *Serrano* v. *Priest*, 96 Cal. 601, 487 P 2d 1241 (1971); *Robinson* v. *Cahill*, reported in *The New York Times*, April 4, 1973, p. 1.

26. *San Antonio School District* v. *Rodriguez*, No. 71-1332 (March 21, 1973).

Appendix A
A Methodological Note on Q
Factor Analysis

In Chapter 10, Q factor analysis was explained in the context of its application to a school referendum situation as a hitherto unused voting research technique. In contrast, the so-called attitude scale is the most widely used and the most carefully designed and tested method for the measurement of attitudes.[1] Several types of scales have been developed, but regardless of differences among them, they all consist of a number of items (stimuli) and a scale of response to these that sorts out respondents along a continuum of valence toward the object measured (the respondents' scores).[2] At least three points are worthy of mention which help to differentiate attitude scaling from Q factor analysis. (1) Scale scores are averaged out for subjects, e.g., "strongly agrees" cancel out "strongly disagrees." The focus is not on response to items within the scale, but on the end score, which in turn determines "how much" of the attitude the respondent has. (2) Since scale scores are therefore normative measures, they are often meaningless unless they are related to some other information about respondents, e.g., categoric groups to which they belong: black-white, urban-rural, etc. (3) The attitude itself—the object "scaled"—is never seen; instead it is left to inference.[3] The assumption is that the scale measures what it purports to measure, an assumption fraught with may potential difficulties, not least of which are those related to the inherent ambiguity of the language of the items of the scale.

No claim is made for the superiority or infallibility of Q factor analysis; rather, this is an alternative approach to attitude measurement which does not necessarily "solve" the problems raised above, but does attack them with different emphases. For example, each respondent's score in Q is preserved as a model of that person's subjective arrangement of the items of the Q sort. In this methodology, the "score" informs the researcher upon which factor the respondent is located and how highly the respondent is loaded on that factor, i.e., how closely the respondent approximates the "purest" model of the attitude represented by the factor. The factor, then, is the attitude; further, it can be argued that because of the way it is extracted, it is "seen," not inferred.[4] In order to assist the "seeing," the focus is on the items within the "scales," because their arrangement suggests what attitudinal configuration has been uncovered in Q sorting. In a sense, when compared to scaling, procedures have been reversed. In scaling, items are selected because they are hypothesized to measure the existence and strength of a predetermined attitude. In Q, items are chosen because they are relevant to a situation under study; respondents rank order these relevant stimuli so that factors appear—perhaps two, three, four, or more, not necessarily guessed in advance of "measurement"—that in turn provide some basis for explaining "what is going on" in the situation being considered. In Chapter 10, the good citizens, the alienates, the ambivalent and cautious, and the caretakers were conceptualized as more than four separate perspectives on the referendum in question, but also as the subjective attitudes of the participants, which consequently *were the event*. Admittedly, that is a great leap of faith. To explain, if not justify, that leap requires a few words on factor analysis and Q technique.

Factor Analysis and Q Technique

Most of the procedures of Q technique are discussed in Chapter 10 using the data of the Q investigation of the Youngstown school referendum, e.g., choosing the P set, constructing the Q sample, sorting statements, employing the forced distribution, and interpreting factors. However, some technical aspects of the use of factor analysis in Q technique were intentionally overlooked. A discussion of factor analysis in Q follows, along with the factor matrix for this investigation and the complete factor arrays.

The goal of factor analysis, regardless of the methodology or technique used, is to reduce data to their most parsimonious explanation. Using the Q investigation of Younstown, with the first P set as a guide, this can be illustrated as follows: 18 subjects rank ordered 54 items for a total of 962 observations. That, of course, is unmanageable as a basis for "explanation." However, since each of the respondents ranked the statements according to the same scale and distribution, with values assigned from 1 to 11, the responses of the 18 subjects can be intercorrelated using Pearson's product—moment correlation coefficient for variables with equal means and standard deviations. In the resulting matrix, there are now 153 numbers (coefficients) which subsume the data instead of the original 962. The number of coefficients (153) can be explained as follows. Assuming that N equals the total number of sorters, then the matrix would read for intercorrelating all sorts: $N \times N$. However, in the diagonals of the matrix, N of these coefficients need not be computed because one of each of the sorts is correlated with itself. Also, because the $N \times N$ matrix is identical below the diagonal as above, we are interested in only half of these; hence the formula: $0.5N(N-1)$. In this instance that is: $0.5 \times 18 \times 17 = 153$. What remains now, according to our definition of factor analysis, is to reduce further the matrix of correlations from 153 to a still more manageable

Table A-1
Rotated Factor Matrix, Q Study of Youngstown

Sorters	Factors 1	2	3	4
1	83x	−17	15	−02
15	53x	−08	18	32
2	50	−11	10	46
7	45x	06	−09	04
9	−07	73x	−03	−02
10	−07	73x	03	02
6	−09	59x	17	16
11	−06	59x	06	14
17	−18	58	−03	53
5	06	35x	08	−13
14	08	33	04	09
13	−04	32	−17	−03
12	−01	17	11	03
4	10	13	83x	20
3	15	−03	06	43x
18	−05	37	06	48
16	07	09	34	42x
8	11	−03	02	04

number, preferably the smallest number of *distinct* and *identifiable* ways to sort the Q sample.

In the initial experiment of the Q investigation described above, centroid factor analysis was used to reduce the matrix, however, in the matrix created by putting together all of the sorts of the three separate experiments of the Youngstown Q investigation, (see below) the principal-components method was used. In that 60 × 60 matrix, ones were placed in the diagonal of the matrix and all factors with Eigen values greater than one were extracted. A varimax (Kaiser) rotation of factors was utilized that approximates Thurstone's simple structure. At that point, then, we have a rotated factor matrix for which factor arrays (described in Chapter 10) can be computed. Table A-1 is from the initial Q experiment of the Youngstown study. It is included to illustrate the origin of the factor arrays, because the all-inclusive factor matrix is too large and unwieldly for explanatory purposes.

Visual inspection of the matrix in Table A-1 reveals at least three important pieces of the explanation that can be extracted from the data at this point in Q factor analysis: (1) the number of factors in the correlation matrix, (2) which subjects are on which factors, and (3) the extent to which the subjects are "loaded" on each factor. However, without the factor arrays, what each factor "means" is as yet unknown.

In the first experiment represented by Table A-1, four factors accounted for almost all of the variance in the matrix. Respondents such as #8 in Table A-1 are not significantly loaded on any factor. The question of significant loadings is not arbitrary. In this Q investigation, the Guilford-Lacey expression for the standard error of a zero correlation[5] was used to determine significant loadings according to the formula:

$$SE = \frac{1}{\sqrt{N}} \quad r = 0$$

With a N of 54 statements significance, at a confidence level of .01 is $\pm$ .351. That is: 7.35 (the square root of 54) divided into 1 = .136; for this study a high significance level was chosen, .01; using the curve of normal distribution for a level of .01, then, 2.58 $\times$ 1.36 = .351. Table A-1 has been arranged so that significant loadings are clustered together. The "x" that follows some of the entries in this table identifies the sorts that are used to compute the factor arrays, in this instance, for each of the four factors.

A factor array is the end product of the computational process; it is *the* Q sort that represents "best" the factors yielded by the rotated factor matrix. The first step in that process is to find those respondents (sorters) who are loaded on but one factor; in Table A-1 it would be those respondents identified by an "x." (Note that #2, #17, and #18 are not so marked for their respective factors.) Using factor one of that Table, #1, #15, and #7 are given greatest weight in determining the response array that is most representative for this factor. Thus the array for factor one consists of a single Q sort that sorter X might have executed with the same result as numbers 1, 15, 2 and 7 "on the average," that "average" being weighted most heavily toward those responses most highly loaded on that factor according to the rotated matrix. This representative Q sort has the property that each of those variates (numbers 1, 15, 2 and 7) will correlate with it by an amount equal to its factor loading with the factor.[6] Consequently, arrays are computed for each factor according to a computer program that weighs the contributions to the array for each factor in proportion to the loading of each completed sort on that factor. This, then, permits the reader to scan the array to check the averaged-out response for each statement factor by factor. Likewise, this permits the kind of interpretative explation undertaken in Chapter 10, designed to "make sense" out of the response of each factor as its response relates to the stiuation under study and to theories of human behavior. Q technique is a tool that can be employed to investigate subjective behavior. It is equally true that the end products of employing Q technique are data (factors) that must be subjectively interpreted, witness our discussion of the four factors in the Youngstown rèferendum explicated in Chapter 10. However, in the light of Q methodology and Q technique, data are collected *and* interpreted according to sound, objective criteria.

Notes

1. David Krech, Richard S. Crutchfield, and Egerton L. Ballachey, *Individual in Society* (New York: McGraw-Hill Book Company, Inc., 1962), p. 147.

2. C. Selltiz, M. Jahoda, M. Deutsch, and S. W. Cook, "Attitude Scaling," in M. Jahoda and N. Warren, eds., *Attitudes* (Baltimore: Penguin Books, Inc., 1966), p. 305.

3. Steven R. Brown and Thomas D. Ungs, "Representativeness and the Study of Political Behavior: An Application of Q Technique to Reactions to the Kent State Incident," *Social Science Quarterly* (December 1970), p. 517.

4. Ibid., pp. 518-519.

5. J. P. Guilford and J. I. Lacey, *Printed Classification Tests,* Army Air Force Aviation Psychology Program Research Reports, No. 5, Washington, D. C.: U.S. Government Printing Office, 1947.

6. William Stephenson, *The Study of Behavior* (Chicago: University of Chicago Press, 1953), pp. 120-122, drawing upon the formula of C. Spearman for factor loadings:

$$\frac{Wb}{Wa} = \frac{fb(1-f^2a)}{fa(1-f^2b)}$$

if *fa* and *fb* are the factor loadings for factor *f* in two variates *a* and *b* respectively, the "weights" for the scores gained by any statement are in the above proportions. In practice, this "weighting" is part of a canned computer program based on the above formula.

Appendix B
School Bond Election Statistics

Table B-1
School Bond Passage Ratios, Fiscal Years 1962-1972

	1962	1963	1964	1965	1966	1967	1968	1969	1970	1971	1972
Alaska	1/1	3/5	4/4	1/1	6/6	5/6	2/3	1/1	1/1	1/1	2/2
Arizona	21/24	23/28	17/19	21/22	5/5	5/6	10/16	7/9	1/1	7/7	10/12
Arkansas	39/39	71/71	31/35	60/68	50/58	50/58	64/77	39/45	36/45	35/48	20/26
California*	115/171	160/245	156/252	153/235	92/166	46/91	57/100	39/111	46/97	18/44	10/54
Colorado	27/35	160/245	19/21	15/27	20/27	10/18	17/23	9/15	13/15	13/22	7/10
Connecticut	10/11	24/25	17/17	36/36	21/22	18/22	15/16	13/15	5/6	17/20	8/14
Delaware	6/6	2/2	3/3	6/9	3/4	3/3	4/6	0/1	1/1	1/1	1/1
Florida	2/2	1/2	6/6	2/2	—	2/6	3/5	1/2	3/4	2/4	2/2
Georgia	4/4	10/11	10/10	6/7	2/2	4/7	7/9	4/8	2/3	5/6	3/6
Idaho*	11/17	8/15	9/9	9/18	13/20	2/4	10/15	3/4	—	2/2	1/5
Illinois	95/134	117/157	94/139	105/120	109/135	119/151	118/182	95/146	61/126	48/93	47/91
Iowa*	50/79	38/100	38/72	46/76	48/75	57/92	57/85	54/88	14/49	9/26	16/47
Kansas	11/12	16/25	4/5	5/5	7/8	28/59	30/54	4/5	2/4	3/3	3/5
Kentucky*	3/3	1/1	—	1/1	1/1	16/17	13/16	0/1	1/1	4/6	4/7
Louisiana	4/4	21/24	37/38	30/31	19/19	4/5	5/6	3/5	4/9	2/5	1/2
Maine	3/3	4/4	6/7	3/3	4/6	2/2	2/3	2/2	—	2/3	—
Maryland	—	4/4		2/3		2/2	2/3	2/2		2/3	2/4
Massachusetts*	20/20	11/12	27/30	16/20	13/16	12/12	9/11	6/8	3/6	7/15	9/11
Michigan	49/71	73/108	94/142	99/139	93/129	72/123	56/98	41/105	34/97	36/104	42/131
Minnesota	44/67	48/71	64/85	56/86	70/108	52/91	69/91	48/90	47/90	22/80	12/36
Mississippi*	5/6	17/23	13/16	15/19	8/13	4/6	5/9	2/4	5/10	0/4	
Missouri*	14/16	26/27	18/20	24/28	10/12	14/19	34/56	7/23	11/26	13/19	17/23
Montana	10/13	17/19	15/19	28/35	13/19	3/5	6/6	2/2	1/1	—	2/4
Nebraska*	37/57	41/59	31/49	35/52	22/28	23/33	29/33	30/39	12/20	14/23	20/33
Nevada	2/2	5/5	2/2	2/3	1/2	1/1	—	1/1	—	2/2	—
New Hampshire*	5/6	7/7	8/9	11/11	5/5	2/5	5/6	2/2	1/4	2/3	2/4
New Jersey	54/73	7/7	79/115	74/92	46/69	73/108	61/91	67/113	59/101	28/68	56/113

New Mexico	12/13	15/17	21/33	14/15	14/14	6/7	18/19	5/5	2/2	4/8	8/12
New York*	36/51	77/110	116/161	84/119	65/81	39/55	24/34	5/16	7/21	14/30	1/11
N. Carolina	2/2	7/9	11/13	7/8	5/6	4/5	1/3	2/4	3/5	1/1	4/5
N. Dakota*	15/28	28/45	24/47	27/46	22/34	12/26	14/27	3/9	13/29	5/8	7/10
Ohio	102/176	77/128	105/171	94/156	127/213	66/125	103/170	46/125	42/104	29/121	36/117
Oklahoma*	20/25	87/101	105/120	67/81	63/80	52/69	66/78	36/49	58/72	34/50	47/69
Oregon	33/42	46/61	30/46	46/56	30/40	31/45	25/43	8/13	12/27	6/22	11/27
Pennsylvania	2/2	4/4	4/5	4/4	1/1	1/1	3/3	4/6	1/1	—	0/1
Rhode Island	3/4	9/10	11/13	13/13	8/10	13/14	4/4	4/6	8/8	3/5	4/9
S. Carolina	—	1/1	1/1	4/4	1/1	—	—	1/1	—	0/1	—
S. Dakota*	16/14	14/23	15/26	17/25	14/21	16/30	10/17	9/17	5/15	1/10	1/17
Tennessee	2/3	4/4	—	8/9	12/15	—	1/2	1/1	—	—	—
Texas	103/127	153/180	161/186	163/204	126/154	123/171	107/142	98/141	96/138	86/137	103/169
Utah	4/6	4/4	10/10	5/5	3/3	3/3	2/3	—	3/4	3/4	2/2
Vermont	6/8	5/8	9/16	12/15	10/12	15/19	11/20	15/23	0/2	7/12	1/4
Virginia	3/4	10/12	7/8	5/5	4/8	4/7	6/10	3/6	4/5	2/4	5/8
Washington*	16/18	42/59	23/34	55/70	39/47	45/54	53/72	16/21	11/18	4/9	4/16
W. Virginia*	1/3	0/3	2/8	4/6	3/6	0/1	3/7	3/3	0/1	0/1	1/2
Wisconsin	10/11	26/42	29/40	28/38	27/34	21/38	33/54	19/44	21/50	6/37	8/31
Wyoming	6/9	8/11	12/17	7/9	10/10	3/4	10/14	1/2	1/3	9/17	4/6
Total	1034/1432	1482/2048	1501/2071	1525/2041	1265/1745	1082/1625	1183/1750	762/1341	647/1216	507/1086	542/1153
Supramajority states*	364/514	557/830	585/853	564/807	428/605	342/497	376/560	215/395	140/271	105/200	126/248
Simple majority states	670/918	925/1218	916/1218	961/1234	847/1140	758/1128	805/1190	547/946	507/945	402/886	416/905

Note: Data are for fiscal years, e.g., 1971 is July 1970 through June 1971.

* States that require a supramajority vote; Californaia before 1970.

**Totals include two successful elections in Indiana in fiscal years 1963, 1964, and 1965; and three in Alabama in 1970.

Source: National Center for Educational Statistics, U.S. Office of Education, "Bond Sales for Public School Purposes," annual reports.

Table B-2.
Ten-Year Summary of School Bond Elections, Fiscal Years 1962-1971

	Number of Elections				Par Value of Bond Issues (in millions of dollars)			Approved	
	Held	Approved	Defeated	Percent approved	Proposed	Approved	Defeated	Percent	Dollars Per Capita*
Alaska	29	25	4	86.2	$ 166	$ 149	$ 17	89.9	$497
Arizona	137	117	20	85.4	238	172	66	72.4	97
Arkansas	544	475	69	87.3	227	177	50	78.0	92
California	1522	882	640	58.0	5952	3157	2795	53.0	158
Colorado	223	157	66	70.4	517	349	167	67.6	158
Connecticut*	190	176	14	92.6	509	443	66	87.0	146
Delaware*	36	29	7	80.6	43	35	8	81.6	63
Florida	33	22	11	66.7	460	233	227	50.6	34
Georgia	67	54	13	80.6	298	242	56	81.2	53
Idaho	104	67	37	64.4	80	52	28	65.1	75
Illinois**	1383	961	422	69.5	1880	1162	718	61.8	105
Iowa	742	411	331	55.4	614	300	313	48.9	106
Kansas	180	110	70	61.1	275	160	116	57.9	71
Kentucky**	7	6	1	85.7	37	34	3	93.2	11
Louisiana	160	148	12	92.5	439	377	63	85.8	104
Maine**	51	38	13	74.5	154	138	17	89.3	139
Maryland**	17	14	3	82.4	295	284	12	96.1	72
Massachusetts**	150	124	26	82.7	309	210	99	67.9	37
Michigan	1116	647	469	58.0	3061	1554	1507	50.8	175
Minnesota**	859	520	339	60.5	1303	768	535	58.9	202
Mississippi	110	74	36	67.3	119	66	53	55.2	30
Missouri	246	171	75	69.5	608	296	312	48.7	63

Montana	119	95	24	79.8	68	53	15	77.7	76
Nebraska	393	274	119	69.7	320	232	88	72.5	156
Nevada	18	16	2	88.9	129	124	5	95.9	253
New Hampshire**	58	48	10	82.8	53	38	15	71.4	51
New Jersey**	942	616	326	65.4	1655	926	729	55.9	129
New Mexico	122	111	11	91.0	157	143	14	91.3	141
New York**	712	491	221	69.0	1710	1004	706	58.7	55
N. Carolina	56	43	13	76.8	342	299	42	87.6	59
N. Dakota	299	163	136	54.5	97	51	46	52.5	83
Ohio	1489	791	698	53.1	2392	1234	1158	51.6	116
Oklahoma	725	588	137	81.1	295	223	72	75.5	87
Oregon	395	267	128	67.6	481	266	215	55.4	78
Pennsylvania**	27	24	3	88.9	398	305	94	76.5	26
Rhode Island	87	76	11	87.4	188	145	44	76.9	153
S. Carolina**	9	8	1	88.9	30	28	2	92.4	11
South Dakota	208	117	91	56.3	100	50	49	50.5	76
Tennessee**	34	28	6	82.4	86	61	25	70.5	15
Texas	1580	1216	364	77.0	2648	2105	543	79.5	188
Utah	38	34	4	89.5	152	145	7	95.5	137
Vermont	135	90	45	66.7	142	72	70	50.9	163
Virginia**	69	48	21	70.0	520	398	122	76.5	86
Washington	402	304	98	75.6	636	481	154	75.5	141
W. Virginia	39	16	23	41.0	167	71	96	42.5	41
Wisconsin**	388	220	168	56.7	762	462	301	60.6	105
Wyoming	96	67	29	70.0	78	45	33	57.4	135
Total***	16,355	10,988	5,367	67.2	$31,207	$19,334	$11,873	62.0	$ 95

*Per capitas are based on 1970 census.

**Voter approval not required of all school systems.

***Total includes three elections in Alabama and six in Indiana.

Source: National Center for Educational Statistics, U.S. Office of Education, "Bond Sales for Public School Purposes, 1970-71."

Index

About the Authors

Howard D. Hamilton is Professor of Political Science at Kent State University. He has been on the faculty of Indiana State College and Bowling Green University and has been a visiting professor at Albion College and Indiana University. He has been a consultant for groups and government agencies in Indiana, Michigan, and Ohio. Professor Hamilton's research has appeared in articles in the *American Political Science Review*, *National Municipal Review*, *National Tax Journal*, *Public Administration Review*, *Public Finance*, *Social Science Quarterly*, *Western Political Quarterly*, and other professional journals. His previous books were *Political Institutions*, *Legislative Apportionment: Key to Power*, and *Reapportioning Legislatures: A Consideration of Criteria and Computers*.

Sylvan H. Cohen is Chairman of the Department of Political Science at Slippery Rock State College. He received the B.A. from Ohio University, the M.P.A. from the University of Pittsburgh, and the Ph.D. from Kent State University. Professor Cohen is coeditor (with Richard A. Gabriel) of *The Environment: Critical Factors in Strategy Development*, and the author of articles on voter attitudes in school referenda, program evaluation, and police-community relations.